INTERNATIONAL CRISIS AND CONFLICT

Also by Richard Clutterbuck

ACROSS THE RIVER (*as Richard Jocelyn*)
BRITAIN IN AGONY
CONFLICT AND VIOLENCE IN SINGAPORE AND MALAYSIA
THE FUTURE OF POLITICAL VIOLENCE (*editor*)
GUERRILLAS AND TERRORISTS
INDUSTRIAL CONFLICT AND DEMOCRACY
KIDNAP AND RANSOM
KIDNAP, HIJACK AND EXTORTION
LIVING WITH TERRORISM
THE LONG, LONG WAR
THE MEDIA AND POLITICAL VIOLENCE
PROTEST AND THE URBAN GUERRILLA
RIOT AND REVOLUTION IN SINGAPORE AND MALAYA
TERRORISM AND GUERRILLA WARFARE
TERRORISM, DRUGS AND CRIME IN EUROPE AFTER 1992

International Crisis and Conflict

Richard Clutterbuck
Security and Political Risk Consultant
and Honorary Research Fellow
University of Exeter

150th YEAR
M

St. Martin's Press

First published in Great Britain 1993 by
THE MACMILLAN PRESS LTD
Houndmills, Basingstoke, Hampshire RG21 2XS
and London
Companies and representatives
throughout the world

A catalogue record for this book is available
from the British Library.

ISBN 0–333–59192–5 hardcover
ISBN 0–333–59193–3 paperback

Printed in Great Britain by
Ipswich Book Co Ltd
Ipswich, Suffolk

First published in the United States of America 1993 by
Scholarly and Reference Division,
ST. MARTIN'S PRESS, INC.,
175 Fifth Avenue,
New York, N.Y. 10010

ISBN 0–312–10188–0 (cloth)

Library of Congress Cataloging-in-Publication Data
Clutterbuck, Richard L.
International crisis and conflict / Richard Clutterbuck.
p. cm.
Includes bibliographical references and index.
ISBN 0–312–10188–0 (cloth)
1. World politics—20th century. 2. World politics. 3. Crisis management. I. Title.
D445.C89 1993
909.82—dc20 93–4375
CIP

Contents

PART V TODAY AND TOMORROW

List of Tables

List of Maps

Preface

The wars of the twentieth century were the bloodiest in history. The purpose of this book is to study why this was so, and how we can handle future crises better. Paradoxically, the end of the Cold War has left the world more unstable than it has ever been since Stalin's time, so there will be many crises to come.

Civil wars may start from small beginnings, usually ethnic or religious passions aroused by militant local leaders; sometimes they build up into bigger wars. But the big wars are often begun by the decisions of one or two individuals: Bismarck, Napoleon III, the Kaiser, Hitler or Saddam Hussein. Though these individuals have national interests in mind, their primary motivation, consciously or otherwise, is to retain their position as leaders. The same applies to the local leader of an insurgency or civil war, whose prime motivation is to arouse the patriotic passions of his supporters so that they will continue to follow him.

After taking part in one big war and several smaller ones, I ended my 35 years in the army teaching at the Royal College of Defence Studies in London, where Brigadiers prepare to be Generals, Captains to be Admirals and Foreign Service officers to be Ambassadors. As practitioners for many years, they needed to learn 'why' rather than 'how'. We exposed them to top decision-makers in every field – political, diplomatic, military, police, legal, social, technological, industrial, commercial, cultural – and the mass media – with at least as long to ask questions as to listen. The cross-examination was so lively that these people all found it worthwhile to come: Prime Ministers, bankers, scientists, Trotskyists. Two years organizing this course taught me a lot about what makes people tick and why they take the decisions they do.

This also provided an ideal transition from the actuality of wars to teaching International Relations and Political Violence at the University of Exeter. University students want to get to grips with the real world, so my 'International Crisis and Conflict' course was invariably oversubscribed: I had to run it twice, in parallel, each year, and in one year three times. It is on that course that this book is based.

Though dealing mainly with contemporary and future conflicts, the book is set in a historical perspective. It looks at how our present international systems were developed and at how wars were avoided or limited so successfully in the nineteenth century; at how that era was ended in 1914 by the worst display of crisis management in history; at how the Treaty of Versailles created Hitler and the Second World War; at the Cold War and the successful resolution of the Cuban Missile Crisis in 1962; at the Arab–Israeli wars and a number of other crises leading up to the astounding series of revolutions in East Europe in 1989–92 and the disintegration of the USSR, all with very little bloodshed; in contrast, at the bloody civil wars – e.g. in Bosnia – to which these changes gave birth; and at Saddam Hussein's invasion of Kuwait in 1990–91.

Case studies play an important part in the book; this is not to teach ready-made answers to future problems – we don't even know yet what the problems will be, still less the answers. But the process of analysing past and contemporary experience gives practice in how to handle such problems; what one famous teacher in a fast changing field called 'dynamic comprehension'.

Some of the case studies are classics – Bismarck's wars, July 1914, and the rise of Hitler in Part II. Then in Part III there are 12 from the Cold War era – there were at least 100 to choose from.[1] Part IV examines the East European revolutions of 1989–92, the creation of 25 new and often unstable democracies seeking market economies, and the coming of age of the United Nations in the Gulf Crisis of 1990–91.

Part V assesses the patterns of future conflict, generated by nationalism, ethnic hatreds and religious fundamentalism, again with case studies of the ongoing peacekeeping operations in Cambodia, Somalia and Bosnia; it considers how we can develop our crisis management techniques and adapt our institutions, such as the UN and NATO, to resolve these future conflicts without bloodshed, as we have so dismally failed to do in the past 80 years.

Exeter RICHARD CLUTTERBUCK

List of Abbreviations

For foreign acronyms and in other cases where it is judged to be more helpful to the reader, an English description (in parenthesis) is given instead of spelling out the words.

ACC	Arab Cooperation Council
Agit-prop	Agitation and Propaganda (revolutionary teams)
APC	Armoured Personnel Carrier
BR	(Red Brigades) (Italy)
CF	Civic Forum (Czechoslovakia)
CIA	Central Intelligence Agency (USA)
CIS	Commonwealth of Independent States
CP	Communist Party
CSCE	Conference on Security and Cooperation in Europe
DC	(Christian Democrat Party) (Italy)
DF	(Democratic Forum) (Hungary)
ECOWAS	Economic Community of West African States
ECSC	European Coal and Steel Community
EOKA	(Cypriot organization for union with Greece)
ETA	(Basque terrorist movement) (Spain)
ExCom	Executive Committee (USA 1962)
FD	(Free Democratic Party) (Hungary)
FIS	(Islamic Salvation Front) (Algeria)
FUNCINPEC	(Political party led by Prince Sihanouk's son) (Cambodia)
HE	High Explosive
ICBM	Intercontinental Ballistic Missile
ID Card	Identification Card
IRA	Irish Republican Army
IRBM	Intermediate Range Ballistic Missile
IRC	International Red Cross
KPNLF	Khmer People's National Liberation Front (Cambodia)
KR	Khmers Rouges (Cambodia)
MRBM	Medium Range Ballistic Missile
MSF	*Médecins sans Frontières* (French-based charity)

NACC	North Atlantic Cooperation Council
NGO	Non-Government Organization
NSF	National Salvation Front (Romania)
OAS	Organization of American States
OECD	Organization for Economic Cooperation and Development
OEEC	Organization for European Economic Cooperation
PAV	(Slovak political party)
PCI	(Communist Party of Italy)
PF	Patriotic Front (Liberia)
PFLP-GC	Popular Front for the Liberation of Palestine – General Command
PKF	Peacekeeping Force
PKK	(Kurdish Workers Party)
PLF	Palestine Liberation Front
PLO	Palestine Liberation Organization
PPP	People's Progressive Party (Pakistan)
RAF	Red Army Faction (Germany)
SA	(Stormtroopers) (Germany 1923–34)
SACEUR	Supreme Allied Commander in Europe
SAM	Surface-to-Air Missile
SAS	Special Air Service Regiment (UK)
SCF	Save the Children Fund
SHAPE	Supreme Headquarters Allied Powers in Europe
SL	*Sendero Luminoso* (Shining Path – Peru)
SLBM	Submarine Launched Ballistic Missile
SNC	Supreme National Council (Cambodia)
SSM	Surface to Surface Missile
UAE	United Arab Emirates
UDF	Union of Democratic Forces (Bulgaria)
UN	United Nations
UNEF	UN Emergency Force (Sinai)
UNHCR	UN High Commissioner for Refugees
UNICEF	UN Children's Fund
UNPROFOR	UN Protection Force (Croatia and Bosnia)
UNSCOP	UN Special Commission on Palestine
UNTAC	UN Transitional Authority for Cambodia
UNTSO	UN Truce Supervision Organization
USC	United Somali Congress

Part I

Introduction

1 International Power and Crisis Management

THE LUNACY OF WAR

War is mass lunacy. The world accepted 8 million deaths in the First World War, and estimates vary from 35 million to 60 million in the Second. At least 1 million died in the Iran–Iraq War of 1980–88. Killing in war is now mainly impersonal, like spraying insecticide, and is covered by laws quite different from those covering any other kind of killing. Yet wars continue. There were more than 30 in progress at the time of writing.

The phenomenon is easier to comprehend at the lowest level. In what was Yugoslavia, Croats and Bosnians in 1992 would kill and risk death rather than allow Serbs to oust them from their villages, in the hideous process of 'ethnic cleansing'. This same intensity of feeling, on a national scale, led French people to flock to the colours three times in 70 years to stop Germans over-running their country, and millions of them died. Less directly, few outside Iraq would question that it was morally and politically right to fight to reverse Saddam Hussein's invasion of Kuwait in 1990–91, and to block Hitler's intention to subject the whole of Europe to a Nazi master race in 1939. Most believe, rightly or wrongly, that the people of the world would have suffered more in the end if they had not done so.

We shall never be wholly free from wars, but they are still an appalling way of solving disputes, not only because of the waste of lives and economic resources, but also because of the misery suffered by millions of families displaced from their homes. Many wars could have been avoided if the crisis from which they exploded had been better managed. The war in 1914 need never have happened. By contrast, the dangerous confrontation in Cuba in 1962 was successfully resolved without fighting.

THE POWER AND MOTIVATION OF NATIONAL LEADERS

However complex and deep-rooted the causes of war and lesser conflicts may be, they are actually started by the decisions of one or more national leaders who are in a position to carry people with them. The art of predicting and handling crisis situations lies in predicting the motivation and behaviour of these leaders.

The primary motivation of any leader is to remain in power. Otherwise he cannot achieve his second aim, which is to advance what he perceives to be the interests of his nation or group.[1] So, predicting what he thinks will best keep him personally in power is a good starting-point.

If he is a military dictator or the ruler of a one-party state, whether or not he maintains a fraudulent façade of democracy and freedom of the press, his primary concern will be to maintain the submission of his henchmen who, collectively, could oust him from power. The art of tyranny lies in giving these henchmen privileges and rewards for loyalty which they do not wish to lose, and convincing them that they will hold their own positions only if he keeps his; the more ruthless the tyranny, the easier this is, because the henchmen may also have a guilty fear of what the people might do to them if their frustration were unleashed. The desperate resistance of some of the secret police in Romania in 1989, up to and even after President Ceauçescu's death, gave an example of this. In a tyranny, retention of power is made easier because even those in humble positions know that they are engaged and fired at the whim of the leader or his hierarchy. Since this goes for editors of newspapers, radio and TV, they can be relied upon not to go further than the cosmetic criticism needed to give them credibility.

To retain power in a pluralist democracy, the leader's decisions will be influenced primarily by his judgement of whether it will gain or lose him votes in the short and long term – votes of the electorate for himself and his party, or votes within that party for him as leader. The factors affecting re-election may be complex, including the macroeconomy (the leader will have few options without national wealth) the microeconomy (the strongest influence on individual voters is how they judge the prospect of their personal prosperity), and the media (the joker in the pack;

they will take the line best calculated to attract readers and viewers amongst their target sections of the community).

But one factor is common to both dictators and elected leaders: there is nothing so certain for attracting popular support as arousing national or ethnic passions. This ensures that advancement of what he perceives to be the national interest comes close behind retention of personal power in the decision of both a dictator and an elected leader. And to make the decision he wants, he needs international power.

Power is best seen in terms of options: the option to do what he wants and not have to do what he does not want, and the option to induce his adversaries or rivals to do what suits him, and not to do what does not suit him.

Thomas Hobbes, in his seventeenth century *Leviathan*, described man's primary motivation as his quest for power, adding that a state's quest for power is a natural extension of this. Man in his natural state, where there is no rule of law, fights every other man for the safety and prosperity of himself and his family, like the non-gregarious animals. Nations, subject to no effective international law, fight or threaten to fight to get what they want.[2]

Machiavelli, in *The Prince*, warned that a ruler must not base his public actions on private morals, since his rivals will do no such thing. Hegel said that a state's highest duty is self-preservation. Hans Morgenthau considered that states pursue secondary aims, other than national survival, at their peril, and increase the risk of conflict by doing so, because the risk is greatest when states predict each other's behaviour wrongly. If they assume that self-preservation is their adversary's primary aim, their prediction of his behaviour is more likely to be right.[3]

THE FOUNDATIONS OF INTERNATIONAL POWER

What are the weapons that a statesman needs to exercise international power, that is, the power to realize his own chosen options and to control the options available to his adversaries – and to his allies? First, his nation must have sufficient economic and military strength to persuade others that they have more to gain from cooperation with him than from conflict. Second, he must be able to convince them that he will, or at least might, be prepared to use these powers. Kennedy's handling of the 1962 Missile Crisis in Cuba (see Chapter 8) provided a good example of this. Third, he must have the moral and political strength to convince his allies and adversaries that he will be able to carry enough of the world's governments with him, either to support his case or at least not to oppose it. Fourth, he must be perceived by them to be likely to be able to carry his own party and his own people with him throughout the course of action on which he embarks.

This internal strength may be gained from a mixture of voluntary support and coercive apparatus. Where he is democratically answerable to universal suffrage, foreigners' perception of his strength will depend on how they rate his chances of holding his power. In the case of the leader of a single party state, the record and credibility of state or party apparatus for enforcing compliance, including control of the media, will be paramount in judging his strength.

In 1990–92 the transition of the Soviet Union and Eastern Europe from Communist Party rule to democratic pluralism made long-term judgements of their internal stability very difficult. It was quite feasible that politicians and officials, frustrated by their inability to solve their country's problems, might revert to more authoritarian methods (whether labelled as 'left' or 'right'); and that their peoples, exasperated with the failure of democratic and market institutions to fulfil their expectations of rising prosperity, might welcome or at least accept their reversion. On the other hand, their former NATO enemies had a strong interest in assisting the survival of their pluralism, and were willing to go a long way in supporting the evolving governments in maintaining stability, especially in understanding the need for patience in resolving the problems of national minorities, both in the peripheral republics of the USSR and within almost all the East European states. This gave the new governments greater political strength (see Chapter 13).

IDEOLOGY, RELIGION AND POWER

Ideology, usually harnessed with personal ambitions for power and prosperity, has often been a major driving force behind the seizure of internal power and the international spread of that power. The commonest ideologies have been religious ones, joined only in the last two centuries by purely social ideologies such as the brotherhood of man and Communism. Prior to the emergence of Christianity (first century AD) and Islam (seventh century AD), ideology seems at first sight to have played only a small part, for example in the development of the Babylonian, Chinese, Indian, Persian, Macedonian and Roman Empires. It is possible that this impression may be a false one: religion may well have played more of a part in these ancient civilizations than history has recorded. In the last 1400 years, the Arab expansion before and during the Middle Ages, and the concurrent and rival expansion of the Holy Roman Empire, were motivated primarily by religion which was used, either sincerely or cynically, to encourage soldiers to die rather than fail to achieve their aims – the expectation of eternal bliss in a life after death being a paramount factor. It is not surprising that such soldiers prevailed. Even in a personal conflict between evenly matched or armed protagonists, if one is prepared to die rather than yield and the other is not, the first is likely to win.

Expectation of eternal life, however, has not been an invariable ingredient of greater readiness to die. Communism, offering no such promise, has often evoked just as much dedication and self-sacrifice;[4] so have national and racial pride.

Genuine religious or other ideological motivations have often played an honourable part in the initial pursuit of power, but have later been used quite cynically to rationalize the pursuit of national ambitious or commercial activities; also as a weapon for the exercise of that power by arousing or enforcing belief or at least compliance by the population – usually through fear of the consequences of non-compliance in this world or the next. This was commonplace in Europe from the time of its conversion to Christianity up till the seventeenth century, as well as in Stalin's USSR and Mao's China. While Khomeini may have remained genuine in his motives right up to his death in 1989, some of his henchmen were certainly quite cynical, and there have been many occasions to question the sincerity of Colonel Gadafi.

CRISIS MANAGEMENT

The term 'crisis management' came into general usage after the Cuban Missile Crisis in 1962. President Kennedy seemed to have handled a dangerous situation successfully without going to war, and the next few years saw a succession of analyses of how it was done and why it succeeded.

The purpose of crisis management is to resolve a dangerous confrontation without fighting, but with vital interests preserved. This usually involves leaving room for some flexibility. As Coral Bell puts it, the aim should be to 'write the peace treaties without first fighting the wars'.[5]

To negotiate successfully requires good intelligence of the adversary's capabilities and intentions including some indication of how he is likely to react to various scenarios. Kennedy had exceptionally good intelligence in 1962. This makes it easier to see the situation through the adversary's eyes, another vital ingredient. It was argued by President Eisenhower in 1959 that the more the adversaries knew about each other, the less the likelihood of war,[6] and he proposed the 'open skies' principle that high-flying spy-planes (and later satellites) should range freely over each other's territory. Cynics (including the Soviet government, which did not accept the idea) were aware that the USA had by far the best reconnaissance capabilities, but there was much strength in Eisenhower's proposal.

It is important to keep communications open – direct and indirect. There were none between the USA and China over Korea in 1950. They were good between the USA and the USSR over Cuba in 1962.

The standard indirect method of communication is by crude signals – commonly by mobilization and movement of troops and warships. There is usually an element of bluff and counter-bluff. If the signals are interpreted to indicate that one side wants 'peace at any price', the other is likely to grab what he wants. Hitler was willing to fight in 1936–39 and he was convinced that Chamberlain and Daladier were not, so Europe endured crisis after crisis until even the most dove-ish decided that it had to stop.

> Pale Ebenezer thought it wrong to fight
> But Roaring Bill who killed him thought it right.[7]

The US government signals were interpreted by Saddam Hussein in this way in 1990 so he felt it a sound risk to invade Kuwait (see Chapter 14).

However, the art of brinkmanship is dangerous. If a leader commits himself so far that he leaves no way out without humiliation, he may hope that his adversary will be scared off, but he may find he has provoked a war. Nasser did this in 1967 (see Chapter 9). Sometimes a leader may create a 'pseudo-crisis', as President Johnson did in 1964 over the incidents in the Tongking Gulf, to give himself a pretext for making a threat which he thought it would be useful to make.[8]

Coral Bell described this as a 'crisis slide' – when one of the adversaries sees no way out other than war.[9] If the two sides have an evident common interest in avoiding war, it will probably be avoided (as it was in Cuba in 1962); Coral Bell called this an 'adversary partnership'. But if a leader, however anxious to avoid war, perceives that climbing down will result in him being ousted from political power, he will probably convince himself that he should go on towards the brink.

Rigid plans constitute another danger. Military plans must always be subordinated to political control, and a vital capability for military chiefs is to understand the realities of politics. The most extreme case was the German Schlieffen Plan in 1914, which was perhaps the biggest single cause of that crisis becoming a world war and not just another Balkan conflict (see Chapter 4).

Crisis managers should be ready to use all methods of applying persuasion, not only diplomacy, warlike signals and war. They can use or threaten economic sanctions, refer to international law, bring in institutions such as the UN, and use intermediaries. And the credibility of a threat matters more than its actual potential strength or effect.[10]

After the Cuban Missile Crisis an American diplomat, Harlan Cleveland, wrote an excellent analysis of Kennedy's handling of the 1962 Cuban Missile Crisis,[11] in which he listed a number of recommendations, including: 'keep your objectives limited' and 'decide how far you would go'. These and his other principles are discussed in Chapter 8. He could well have added 'keep your options open' and 'leave your adversary a tolerable way out, so that he will not lose his job'.

On a broader canvas, Sir Norman Angell aroused much controversy before the start of the First World War by expounding the 'Interdependence Theory',[12] that is, that the European powers had become so economically interdependent that they would not be so stupid as to go to war with each other. He proved wrong, but he should have been right. They *were* unbelievably stupid. Nevertheless, his theory certainly influenced Adenauer, Monnet and Schumann in founding the European Coal and Steel Community (ECSC) leading to the European Economic Community (EEC) with that precise intention – to make France and Germany, enemies for centuries, so interdependent that neither could make war except in alliance with the other.

This is the most promising direction in which world leaders should be looking in the future.

Part II
Power in History

2 Historical Roots of International Conflict

CIVILIZATION AND HUMAN CONFLICT

The 'naked ape'[1] emerged from the jungle about 2 million years ago. Those of our ancestors who survived this move were the ones who learned to use their superior brains not only to combine with each other in hunting groups, which wolves and many other animals did, but also to throw missiles, which very few other species do. They later learned to fashion weapons to compete with the animals who ranged over the open plains, fleeter of foot and more powerful in tooth and claw. Humans who failed to master these cerebral arts either died of starvation or were caught and eaten by other carnivorous animals.

At the same time, indeed millions of years before them, the highly organized societies of ants and bees had already surpassed what were to be the highest of human civilizations in their efficiency and in their ultimate prospects of survival as a species. As disciplined societies they are most impressive. One has only to lay bare an ants' nest by unwittingly lifting, say, the paving stone that provides its roof, to reveal the top layer of something like the London Underground system, with other tunnels delving deeper from it. In the channels thus uncovered are several thousand ants and several thousand eggs. Suddenly exposed to the sunlight and the birds, every ant instinctively seizes an egg and drags it out of sight into the nearest surviving tunnel. After a few minutes of frenetic activity, there is not an egg to be seen, and very few ants. Yet they require no sergeant-major ants to organize this, and no police ants to arrest those who do not conform to the law; every ant knows what to do and does it.

Very occasionally, when a village community is faced with a sudden disaster, such as an aircraft crashing onto it (as at Lockerbie in Scotland in 1988), or a flood or an earthquake, it can galvanize human beings into similarly dedicated and spontaneous activity, but the ants and bees apply it to their routine tasks day after day.

Various human overlords have yearned to organize their people into similar efficiency – most recently the puritanical Marxists and Fascists, and some of the religious fundamentalists. But humans have independent brains and, perversely, will not conform as obediently as ants; so all these attempts have failed before they have gone a fraction of the way towards the perfection of the ant-hill society.

The peculiarly human form of civilization emerged from the discovery of agriculture, of the ability of the human to grow crops of his own choice and to rear domestic animals to provide food and clothing. This began about 10,000 years ago, and it at once introduced a new dimension (new to man, that is; the ants had had it for ages). Agriculture needed a secure base, in which the crops and stock could mature, protected from the marauders (humans and other animals) who would gladly steal the food without doing the work. So agriculture gave birth to villages, with provision for external and internal security. Village security required organization – and people to do the organizing. Human hunting groups – like wolf packs – had for thousands of years had their chiefs and many had also organized cooperative care and protection of their young. But the village needed more than that, if crops and domestic animals were to be secure, day and night, during the many months they needed to ripen or mature; secure not only against outside marauders but also against the greed of others within the village community, numbering hundreds rather than the handfuls in the hunting groups. So there was a common desire, not only for organization of security, but also for a rudimentary rule of law, and this required a chief and a hierarchy. Whether its authority was derived from majority support or from *force majeure*, this hierarchy was generally accepted by a consensus as better than having competing factions or having no organization at all.

The lives of these first villagers and the origins of collective human conflict are nowhere better illustrated than in the topographical pattern of the uplands of Kurdistan in south-eastern Turkey as seen from the air. The upper tributaries of the great Tigris and Euphrates, at this point, are generally dry water-courses carved through clefts in a barren plateau. On the edges of these clefts are little flat triangles of green where the rainwater settles during the brief periods of rainfall, forming shallow reservoirs from which it spills over into the ravines and along the rocky river bed. Only in these triangles does it sink in and settle for long enough for the soil to nurture rich vegetation and create humus; all around them there is, at best, the sparsest of grazing for the herds of a few nomadic desert tribesmen. These tribesmen, or hunting groups before them, will have been there for a million years, but the shape of the land and the green triangles for millions of years before that. With the discovery of agriculture (and there is evidence that this did occur first around the Tigris and the Euphrates), those fertile green triangles will have become the villages (as they still are) offering a vastly more comfortable lifestyle than that of the nomads who no doubt tried to invade and take them over. The survival of the villagers will have depended on their ability to present a coherent static defence to hold their highly prized land. These were probably the first recognizable battlefields, with organized bodies up to several hundred strong fighting at the perimeters on either side.

CITIES, STATES AND EMPIRES

Static defence begat walls, and the need for sufficient numbers to repel concentrated attacks begat bigger and bigger villages. Further down the rivers, in the great plains of what became Babylon, the green triangles gave way to large fertile fields, some with contrived irrigation, alongside easily navigable river highways. Here, walled villages developed collective and aggressive defences, no longer purely static but making forays to sweep the marauders also from their cultivated fields outside the walls.

When the largest villages became cities, their defences, their hierarchies and their organized armies became larger. Around their chiefs or kings, a rich and privileged elite emerged, able to enjoy better food, better clothing, better housing and greater security. Leisure, culture and stability would develop for these elites, and what became known as civilization. The earliest cities of this kind are believed to have been on the banks of these two rivers, probably dating from 5000 to 6000 years ago (4000 to 3000 BC). By 3100 BC, this culture had produced a pictorial script, and syllabic scripts on tablets of clay have been dated around 2500 BC. From the same period, the tombs of kings and queens have revealed that they enjoyed a luxurious and privileged lifestyle, wearing rich clothing, gold and jewellery, surrounded by incredibly beautiful artefacts. Each was served by as many as 50 or 100 personal servants and guards, whose loyalty was assured by a degree of luxury and security, which, though less than that of the king or queen, was still far above that of the citizens outside. Next down the scale were the inhabitants of the guarded agricultural villages, their security reinforced by the availability of the king's armies from the cities; and finally, with little comfort and precarious security, there were the nomads out beyond the cultivated lands.

In common with others through the ages, most of these people refused to accept the finality of death, preferring to believe in an afterlife to which they could take their cherished belongings; whether this belief was spontaneous, or fostered by the elite to maintain their authority and secure obedience, most civilized peoples have independently built temples in which to worship a superhuman deity to whom they believed they owed both present and future blessings.

Similar developments since 2500 BC resulted in other civilizations in south and east Asia, later spreading into Europe, Africa and the Americas. These civilizations appear to have originally developed independently, though some of their remarkable similarities suggest that migration and then trade promoted the exchange of ideas. Cities, with their dependent hinterlands, joined forces into states for trade and security, the stronger states dominating the weaker, culminating in the mighty empires of Persia, India and China, then of Greece and Rome, and on into the Holy Roman, Islamic and Mongol Empires. Almost every development was accompanied by armed conflict, genocide and enslavement, up to the most horrific slaughter of all in the twentieth century.

Civilization came to Europe from two quarters, south-west Asia and Crete (one of those which had developed its own civilization) from about 2500 BC onwards, initially into Greece, which by 750 BC was itself expanding into Italy and back into south-west Asia. In 334 BC, Alexander began his astounding advance to take over almost all the Persian Empire as far as India. In historical terms, the Greek Empire was shortlived, and Greece itself was part of the Roman Empire by 146 BC. The Roman Empire, extending to the whole of western Europe, north Africa and south-west Asia beyond the Tigris and Euphrates, was in turn overwhelmed by south and east Asian invaders in the fifth and sixth centuries. But the 'barbarians' were attracted not only by the prospects of loot, but also by the desire to absorb and emulate Roman civilization. The powerful force of Christianity, which had by then permeated the Roman Empire, also survived, and it was the Graeco-Roman civilization that developed into the European civilizations which spread over the world, not only in political control and influence, but also through its economic philosophies, which, to this day, form the foundation of almost all the most powerful states in the world. The Spanish, Portuguese, Dutch, British and French Empires spread their control to a quarter of the world. Though they all came and went within 500 years, their philosophy remained and continued to spread.

A rival European philosophy – Marxism – and the Russian Empire it took over, was the shortest lived of all. In future, the challenge to democracy and market economics may well come from the revival of Islam, which had grown through the seventh to the nineteenth centuries, and has been revived by oil wealth. It is more likely, however, that the burgeoning capitalist states of east Asia, led by Japan with a fast industrializing China, will dominate the world in the twenty-first century. The history of the world, and especially that of the bloodstained twentieth century, suggests that to accommodate such changes without armed conflict will require a system of international relations and feats of crisis management which have thus far never been achieved.

THE GROWTH OF EUROPEAN POWER

The modern system of international relations has developed over the eighteenth, nineteenth and twentieth centuries in the course of attempts – almost invariably fruitless – to contain the rivalries between the increasingly rich and powerful European countries. Their phenomenal growth stemmed from a number of causes: population growth arising from better food, hygiene and medicine; maritime exploration, trade and settlement in the New World; an agricultural and mineral revolution leading to the industrial revolution starting in Britain in 1760; further acceleration of population growth; and the second phase of colonial expansion into what has now become the Third World, spurred by political and economic ambitions and missionary zeal. European power reached its peak at the end of the nineteenth century,[2] whereupon the rival European powers set about tearing each other apart in what were called world wars but began as self-destructive intramural European wars. Attempts to avert this in the nineteenth-century balance of power system and the League of Nations in the 1920s and 1930s failed. The United Nations from 1945 to 1989 played less part in averting a third world war than the 'balance of terror' provided by nuclear weapons, but it is too early to say whether the collapse of this balance and the apparent coalescence of the United Nations in 1990 will bring a more peaceful world or a growth in the small but often bloody local and regional conflicts which plagued the second half of the twentieth century. The decisive turning back of Iraq's invasion of Kuwait in 1991 perhaps gives a glimmer of hope that, if the United Nations can develop a united will to contain aggression, there may be fewer wars in the twenty-first century than in the twentieth. But its failure to stem the massive loss of life and human disruption in the small and localized conflicts arising from the disintegration of Yugoslavia and civil wars in Africa is deeply discouraging.

The expansion of European power in the nineteenth century which sowed the seeds of its disastrous self-destruction in the twentieth and the consequent growth of US and Japanese power was largely generated by four driving forces: industrialization, imperialism, nationalism and radicalism. All of these were spurred on, or in some cases used, by the desire for international power in terms of options described in Chapter 1 (pp. 5–6).

INDUSTRIALIZATION

Industrialization had been developing slowly since the dawn of civilization, gradually gathering momentum, but it has burgeoned explosively in the past 250 years. The exponential growth began in Britain and was soon pursued by Germany and other European powers, followed by the USA (largely primed by capital generated in Britain), by Japan and, belatedly, by tsarist Russia. It has lurched forward in cycles of booms and slumps, with very roughly 50 years between peaks, though there were lesser waves of growth and recession superimposed on the bigger waves of the cycles. The peaks can be associated with five recognizable technological phases: mechanized factory production, water and steam instead of muscle power, burgeoning to meet the military and economic demands of the wars against Napoleon (1790s and early 1800s); then the railway boom (1850–75); then the chemical and electrical boom, led by Germany (early 1900s); then air transport, energy and electronic communications (1950s and 1960s); and currently microelectronics, especially robotics and information technology (probably peaking around 1995–2000). After each boom came a slump (1820s, 1860s, 1920–30, 1970 to mid-1980s) when rising expectations caused wages and salaries to outstrip productivity. Each slump spurred technological research to find new ways to increase productivity, leading to the next boom.[3]

Still in projection of Thomas Hobbes's motivation of man (p. 5) these fluctuating industrial expansions were manifestly generated by a desire for power in terms of options at every level; at working level by industrialists and trade unions; and at national level by political leaders seeking internal power and international options.

IMPERIALISM AND NATIONALISM

British imperialism after 1600 was generated by the urgent need for trade by an island already populated by many more people than it could feed, creating a requirement for a network of ports and naval bases; also by pressure for emigration by frustrated people who saw a better chance of making their fortunes overseas. The migratory pressure grew as the industrial revolution gained momentum, not so much amongst the new unskilled workers in the factories, but amongst skilled craftsmen who saw their prosperity, job satisfaction and prospects for advancement being eroded by the machines. So it was from the more able and ambitious artisans that most of the migrants to the new empires came, notably the British, the Dutch and the French.

This ensured that the long-standing rivalry between Britain and France continued. Following their prolonged wars through the Middle Ages and the Tudor period, their competition continued through the seventeenth and eighteenth centuries in their first attempts at empires in North America and India, and then through the nineteenth century in the Middle East and Africa. Nationalism, with its popular manifestations of chauvinism and jingoism, was rife.

At the same time another form of nationalism was burgeoning in Europe, amongst fragmented peoples with a common culture: the 22 German states and the mass of Italian principalities largely dominated by the Austro-Hungarian Empire. This surge of nationalism created two new united countries in the second half of the nineteenth century, both of which developed ambitions that were to be a major cause of the First and Second World Wars in the first half of the twentieth century.

REVOLUTION, SOCIALISM AND DEMOCRACY

Running in tandem with these trends was a tide of radicalism in the industrializing countries of Europe. This first took shape in the French Revolution of 1789, and gained strength through the 'Year of Revolutions' in 1848 and an attempted revolution in Paris in 1871. It reached its climax in the Russian Revolution of 1917, whose repercussions proved to be the dominant cause of international conflict for the next 70 years.

Alexis de Tocqueville, in his classic analysis of the French Revolution,[4] points out that revolutions begin, not when the *ancien régime* is at its most repressive, but when, concerned about economic failure and social dissent, it starts to make reforms. This raises a real hope among the dissenters that the ruling elite is no longer invincible, and that they can take risks to overturn it. The conservatives then become alarmed and, if the government fails to take repressive action, they may take the law into their own hands. Public confidence in the goverment declines; so too does the confidence of the government in itself. The police and other public officials begin to doubt whether they will be supported if they take decisive action; as law and order collapses, the police and soldiers get worried about what will happen to them if the mob prevails, and try to placate them by pulling their punches. This leads to what the Russian revolutionary, Tkachev, called a public sense of impunity – so they take bigger chances still.

Starting from de Tocqueville's premise, Crane Brinton analysed what happens after the *ancien régime* is overthrown.[5] To achieve this against the armed power of the state, the poorly armed revolutionaries of all complexions, moderate and extreme, have to cooperate. Because most of the public fear the insecurity that would follow extreme change, it is usually the moderates who are carried to power (e.g. Mirabeau in France, Kerensky in Russia) but they try to placate the extremists by giving them a share. The moderates are, however, committed to dismantling the tools of repression. The extremists (the Jacobins in France, the Bolskeviks in Russia) take advantage of this to oust the moderates. They, however, then find that they cannot carry their people with them so they introduce the third phase – terror (Robespierre in France, Stalin in Russia). This eventually sickens the people so there is a conservative reaction in response to a public yearning for order and security. (The Thermidorean Reaction was followed by Napoleon's dictatorship in France.) There was a variant in Russia with Stalin purging 19 million of his own people to establish his power, thereafter himself becoming the most feared right-wing dictator of modern times.[6]

True to form, the French Revolution started as a middle-class revolution, which survived three years before it was ousted by the Jacobins who, a year later, calculatedly and avowedly ruled by Terror (1793–4). The conservative reaction that ousted the Jacobins soon led to a populist dictatorship by Napoleon, initially as First Consul (1799) and then as Emperor (1804–14). He conquered most of Europe before he overreached himself. After several more lurches, the bourgeois revolution was consolidated in 1830 (41 years from 1789) under a constitutional monarchy. This in turn became a republic in 1848 and – once again – a dictatorship under Napoleon III (massively endorsed by a plebiscite in 1852), which ended ignominiously in the Franco–Prussian War in 1870–71. Since then, after the failure of the brief and bloody attempt to set up a Commune in Paris, France has remained a parliamentary democracy.

The British Parliament and middle classes pre-empted revolution by evolutionary political and industrial change. In 1832 the electorate was widened (though still with a property qualification) and the right of workers to organize and legally exert collective power followed gradually. Universal male suffrage was achieved in 1884, with virtually no bloodshed, in contrast to France. Even then, due mainly to middle-class economic control both of employment opportunities and of the emerging popular press, much of the 'power of the people' was still illusory.

The idea of universal popular control of both political and economic power had developed in the early part of the nineteenth century in two separate streams – the evolutionary and the revolutionary. A British mill-owner, Robert Owen, pioneered the evolutionary stream, by turning his mill into a (limited) workers' cooperative in Lanark in 1808, and he also later introduced trade unions, initially in the form of the London Corresponding Society. It is easy to sneer at him as a 'paternalist' but he gave more genuine rights and benefits to his workforce than any other employer of his day; even if some of his ideas turned sour, they probably launched more of the significant changes in workers' rights in the nineteenth century than any of the radical theorists.

At the same time as Owen was making his early experiments in practical socialism and workers' power, two French philosophers, the Comte de Saint-Simon (1760–1825) and Charles Fourier (1772–1837), were developing socialist theories: Saint-Simon expounded socialism as a religion, and Fourier commended the organization of communal associations in place of the wastefulness of competitive capitalism. In the same period the German philosopher, G. W. F. Hegel (1770–1831) was developing his analysis of the progress of human thought in the form of a dialectic in which a thesis creates an antithesis which synthesizes into a new thesis, as a continuing process. Hegel was a fascist rather than a socialist, believing (like Robespierre and Stalin) in the absolute right of the state to exercise power, but Hegel's dialectic was the theory whereby Karl Marx analysed the progress of tribalism to feudalism to capitalism to socialism to communism.

It was, of course, Karl Marx, who, with Frederick Engels, launched the 'revolutionary' stream of socialism in the 1840s. There was a perplexing element of (perhaps unconscious) hypocrisy in both. Engels was a very rich and successful capitalist running the English subsidiary of his father's Rhineland-based cotton-exporting firm; then, after he sold it, he lived the life of a prosperous Victorian gentleman on the interest of the capital he had acquired. In his spare time he wrote and campaigned, advocating a Communist revolution and arguing that England, as the most developed industrial country, was its most promising venue. Like many prosperous revolutionaries, he may have pursued this with the inner confidence that it was in fact unlikely to happen in time to affect his own comfortable lifestyle. In 1845 he published *The Condition of the Working Class in England in 1844* and, when Marx was exiled from German to England, Engels financed Marx's research and joined him in writing the *Communist Manifesto* (1848).

Marx could be described as 'a brilliant prophet of the past'. He analysed the social and economic march of history from nomadic hunting groups through agricultural settlements to city states and nation states; then to feudalism, in which the extension of ownership of agricultural land created a strong and stable society of kings, barons, squires, tenants and landless peasants with, at the bottom of the pile, slaves, who were bought and sold as property, along with their children. The growth of trade and empires not only enriched the landowners but also developed (at a growing rate from the sixteenth century) a middle class, which burgeoned with industrialization from the late eighteenth century. It was this class – the bourgeoisie – which created the capitalist revolution that eroded the power of the feudal aristocracy, especially in Britain and France and later in the rest of Europe.

Hereafter Marx's predictions proved increasingly wrong. The revolution of the new industrial proletariat to oust the capitalists and the birth of the socialist state did not occur where he had forecast – in Britain or Germany. Indeed, Engels remarked ruefully in 1874 that the most revolutionary body in Europe in the past 30 years had been the British House of Commons. The nearest approach to Marx's revolution occurred where he had least expected it – in Russia in 1917; even here it was a travesty which must have made him turn in his grave. The 'public ownership of the means of production, distribution and exchange' proved to be just as illusory in the USSR as in the European democracies, for the ownership was by a state authority controlled by a privileged party elite (Lenin's 'vanguard of the revolution'). This was much more rigid and powerful than the socio-economic elites who controlled Western parliaments and industries, where the workers defied Marx's prediction, and did not get poorer, but richer. Moreover, nowhere did the socialist state wither and make way for Marx's ideal Communist society. On the contrary, within 10 years, the 1917 Revolution had led in various stages to totalitarian Fascism of which, with hindsight, Lenin's successor, Josef Stalin, was the most ruthless exponent of all. The brief alliance of these totalitarian states (Germany, Italy and the Soviet Union) in 1939 precipitated the Second World War from which only the USSR – by being thrown against her will into the democratic alliance – emerged intact, and her influence, totalitarian in the name of Marx, spread to Eastern Europe by conquest, to China and to many ex-colonies, anxious to find an alternative to reliance on their former masters. Finally Soviet Communism blew itself out in the most astounding of all the years of revolution in history, 1989. The Berlin Wall came down almost to the day on the Soviet Union's 72nd birthday – roughly the biblical lifespan of one man.

The strains between rival industrial states, and later between democratic and totalitarian, brought about the two bloodiest wars in history, resulting in the loss of at least 40 million European lives. The more immediate circumstances of the outbreak of these wars, and the political mistakes that caused them, will be examined later in this book. Historically, however, they will be seen as two disastrous European civil wars. At the turn of the century, 'the mighty continent' of Europe, comprising by then 10 per cent of the world's population, was responsible for well over half its annual wealth creation.[7] Consequently its people enjoyed a standard of living vastly higher than anywhere else in the world except the settler states formed in the previous two centuries on the European model – the USA, Canada, Australia, New Zealand and South Africa. In just 31 years (1914–45) Europe had squandered its means of wealth creation and millions of its most able people in inter-European slaughter on the battlefields, and in genocide of millions more inside Germany and Stalin's Soviet Union. These appalling conflicts left two so-called superpowers but one, the USA, was dominant for the second half of the twentieth century. Though it is conceivable that a United Europe (paradoxically German-led) might emerge again to dominate the world in the twenty-first century, it is far more likely that the centre of gravity will shift to Japan and China.

Europe's attempts to avoid its own self-destruction in the nineteenth century, by means of a balance of power, and its disastrous failure to do so in 1914 and 1939, are the subject of the next three chapters.

3 The Balance of Power

THE CONGRESS OF VIENNA

The French Revolution and the consequent 23 years of the Napoleonic Wars totally transformed the attitude of European countries towards international security. Only the rise of Stalin and Hitler (see Chapter 5) has been comparable in its effects. Both times, as the dust settled, there was a sigh of relief and a cry of 'never again'; both prompted an anxious search for collective security.

At the Congress of Vienna, in 1814, the purpose was to prevent not only invasion but also revolution. The biggest shudder amongst France's neighbours came when the French Revolutionary government had launched its armies in 1792 with the declared intention of overthrowing all European monarchies and the societies over which they reigned. The arrest of King Louis XVI while attempting to escape in 1791, his execution in 1793 and the Terror in 1793–94 left them in no doubt of the fate that awaited those who held the power if they failed to defend themselves. When the 26-year-old General Napoleon Bonaparte overran Austria's southern dominions in 1796, routing her professional armies with what they saw as a band of scallywags incited by the promise of loot in the cities they overran, the alarm increased. And when Napoleon became Emperor in 1804, still proclaiming populist government, and overran Europe from Madrid to Moscow, his domination seemed to be complete; but he had overreached himself. The relief of the European governments at his defeat and abdication in 1814 was tempered by the stark recollection of the spectrum of threats against which they would still have to guard themselves. Their system of collective security kept the peace (apart from Napoleon's 100–day attempt at a resurgence in 1815) for 40 years until 1854; in fact, it prevented anything approaching the scale of the Napoleonic Wars for 100 years, until 1914.

The Congress of Vienna formed a Quadripartite Alliance of the kingdoms of Austria, Britain, Prussia and Russia (see Table 3.1). This was widened in 1818 by the inclusion of France under her

Table 3.1 Outline chronology, 1814–1914

1814	Congress of Vienna: Austria, Britain, Prussia, Russia form Alliance
1818	Congress of Vienna: Alliance joined by France
1820–30	Alliance intervenes in liberal revolutionary attempts all over Europe Austria generally favoured repression Britain tried to encourage constitutional monarchies
1848	Liberal revolutionary attempts in Austria, France and Prussia Most ended with conservative reaction
1854–5	Crimean War: Britain, France and Turkey against Russia
1859	France and Sardinia drove Austria out of Lombardy
1859–61	Unification of Italy
1864	Bismarck's first war, against Denmark
1866	Austro–Prussian War, New North German Confederation excludes Austria
1870–71	Franco–Prussian War, German unification, Paris Commune crushed
1878	Congress of Berlin meets to restrain Russia after victory over Turkey
1879	Austro-German Alliance
1884	Berlin Conference on Colonies in Africa
1890	Kaiser Wilhelm II dismisses Bismarck
1894	Franco–Russian Alliance
1898	Fashoda Incident (Britain and France) in Sudan
1898	German naval expansion seen as threat to British navy
1902	Anglo–Japanese Naval Alliance
1904–5	Russo–Japanese War
1904	Entente Cordiale (to avert Anglo–French colonial disputes)
1905	Liberal revolution leads to Parliament in Russia
1908	Austria annexes Bosnia
1912–13	First and Second Balkan Wars
1914	Outbreak of First World War

restored Bourbon monarchy. In fact, this Alliance, unlike most, was no longer focused on a common enemy as such, but rather on the concept that a revolutionary explosion and the disruption and suffering which followed from it was the common enemy. This concern was especially apparent in the attitudes of Austria and

Russia, but an attempt to commit the Alliance to joint action against international revolutions was frustrated by the British Foreign Secretary, Castlereagh, who was well aware of his Parliament's reluctance to allow a precedent of successful international interference in any country's domestic affairs.

The first test of this came in 1820, when a liberal revolt in Madrid forced the King of Spain to accept a new Constitution and Castlereagh strongly opposed intervention. The revolt spread to Portugal and Naples.[1] At this, Austria, Prussia and Russia signed the Troppau Protocol, denying that any people had the right to overthrow their rulers. Metternich, the Austrian Chancellor, in face of British protests, sent in troops to suppress the rebellions in Piedmont and Naples. In 1822 the Congress of Vienna was summoned again to discuss problems arising from the Greek rebellion against Turkish rule in 1821, but the revolt in Spain was spreading and, despite eloquent objections from Canning (who had succeeded Castlereagh at the Foreign Office) the other powers urged France to send troops into Spain in 1823 and the rebellion was crushed.

Castlereagh and Canning, though very different in style, were both convinced that constitutional government must come to the European monarchies (as it already had, 150 years earlier, to Britain) and that its ruthless suppression would be likely to lead to another explosion like the French Revolution.

Britain's foreign policy throughout the nineteenth century was to maintain a Balance of Power, so that no single one of the five Great Powers, and no alliance amongst them, could dictate the affairs of Europe at the expense of the others.

Until 1814–15, the threat had come from France. In the 1820s, Britain's concern was at the repressive power (and attitude) of Austria, made especially dangerous if she carried Prussia, Russia and France with her – and now also the restored monarchy in Spain. Canning's next trial of strength came in 1823–25, when the other four powers were anxious to restore Spanish sovereignty to the South American colonies which had declared their independence. Canning joined forces with President Monroe of the USA, who sent a 'message to Congress' in 1823 (thereafter known as the Monroe Doctrine) warning Europe not to interfere. Britain also cooperated with Russia and France in giving military assistance to the establishment of Greek independence from Turkey in 1827–28, much to the chagrin of Metternich.

THE REVOLUTIONS OF 1848

Despite the efforts of Metternich, the internal pressures for liberal and populist revolutions built up all over Europe. Only in Britain were they effectively contained, by evolutionary changes towards widening both industrial and political democracy, for example the development of trade unions, the legalizing of collective action by workers against employers in 1824, and the Reform Bill of 1832 which enfranchised large numbers of petty bourgeois householders and smallholders.[2] Demands for universal suffrage (which did not come even for males until 1884) did lead to some rioting but even in the worst case ('Peterloo' 1819) no more than eleven were killed. This number would have been regarded as trivial in continental Europe, where deaths in civil disturbance were more commonly measured in thousands or tens of thousands. The outrage it caused in Britain was significant in itself. The Peterloo eleven were killed by young country-based equestrian volunteers serving in the Yeomanry whose overreaction brought widespread condemnation and accelerated rather than delayed the process of change.[3]

Following Peterloo, the London Metropolitan Police (1829), and later other police forces,[4] were formed and trained to handle disturbances without the use of weapons. In 1848, with Europe ablaze with revolutions, a Chartist march on Parliament was controlled by a massive public response to the Metropolitan Police Commissioner's appeal for volunteer Special Constables, who outnumbered the demonstrators by six to one. The march was blocked without violence south of the River Thames and two spokesmen were heavily escorted across the bridge to deliver their petition.[5]

Elsewhere in Europe, however, revolutionary activity was not so peaceful. Austria remained dominant both in her own Empire and over most of the German and Italian states, and deterred them from accepting liberal constitutions. A revolution in Poland was successfully sealed off by Austrian and German troops in 1830 and other attempts in Italy were repressed. Improvements in medicine and hygiene, however, were causing a rapid rise in population. In the Austrian dominions, for example, the population rose by 30 per cent in the first half of the nineteenth century.[6] Unrest grew in urban areas amongst the frustrated middle class, intellectuals (especially students) and former peasants whose desperate migration into the cities in search of food and work merely increased their hardship.

One of the leading spirits in harnessing this discontent was Guiseppe Manzini, whose *Risorgimento* and Young Italy movements grew rapidly in the 1830s. His followers struck the first blow at Palermo in January 1848 and by the end of the month autonomy had been granted to Naples and Sicily. This spread to Piedmont, Tuscany and Rome in February, and the Austrian puppet rulers were driven from Parma and Madeira in March when the King of Piedmont also successfully prevented Austrian intervention in Milan and Venice.[7]

In the same months, in Vienna itself, the government was forced to approve the election of an Assembly (which, as in France, the liberal middle class managed to dominate at the expense of more revolutionary members). Hungary obtained self-government. Metternich resigned.

Also in March, King Friedrich Wilhelm of Prussia was forced to concede a liberal Constitution, and the movement towards a united Germany gained momentum. The newly elected governments in Berlin, Vienna and other German capitals set up a German National Parliament in Frankfurt, elected by universal male suffrage. This met in Frankfurt in May, but in the event proved a disappointment. Torn by powerful and conflicting Protestant and Catholic groups, and by local patriotism, it was unable to make or carry out laws which national governments would accept[8] (rather as the European Parliament found in the 1970s and 1980s).

By the end of 1848, the revolutions had largely petered out and the reaction set in; the King of Prussia dissolved the new Constitution in December and banned public meetings. In Austria, a Czech rising was put down in June and in December the Emperor abdicated in favour of a young nephew, Franz-Joseph, who appointed a conservative chief minister.[9] The Hungarian rebellion continued but was crushed in August 1849 by Russian armies which had come to the aid of the Austrian government. By September 1849 the Frankfurt Parliament had collapsed, rejected by all its national governments. The European revolution had ended in a complete restoration of the old order.

Russia (politically and militarily) and Britain (politically and financially) had opposed the revolutions. So too had France –

though she herself went through perhaps the greatest turmoil of all between 1814 and 1852.

FOUR MORE FRENCH REVOLUTIONS

On his restoration in 1814, King Louis XVIII had granted a liberal Constitution, wisely preserving what was best from Napoleon's efficient administration. In 1824, a strongly conservative Assembly rejected the Constitution, and supported a palace *coup d'état* by Louis's brother Charles, Count of Artois. Crowned as King Charles X, he attempted to reverse all the constitutional developments emanating from the original revolution which had established the power of an elected Assembly in 1789; he reimposed total censorship of the press and reduced the electorate to a mere 25,000 of the richest people in France. This led inevitably to a middle-class reaction in which Adolphe Thiers – who was to play a leading part in French politics over the next half century – was a leading figure. Rioting became out of control and Charles X abdicated in 1830.

By the skin of their teeth, the middle-class politicians managed to avert the disaster of another Jacobin seizure of power with the presumed risk of another Terror, and secured the support of the assembly for their candidate as a constitutional monarch – Louis Philippe, Duke of Orleans, descended from a younger brother of Louis XVI. Louis-Philippe's 'bourgeois monarchy', however, led to a growth of corruption amongst politicians and officials, and of an insistent demand for a republic with universal suffrage. Once again, the government lost control of the streets. Louis-Philippe abdicated in February 1848 and a government was formed by a coalition of liberals and moderate socialists drawn from the old Assembly. They called an election for a new Republican government based on universal suffrage, increasing the electorate at a stroke from 250,000 to 9 million. As so often after a period of turmoil and insecurity, the electorate returned a conservative Assembly.[10] Of its 800 members, most were moderate royalists and liberal republicans, the Socialists getting only 100 seats. The Socialist revolutionaries reacted violently on the streets in an attempt to reverse the verdict of the election, and this was suppressed with the loss of 16,000 killed and wounded. This led to a strengthening of the conservative reaction amongst a thoroughly alarmed population, and the government proposed a new Constitution with a powerful President elected by popular vote. Napoleon's nephew, Louis Napoleon Bonaparte, stood as a 'guardian of order' and was elected with nearly 75 per cent of the 7.5 million votes cast.[11]

His majority consisted largely of small independent farmers who made up most of the French electorate,[12] feared the seizure of their lands in a socialist revolution, and distrusted the intellectual politicians in Paris, whether liberal or socialist. The name of Bonaparte was an irresistible draw and further disorders merely increased Louis Napoleon's popular support. In 1852 he introduced a new Constitution under military law and assumed the title of the Emperor Napoleon III, endorsed by a massive majority in a plebiscite. For the time being, the French people had had enough of democracy, and rallied to a new dictator.

CAVOUR, BISMARCK AND NAPOLEON III

In the second half of the nineteenth century and through to 1914, the five major powers in Europe redirected their main focus from revolution (which seemed to have largely blown itself out) to collective security to prevent any one power dominating the continent. This had, in fact, always been Britain's main concern. Failure to operate effective alliances had allowed Napoleon I to overrun most of Europe by 1812. Who could tell where the new Emperor might lead the French? Both the Austrians and the Russians – and sometimes also the Prussians – had used their armies outside their own borders, albeit in the name of counter-revolution, but they might next time use them to extend their own power. They had sometimes joined forces to produce a strength which Britain did not like to see.

Britain's self-imposed task of maintaining the Balance of Power in Europe was carried out by throwing her weight against any combination of powers which seemed to be getting dangerous. She had only a small army (in any case dispersed on imperial policing) so her weight was economic, industrial and maritime. Since the Battle of Trafalgar in 1805, Britain's navy had been supreme on the oceans of the world, and this supremacy grew throughout the century. Britain developed her maritime power – mercantile as well as naval – to outstrip France and other colonial powers in extending her overseas naval and trading bases.

The first manifestation of this came only six years after the suppression of the European revolution in 1848, when France and Britain joined forces in the Crimean War of 1854–55 in order to check what they saw as an unhealthy extension of Russian power at the expense of Turkey. Despite many blunders it was, in the end, ability to launch and maintain an army by sea that prevailed. (Further attempts to contain Russian expansion were to continue throughout the century culminating in decisive victory of another emerging maritime power in 1904–5 – Japan – using a navy largely equipped and trained by the British.)[13]

At the same time, there was a realization that the movement towards the unification of the Germans and of the Italians was unstoppable and could lead to the emergence of at least one unhealthily powerful actor in Europe: certainly Germany, and perhaps Italy as well. Moreover, centuries of European conflicts and treaties had left large numbers of dissenting ethnic minorities on the wrong side of the frontiers, notably of Austria, Russia and Turkey – always creating a danger of aggression on behalf of 'our brothers being persecuted across the border'.

The unification of Italy under King Victor Emmanuel of Piedmont was achieved for the most part in 1861 (see Map 3A). The process began in 1858 with a cynical deal between Piedmont's Prime Minister Cavour and Napoleon III. Cavour engineered a brief war with the Austrians, to drive them out of Lombardy in 1859, which Napoleon III agreed to join in exchange for the cession of Nice and Savoy from Piedmont to France. Napoleon enraged Cavour by making a secret deal to leave Austria in possession of Venetia, but Parma, Tuscany and Modena all voted overwhelmingly to join Piedmont in March 1860. Meanwhile, Garibaldi's rising in Sicily and his conquest of Naples in September 1860 alarmed both Cavour and Napoleon, who again cooperated in allowing Piedmontese armies to move into the Papal states (garrisoned mainly by French troops) and into Naples, upon which Garibaldi handed over his conquests to the new Kingdom of Italy. Italy joined the Austro–Prussian War in 1866 to secure Venetia, and France withdrew its troops from the Roman Republic in 1870 to allow the King to rule the whole of Italy and move his capital to Rome.[14]

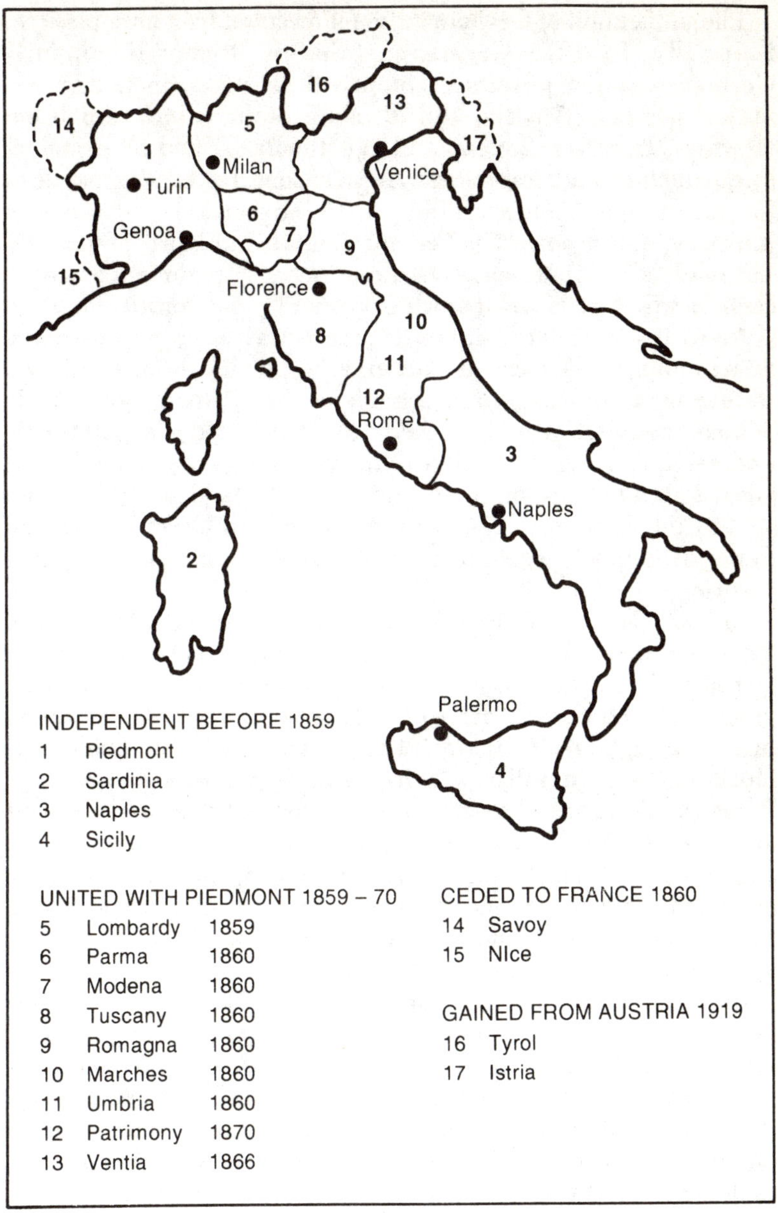

Map 3A Unification of Italy 1859–70 (plus 1919)

The unification of Germany also followed a tortuous course (see Map 3B). In 1815 Germany – that is, the predominantly German-speaking peoples – comprised 39 states, including two major powers (Austria and Prussia), four minor kingdoms (Bavaria, Hanover, Saxony and Württemberg) and 33 principalities, duchies and free cities. At the Congress of Vienna, they formed a loose confederation, with no central executive or judiciary, and a powerless Federal Diet at Frankfurt, not elected but made up of representatives nominated by the member states, each of which retained its own sovereignty and constitution.[15]

As with the Italians, however, there was a strong emotional desire amongst the German-speaking peoples for the strength and stature conferred by unity, though neither Austria nor Prussia wished to unite with the other (and never did, except briefly under Hitler). Just as Italian unity was built around Piedmont, German unity was built around Prussia. As described earlier (p. 29) the attempt in 1848 to form an elected German National Parliament quickly collapsed in the face of local and religious rivalries.

In 1862 Otto von Bismarck (until then Prussian Ambassador in Paris) became Prime Minister. Within nine years he had unified Germany in a series of short sharp wars which, since the German people suffered little from them, aroused powerful patriotism and pride throughout Germany. The first, in 1864 in Schleswig-Holstein, was in alliance with Austria against Denmark.[16] Prussia and Austria, however, quickly fell out over their spheres of influence. At this stage Bismarck showed the diplomatic skill and sense of timing which he was to display in every crisis; he exploited the fact that the other European countries expected an Austro-Prussian war and were planning to use it for their own advantage.

In October 1865 Bismarck met Napoleon III (whom of course he knew well from his time as Ambassador in Paris) in Biarritz, and gave some general promises of benefits to come if France remained neutral in the event of an Austro-Prussian war. Napoleon readily agreed, since he was sure that French security and influence would be increased if Prussia and Austria exhausted each other in a war. Bismarck then secured the support of Italy, with the promise that she would acquire Venetia from Austria. Bismarck then provoked a crisis by proposing the dissolution of the Confederation and the creation of a new German Constitu-

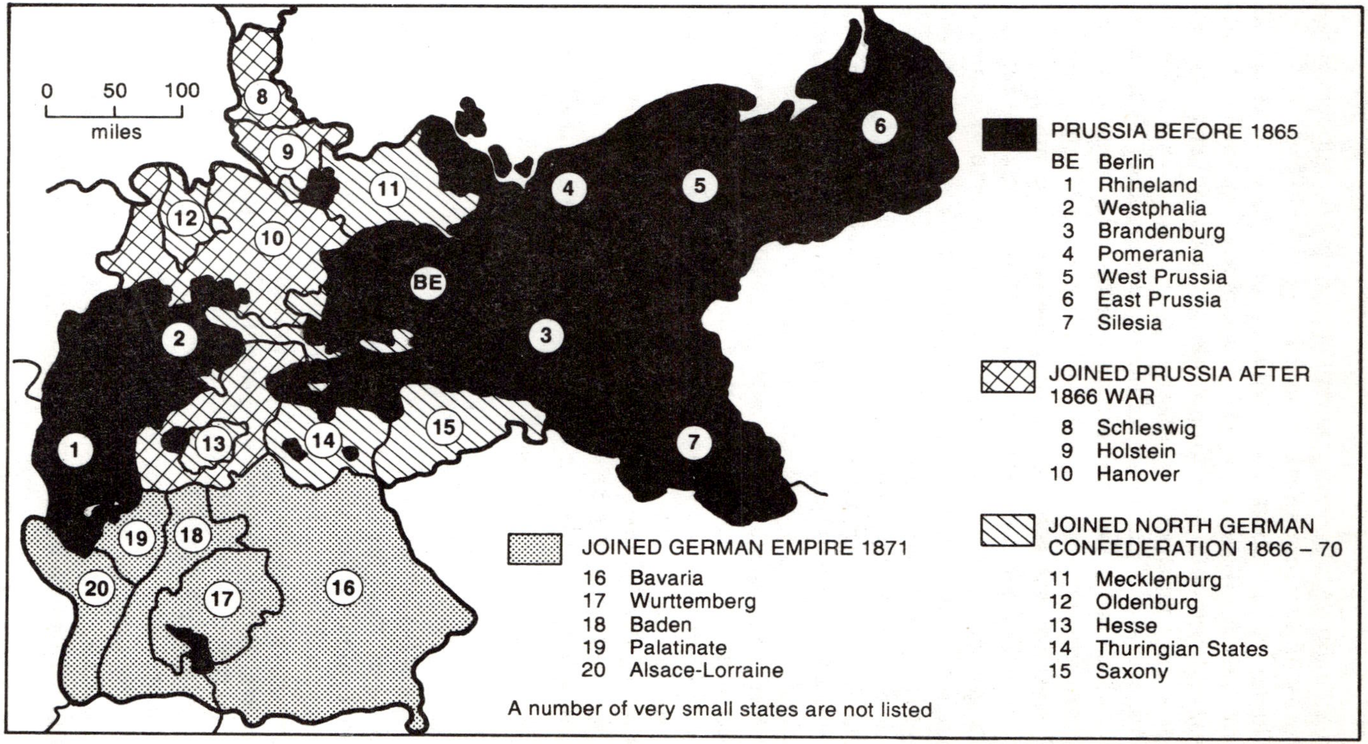

Map 3B Unification of Germany 1864–71

tion excluding Austria. Austria refused, gaining the support of the majority of the German states, and began to mobilize.[17]

The timing of mobilization played a crucial part.[18] Prussia had outstripped Austria in industrial development, especially of railways, and was thus able to mobilize and deploy her armies in three weeks compared with Austria's six. Austria was well aware of this, and also of the danger of the Italians invading Venetia, so she had to order full mobilization on both her northern and southern fronts.

Everything was going exactly as Bismarck had intended; he took no action for two weeks, to ensure that Austria was seen as the aggressor.[19] He was still able to mobilize in time to be ready when the Austrians were, and he ordered his army to move towards the Austrian frontier through Saxony, using the German Confederation's denunciation as his justification.

The Austrians declared war on 17 June 1866. The fighting was over in seven weeks, thanks to a decisive victory for the Prussians at Sadowa. Prussia was able to declare the Confederation dissolved and instead formed a North German Confederation[20] which excluded Austria, but gave more power to a Central Federal Council that Prussia was able to dominate, as the other 21 North German states were pygmies in comparison. The predominantly Catholic German states south of Frankfurt and the River Main, including Bavaria, remained separate, until they too were brought in by the Franco–Prussian War in 1870–71.

THE FRANCO–PRUSSIAN WAR

The spark that caused the war in 1870 would never cause a war today, but the story is worth telling because it illustrates the decisive influence of the leaders' personal perceptions of each other on whether a crisis will lead to war or not. This factor was to prove equally decisive in, for example, the First World War (Chapter 4), the 1962 Cuban Missile Crisis (Chapter 8), the Falklands War in 1982 (Chapter 12) and the invasion of Kuwait in 1990 (Chapter 14).

Bismarck was a strong believer in Prussia's constitutional monarchy, and he and King Wilhelm I had a good working relationship. The King was liberally minded and conciliatory, and Bismarck had often to apply persuasion when he wanted him to take a tougher line in his foreign policy. Bismarck was essentially conservative, but did carry out, in his 28 years as Prime Minister and Chancellor, some of the most liberal reforms in Europe, in fields such as industrial relations and welfare. He was therefore well able to carry a liberal Parliament with him. In his foreign policy, he also realized that he still had to live with his defeated enemies, and was generous in his peace terms. Also, after his first triumphant nine years in which he won three wars and united Germany, he realized that Germany would prosper best in a peaceful Europe. In his remaining 19 years from 1871 until his dismissal by the young Kaiser Wilhelm II in 1890, he went to great lengths to resolve conflicts and remove the seeds of war.

During 1862–71, however, he was driven by his mission to unite Germany, determined to be remembered for this in history, and to remain in power until this task was completed. To this end he was ruthless, shrewd and cunning, but at the same time practical, realistic and diplomatic. These qualities had all been apparent in his handling of the Austro–Prussian War in 1866 when he united the 22 North German states and destroyed the rival Austrian influence over them.

He realized that the way to complete the unification of Protestant North and Catholic South of Germany was to exploit the age-old antagonism to France to arouse German nationalism; this could be achieved only by proving his domination over Napoleon III, going at least to the brink of war, and probably having to fight and win it. To achieve this result (and to carry the King, Parliament and the public with him) he considered it essential for France to be seen as the aggressor. Knowing Napoleon's weaknesses and problems, he was confident that this could be done.[21]

Napoleon III was a very much weaker character. He had been put forward as a presidential candidate in 1848 by hard men of the Fascist-inclined Bonapartist Party; he had the Napoleonic name, he was able to rouse an audience and the hard men were confident that they could control him. France's victorious part in the Crimean War in 1854–55, and then in the liberation of Italy in 1859–60, established his prestige. So too did his colonial expansion in north and west Africa (1857–62). Nevertheless, he had judged wrongly in 1866 that the Austro–Prussian War would exhaust both countries; he was alarmed by Bismarck's rapid and spectacular victory and the subsequent unification of north

Germany under Prussian domination. Internally, France's economy was a mess, and he was under pressure from both sides – his Bonapartist henchmen and an increasingly liberal Assembly. He was also a sick man in 1870 (he was dead three years later). He knew that his army was poorly trained, organized and equipped compared with that of the Prussians, and viewed the prospect of war with some anxiety. Yet he knew that his own political survival depended on him being seen to stand up to the Prussians. He would be doomed unless he kept Germany divided. He hoped, no doubt, to humiliate them by intrigue, but knew well that brinkmanship would be inevitable and that war might well follow.

Bismarck, in anticipation of such a war, secured Russian agreement in 1868 to deploy troops on the Austrian frontier in the event of a Franco–Prussian war to deter Austria from interfering. He also secured British neutrality by revealing proof of French ambitions to expand into Belgium, and Italian neutrality by opening the prospect of them taking control of Rome when French troops were withdrawn to fight the Germans.[22]

The crisis that led to the war resulted from what initially seemed to be an innocuous event in March 1870. The Spanish government, having ousted their Queen in a revolution in 1868, decided that they would do better to have a monarch who was part of the extended family which provided nearly all Europe's interrelated kings and queens. They therefore offered the crown to Prince Leopold of Hohenzollern, a young member of the Catholic branch of the Prussian royal family. Leopold initially declined, but the offer was repeated at the end of June, and this time Leopold accepted, with Bismarck's encouragement. The French press exploded and on 6 July the government announced that, unless Leopold's candidature was withdrawn, France would go to war. King Wilhelm I was conciliatory and, to Bismarck's annoyance, the Hohenzollern family announced on 12 July that Leopold had stood down. The French, however, were determined that Prussia must be humiliated. They instructed their Ambassador to see the King (who was taking the waters in Ems), and to demand an apology and an undertaking that Leopold's candidature would never be renewed. King Wilhelm politely replied that the withdrawal of the candidature had closed the matter and that he had nothing more to say. He sent a telegram from Ems to

Bismarck in Berlin, reporting these exchanges, and authorizing him to inform foreign embassies and the press. Bismarck did so on 14 July, but first he edited out the conciliatory tone and left only phrases which implied that the King had brusquely dismissed the French Ambassador and refused to see him again. The hysterical reaction of the French press and the insistence of the Bonapartists convinced Napoleon that he had no hope of political survival unless he declared war on Germany – which he did on 19 July. As in 1866 Bismarck had so handled the crisis that his enemy was seen to be the aggressor.[23]

The Prussian army was much better equipped, organized and prepared for war than the French and – as against Austria – mobilized and deployed faster. Within six weeks (on 1 September) they surrounded a large part of the French army at Sedan, including Napoleon III himself, and forced them to surrender. Napoleon abdicated and the Assembly formed a Provisional government on 4 September, pledged to continue the war. On 27 October most of the rest of the French army, surrounded in Metz, also surrendered. Paris was besieged and held out until 28 January 1871. While the siege was still in progress (18 January) King Wilhelm I was crowned Emperor of all Germany – Bavaria and the other German states having joined in the war and opted to join the Federation in the patriotic fervour and pride of the German victory, which was Bismarck's prediction and purpose.[24]

The French Provisional government quickly called an election on 8 February which returned a strongly conservative Assembly, of predominantly traditional parties with very few Bonapartists. The veteran Orleanist, Adolphe Thiers, became President of the Third Republic. The Assembly had little option but to ratify Germany's terms for the Treaty of Frankfurt, ceding Alsace and Lorraine, and accepting a German army of occupation until £200 million was paid in reparations.

Socialist leaders in Paris, however, furious at the election of a conservative Assembly,[25] tried to seize power by forming a Commune in Paris at the end of March. Thiers had to move his government to Versailles, and from there he acted decisively. Bismarck agreed to his request to release French prisoners of war to put down the rising. In one of the bloodiest revolutionary conflicts in French history, the Commune was ruthlessly suppressed, and Paris reoccupied, street by street in May; 20,000

Communards were killed.[26] Though widely hailed by Socialists (including Karl Marx) as the first truly Socialist revolution, the Paris Commune made the Third Republic even more conservative, and Thiers led a remarkable recovery and reconstruction;[27] all reparations were miraculously paid off by 1873.[28]

Bismarck, having got what he wanted, became the leading peacemaker in Europe. With the decline of the Ottoman and Austro-Hungarian Empires, Russia expanded fast into the Balkans. Bismarck and the British Prime Minister, Disraeli, were prime movers in bringing about the Congress of Berlin in 1878 where the rest of Europe joined forces to check the Russian expansion.

THE BALANCE OF POWER

Bismarck, unlike Napoleon III, Kaiser Wilhelm II, Hitler and Stalin, had no desire to govern all Europe. He realized that German growth and prosperity depended on prosperous and stable trading partners as his neighbours. He shared the traditional British belief in a Balance of Power. He particularly avoided competing with British colonial expansion, being shrewd enough to realize that colonies were draining British strength, not adding to it; he also avoided challenging British sea-power, convinced that a supreme German army and a supreme British navy, interdependent rather than rivalling each other, would best keep the peace. The German economy grew rapidly and Germany soon overtook Britain in steel, electrical and chemical industrialization.

Internally, Bismarck after 1871 pursued an exceptionally progressive programme of social reform. A revolutionary socialist would argue that he was attempting to outflank Marxism by means of developing a welfare state. Be that as it may, Germany in the early 1880s led the world in social security measures, including sickness insurance, compulsory accident insurance, old age pensions and shop-floor participation in works management.[29]

In the European Balance of Power, Britain preferred to keep out of formal alliances and to keep herself free to throw her weight – especially her naval and industrial weight – where it was needed to maintain the balance.

It was the accession of Kaiser Wilhelm II which led to the dismissal of Bismarck in March 1890. The new Kaiser had colonial as well as European ambitions and did not share Bismarck's readiness to accept the restraint of a predominant British navy. This set in motion the changes in the Balance of Power which led to an explosive instability in Europe, needing only a spark in the Balkans in 1914 to detonate it. This chain of events is therefore discussed in the context of the outbreak of the First World War in the next chapter.

ACHIEVEMENTS OF THE CONGRESS OF VIENNA: 1815–1914

The hundred years after the Congress of Vienna were a period of dramatic industrialization, economic growth and population growth in Europe, but the calculated Balance of Power had largely prevented major European wars. Such as did occur were generally swift and, compared with the Napoleonic Wars and some of the other prolonged conflicts in history, caused *relatively* little loss of life. About 80,000 were killed or wounded in battle in the Crimean War, though many more died of disease. At the Battle of Solferino in 1859, about 30,000 were killed and wounded,[30] about 40,000 at Sadowa (Königgratz) in 1866,[31] and 26,000 at Sedan in 1870.[32] In all, including the Siege of Paris, the Franco-Prussian War claimed 184,000 killed and 244,000 wounded,[33] though to this must be added 20,000–40,000 Frenchmen killed by other Frenchmen in the Paris Commune rising in 1871. The American Civil War lasted four years and was bloodier than any of these, with 50,000 battle casualties at Gettysburg alone.[34]

These figures contrast with those of the twentieth century. In the First World War over 8 million were killed; in the Second World War estimates vary between 35 million and 60 million.[35] So the attempts at collective security in the nineteenth century, planned by the Congress of Vienna and maintained by the Balance of Power, were a great deal more successful than those that followed it. The events described in this chapter (e.g. in 1820–25, 1848, 1854, 1859, 1866, 1870 and 1878) were potentially just as explosive, with the same background of Great Power rivalry, as those that led to the tens of millions of deaths in 1914–

18 and 1939–45, not to mention between 20 million and 30 million more in the genocide practised by Stalin and Hitler in their own countries.

The First World War not only killed 8 million of the best young men in Europe; it blasted Europe's thriving economy into crippling debt; it launched Russia's Communism on its 72-year destabilization of the world;[36] and it sowed the seeds that produced Hitler and the even more devastating Second World War. The nineteenth century statesmen would never have allowed their rivalries, and a relatively small Balkan crisis, to lead to a European war. So the next chapter examines how and why the European international relations system broke down in 1914.

4 The Outbreak of the First World War

AN EXPLOSIVE MIXTURE

As with the Franco–Prussian War of 1870, the spark which set off the First World War was a small one, and statesmen involved must be roundly condemned for allowing it to happen. The American Civil War, the Franco–Prussian War and the development of weapons – of artillery and of the first fully automatic machine-gun (1884) – can have left them in little doubt that heavy casualties would result. They did, however, genuinely envisage warfare in terms of weeks rather than years.

Many historians have concluded that certain countries, notably Germany, actually wanted the war, engineered it and made no effort to resolve the crisis when it came. This is a myth, probably born of the desire during the war itself and in the 1920s and 1930s to prove the war guilt of the Germans – for which they were forced to sign a confession at Versailles in 1919. Though there were some German statesmen and generals who thought they had a better chance of beating the Russians then rather than later, all the evidence is that Germany was *not* fostering or expecting a war in July 1914, and that the Kaiser and his Chancellor made genuine (though belated) efforts to stop it happening. No one wanted a European war, although Austria *did* want a short local war to punish Serbia. The actual outbreak of the war, like a Greek tragedy, arose from the personalities and perceptions of the statesmen and generals involved.[1] Nevertheless, the Greek tragedy would not have happened unless there had been an explosive situation.

Europe had by 1914 settled into a rigid system of formal alliances from which only Britain still kept aloof.[2] Prior to the 1870 war, alliances had been fluid and pragmatic: as described in the previous chapter, Bismarck had allied with Austria in 1864 to take over Schleswig-Holstein from Denmark; then in 1866 with Italy (along with a tacit understanding with France) to drive

Austria out of the German Confederation; then with both north and south Germany, backed by an agreement with Russia, to defeat France in 1870–71. It was when Russian expansion in the 1870s threatened to flow unchecked into the declining Austrian and Ottoman Empires that Bismarck made the first of the formal alliances in the structure which was to influence the march of events so dangerously in 1914 – the Austro-German Alliance of 1879. This was initially a secret agreement, that Germany would give military aid if Austria were attacked by Russia and that Austria would come to the aid of Germany if she were attacked by Russia in concert with another power (by implication, France). In 1887 Bismarck attempted to reassure Russia that his aims were defensive by negotiating the 'Reinsurance Treaty', whereby Germany and Russia agreed to be neutral in any war in which the other were involved except if Germany attacked France or if Russia attacked Germany. He tried particularly to convince them that the Austro-German Alliance itself was purely defensive, and he did not undertake any German support for Austria if she attempted to extend her influence in the Balkans.[3] (Kaiser Wilhelm II, however, certainly took a different line from this when he gave his famous 'blank cheque' to Austria at the very start of the Serbian crisis in July 1914 – see p. 49).

After Bismarck had been dismissed in 1890, the Kaiser's unconcealed ambitions soon provoked a formal Franco-Russian Alliance whereby, if France were attacked by Germany, Russia would come to her aid, while France undertook to mobilize if Austria mobilized. This formally completed the splitting of Europe into two camps – Germany/Austria and Russia/France. Such moves were a malign influence on the handling of the 1914 crisis, although any of these states could have found loopholes to evade action if they thought such action would not be in their national interest. Nevertheless, the fact that action against one of the partners might bring in the other – or even that it might provoke general mobilization – encouraged members of the opposing alliance to steal a march by starting to mobilize first. In theory, of course, these very fears were intended to *deter* the aggressor; there is a school of thought that if Britain had made her intentions clear, particularly regarding her fleet, by a military commitment to France, the war would not have started at all. Analysis of the course of the crisis, however, does suggest that the perception of the alliances opposed to them made all the participants act more rather than less precipitately – making the mixture more rather than less likely to explode.

THE KAISER AND THE GERMAN NAVY

It was not only the anxieties and national sensitivities generated by the alliance system, however, which set in motion the chain of events that led to the First World War; the Kaiser's change in naval policy in 1898 was probably even more significant. Bismarck, having achieved his ambition of uniting the German people, wanted a peaceful Europe in which Germany could find markets for her growing industrial production, which he was convinced would give Germany an unchallenged economic dominance in Europe, and give him all the options described on p. 5. He believed that Europe would accept this economic advance provided that it was not perceived as leading to military dominance, and there would be a manifest restraint on Germany military dominance so long as she did not try to rival Britain's naval supremacy. Ironically today, 100 years after Bismarck was dismissed, although the Kaiser and Hitler in turn led Germany to military disaster, everything he worked for has at last been achieved – a united Germany economically supreme in Europe. A major factor in this was her positive rejection of military dominance since 1945, especially her refusal to become a nuclear power.

But military dominance was just what Kaiser Wilhelm II was seeking. The first German Navy Bill in 1898 was aimed at eventual parity with the British navy.[4] This had precisely the effect that Bismarck had feared: it led Britain to switch from her historic family relationship with Germany to a new partnership with France, since only a combination of the British navy and the French army could now hope to prevent an aggressive Germany from dictating her own terms in Europe. It also led Britain to conclude a naval alliance with Japan in 1902,[5] so that she could withdraw most of her Far East Fleet to strengthen her Home Fleet. This led in turn to the Russo–Japanese War in 1904–5, in which the Japanese navy was equipped largely with British-built ships and assisted by British naval advisers. The Japanese victory was initially welcomed in Europe, because there was growing concern about Russian military expansion and industrialization.

But there was some concern when it precipitated revolutionary risings in Russia, which resulted in some concessions in 1905, and gathered strength as the Russian *ancien régime* was increasingly forced to liberalize,[6] putting in motion the same process as was pointed out by Alexis de Tocqueville in his analysis of the French Revolution (see p. 20).

One British move towards mending fences with France was to try to defuse the rivalry over their expanding colonial empires. There had been some dangerous confrontations, including one in Fashoda in Africa in 1898 between General Kitchener advancing south from Khartoum and Captain Marchand advancing east from Gabon.[7] This was peacefully resolved, despite hysterical press comments in London and Paris, because both sides realized that they needed to stand together against Germany. Primarily to avoid any more such incidents, they negotiated the Entente Cordiale in 1904. This recognized British supremacy in Egypt and French supremacy in Morocco. There was no military commitment in Europe, but it did remove a source of friction which could have prejudiced their cooperation against Germany.

Germany set out to test this cooperation twice in Morocco – in 1905 and 1911 – on the second occasion directly challenging Britain's sea-power by sending a gunboat, the *Panther*, to Agadir to 'protect German interests'. The French seemed ready to negotiate, but Britain, alarmed at the prospect of a German naval presence across the Straits from Gibraltar, gave an indirect but clear signal that this could become a *casus belli*. The Germans withdrew with a good grace. Anger at his humiliation over this withdrawal, however, prompted the Kaiser to announce in 1912 plans for further naval expansion, this time avowedly aimed to achieve parity with Britain by 1920. Meanwhile Austria was having increasing difficulty in controlling her Slav territories in the Balkans, and Germany feared the disruption of the balance of power if the Austrian Empire disintegrated, since this could only invite further Russian expansion.

SARAJEVO

The spark which detonated the explosive mixture consisted of two shots fired on 28 June 1914 in Sarajevo, capital of Bosnia, by Gavrilo Princip, a Bosnian student of Serbian blood; one shot killed the Archduke Franz Ferdinand, heir to the Austro-Hungarian throne, and the other killed his wife. Bosnia, like Serbia, had formerly been part of the Ottoman Empire, and had been annexed by Austria in 1908 as part of an agreement with the Russians (see Map 4A and Table 4.1).

Princip, then aged 20, though born and domiciled in Bosnia, identified himself with Serbia, which had fought for and won its independence in 1912 after 600 years under Turkish rule. The assassination was an impulsive idea of his own, when he heard that the Archduke was to visit Bosnia. He obtained some bombs

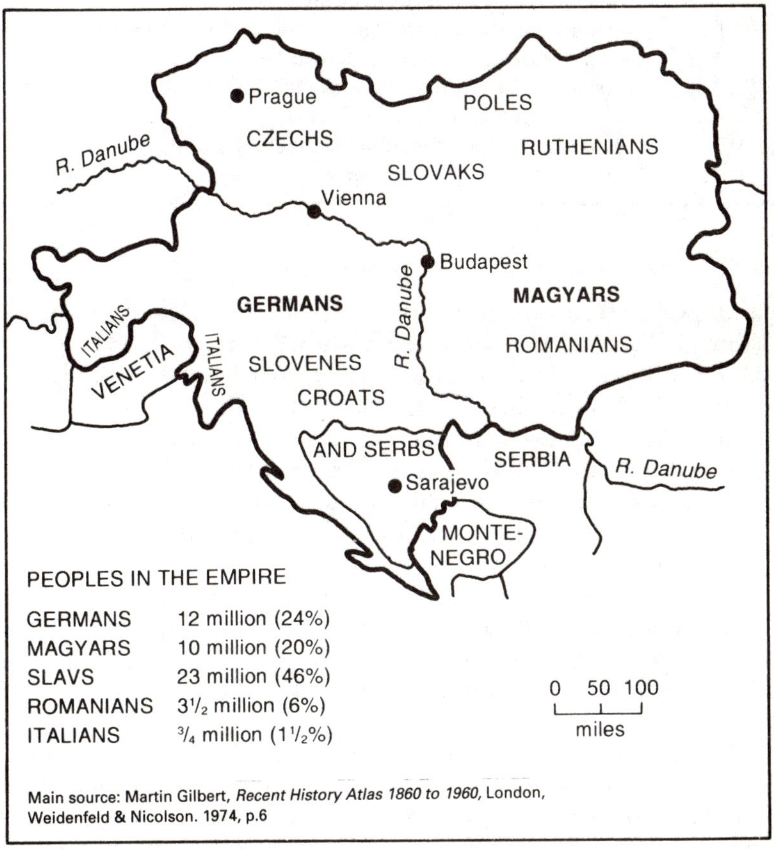

Map 4A The Austro – Hungarian Empire, 1914

Table 4.1 Outbreak of the First World War, 1914

28 Jun	Sarajevo. Assassination of Archduke Franz Ferdinand
5 Jul	Kaiser pledges to support firm reaction ('blank cheque')
14 Jul	Austrian ultimatum held back during Franco–Russian meetings
23 Jul	Austria sends ultimatum to Serbia
25 Jul	Russia recalls technical officers to prepare for mobilization
25 Jul	Serbia replies to ultimatum (almost all accepted)
28 Jul	Kaiser encourages Austria to accept Serbian reply (too late)
28 Jul	Austria declares war on Serbia. Bombardment begun
28 Jul	Kaiser urges 'Halt in Belgrade'
30 Jul	Russia orders general mobilization
31 Jul	Germany orders general mobilization and sends ultimatum to Russia ('stop mobilization')
31 Jul	German ultimatum to France ('do not mobilize')
1 Aug	Germany declares war on Russia
2 Aug	German ultimatum to Belgium('free passage')
3 Aug	Germany declares war on France
3 Aug	Germany invades Belgium (Schlieffen Plan)
4 Aug	British ultimatum to Germany. Declares war

and pistols from an army acquaintance in Belgrade who was (though Princip may not have known it)[8] a member of the Black Hand, a clandestine Serbian movement dedicated to the liberation of all South Slav territories from Turkish or Austrian domination and the founding of a South Slav state – as indeed came about after the war, as Yugoslavia. Princip (who, because he was under 21, was not shot, though he died in prison during the war) is to this day revered as a national hero in Serbia, and has a bridge bearing his name.

There is no evidence that the Serbian government had any part in the plot;[9] when they heard a rumour that weapons had been smuggled into Bosnia, the Serbian minister in Vienna warned an Austrian minister, who surprisingly took no action either to warn the Archduke or to tighten security.

Nevertheless, after the assassination, the Austrian government felt that they had to be seen to react. The very existence of an independent Serbia encouraged Slav minorities in Austria to be rebellious, so nothing less than public humiliation of Serbia would do. The Austrians were confident that the Serbs would grovel rather than risk war and to a great extent they did.

The subsequent crisis provided a classic example of appalling crisis management on all sides. As in the Austro–Prussian and Franco–Prussian wars of 1866 and 1870, government actions were dominated by their calculation of relative times of mobilization and rail movements of troops. All believed that if they stood firm their adversaries would climb down. Some of Kaiser Wilheim II's advisers may have believed that, even if the Russians did not back down, it was worth risking war in 1914 rather than later, since the pace of military training and industrialization was such that Russia would be able to field more troops than Germany within the next few years.

So when the Austrian Ambassador had lunch with him in Potsdam on 5 July, the Kaiser encouraged Austria to take immediate and decisive action against Serbia, assuring the Ambassador that Austria could rely on Germany's faithful support even if this brought her into conflict with Russia. The Kaiser and his ministers were anxious to stem the worrying decline and the prestige and credibility of the Austro-Hungarian monarchy, both internationally and inside their very unstable Empire. He also believed that all the European monarchs should unite in firm action in response to the assassination of the heir to a throne. If this went unpunished, it would encourage the idea of regicide.[10] He believed that Tsar Nicholas II of Russia would see it in this light, and would approve of punitive action against Serbia. Neither the Austrians nor the Germans had any conception at this stage that the situation could lead to a general war. Indeed, the Kaiser and most of his generals went away on holiday immediately after he had given the Austrians their blank cheque.[11]

The effect of this blank cheque on the Austrian Foreign Minister, Count Leopold von Berchtold, however, was electrifying. Until 5 July, he had vacillated in his response to the assassination. While he felt that a firm reaction was needed to prevent disintegration of the Empire as a Great Power, he was reluctant to take military action against Serbia for fear that Russia would intervene and he was uncertain of German support. With the specific guarantee of such support he was convinced that Russia would not dare to risk war. Indeed, the Chief of Staff, Conrad von Hotzendorff, urged immediate mobilization but the Emperor, who was old and tired and dreaded the idea of war, refused. Berchtold, however, set to work to draft an aggressive ultimatum which he was sure that Serbia could not accept, so that Austria could then deal a mortal blow without fear of Russian intervention.[12]

This ultimatum was ready on 14 July, but by this time Berchtold was losing some of his enthusiasm for war. It so happened that President Poincaré of France and his Prime Minister were making a state visit to St Petersburg. Berchtold, very conscious of the Franco-Russian Alliance, was anxious not to provoke a crisis just when the Russians were ideally placed to seek French support for a declaration to come to Serbia's aid. The French President and his ministers were due to leave St Petersburg on Thursday 23 July, so Berchtold decided to wait until they were safely at sea before the ultimatum was delivered.

Its demands were harsh and unyielding: the dissolution of Serbian nationalist groups, the dismissal of certain military officers, the arrest of leading political figures, action against accessories to the assassination and – the ultimate insult – the right of Austrian officers to take a full part in the investigation of the incident and the implementation of these measures on Serbian soil. The Serbs were given 48 hours to indicate total acceptance of all the demands or take the consequences, that is, the deadline was 6 pm on Saturday 25 July.

It had taken the Austrians three weeks to produce this – their first formal reaction – to the assassination. This had lulled the rest of Europe (including Germany and Serbia) into believing that the crisis had petered out. The Serbian Prime Minister, Nikola Pasic, was away on an electioneering tour when the ultimatum arrived. He asked the other ministers to draft a reply and, by the time he was summoned back to Belgrade, they had more or less decided to accept all the Austrian terms. On second thoughts, however, they made a few reservations, especially about the right of Austrian officers to supervise the measures on Serbian soil. This was probably just to play for time for more negotiation.[13]

The Serbian answer was delivered to the Austrian Ambassador, Baron Giesl, five minutes before the deadline, at 5.55 pm. Giesl had instructions to break off diplomatic relations immediately unless the terms were totally accepted. He (and his government) was clearly not expecting this virtually total acceptance: he and his entire staff were packed and ready to leave. In fact, they caught the 6.30 pm train from Belgrade station![14]

The British Foreign Secretary, Sir Edward Grey, attempted to sponsor negotiations between Austria and Serbia, but the Austrians clearly did not want to negotiate and the suggestion probably accelerated their declaration of war,[15] which they announced on 28 July. They began bombarding Belgrade next day (it was only 10 miles from the frontier), but they made no attempt to invade Serbia. In fact they mobilized only the half of their army that was on the Serbian frontier, and did not mobilize the other half facing the Russians, for fear of provoking intervention.

The Kaiser had clearly not taken the crisis seriously, after giving his blank cheque on 5 July, believing that this alone would ensure that the Russians did not intervene. Although he was aware of the general tenor of the Austrian ultimatum, he did not ask to see the text; nor did he look at the text of the Serbian reply of 25 July until the morning of the 28th. On seeing it, he instructed his Secretary of State to congratulate Austria, and to say that, naturally, every cause for war had vanished.[16] But Austria was already in the process of declaring war that day.

The Russians, however, were more alarmed, fearing that the Austrians intended to eliminate Serbia as an independent state. This, and their awareness of Germany's cultivation of relations with Turkey, rekindled their fear of a plot to block their exit from the Black Sea. They also believed that a war between Austria and Serbia would inevitably bring in Russia and Germany, and the terms of Austria's ultimatum convinced them that Austria intended to go to war. Russian mobilization, in such a huge country, was ponderous, so they took a preliminary measure on 25 July: the recall of a number of technical and administrative personnel in readiness to receive reservists and issue equipment.

When Austria declared war, the Kaiser did become alarmed, and told his Chancellor to send a telegram to Berchtold urging the Austrians to halt in Belgrade to avoid spreading the war. (In the event, the Austrians did not succeed in advancing at all in 1914. The first to advance were the Serbs.)

At the same time, the Kaiser sent a telegram to his cousin the Tsar (both were grandchildren of Queen Victoria), offering to mediate. This crossed with a telegram from the Tsar, describing the indignation of the Russian people about Austria's declaration of war, and begging the Kaiser to stop his Allies from going too far, as he would otherwise be overwhelmed by the pressure to intervene and that this could lead to a European war. The correspondence ended abruptly on 30 July, when the Tsar telegraphed that his military measures, decided five days ago (i.e. on 25 July), were in response to Austrian partial mobilization but should not interfere with the Kaiser's mediation.[17] By that time, however, the mobilization machines, and their complex and inflexible railway timetables, had taken charge.

MOBILIZATION TIMETABLES

All the major powers in Europe except Britain had large conscript armies. Each conscript served a period of full-time military training and then served most of the first half of his life on the reserve, with annual refresher training and liability for immediate recall when the order to mobilize was given. All over Europe there were thus millions of men, ready to receive a card ordering them to report at a specified time to a specified depot. These millions of cards were all kept ready for issue, with only the date to be completed.

The regiments in these armies were commanded by a cadre of full-time professional officers and NCOs. Some were kept at full strength with conscripts undergoing their full-time service, and these would be already deployed on the frontiers to deal with any unexpected incidents. Most of the regiments, however, just had their professional cadres and a small complement of full-time conscripts, their ranks ready to be filled with specified reservists, a stated number of hours or days after the order to mobilize. Then, again at a specified time after mobilization, the completed regiment would board a specified train to go to a specified slot in a specified division or corps at a specified place in the deployment for battle.[18]

This involved a rigid railway timetable to make best use of the available lines and rolling stock. The importance of this had been clearly demonstrated in the Austro–Prussian and Franco–Prussian wars of 1866 and 1870 when, as described in Chapter 3, the great superiority of the Prussian organization enabled them to get their armies at fighting strength on the frontiers more quickly than their opponents. The Prussians were well aware of this superiority, and were able to gain a great diplomatic advantage by allowing their enemies to order mobilization first.

These rapid and overwhelming defeats of Austria and France made a deep impression on all countries, including Russia, which had also suffered the humiliation of defeat in the Russo–Japanese War of 1904–5. Every Ministry of War therefore honed its railway timetables to 'get there fastest with the mostest'. Once the mobilization order was given, there was no flexibility for change.[19]

The fear of disrupting the process was particularly intense in a country which had to mobilize armies on two or more fronts, for example Germany against the French and Russian Fronts, and Russia with its Western (German) and Southern (Austro-Hungarian) Fronts. Russia was particularly anxious not only because of the vastness of her distances, both for reservists rejoining their regiments and for regiments moving to the fronts, but also because her railways were much less efficient than those of the Germans.

It was more for this reason that Russia took the first preliminary move in recalling technical and administrative personnel on 25 July 1914, when the Serbians told them the terms of the Austrian ultimatum.

The Austrians mobilized only the southern half of their army on 28 July, but when the Russians mobilized the Austrians changed their order to full mobilization on 31 July.

During these three days, the Tsar and his ministers were vacillating. When he heard, on the afternoon of 29 July, that the Austrians were bombarding Belgrade, the Tsar took the advice of his War Minister and ordered general mobilization. That evening, he received the telegram from the Kaiser begging him not to mobilize and offering to mediate. The Tsar promptly cancelled his order for general mobilization and an order for partial mobilization went out. His generals were appalled and urged the Foreign Minister, Sergei Sazonov, to persuade the Tsar to change his mind again. This he did, and he cancelled the partial mobilization order.[20] Next day (30 July) he again gave the order for full mobilization. Even at this stage the Russians had no intention of making war on either Austria or Germany. They knew that the rest of the world was well aware of the long time that Russian mobilization would take. Their order to mobilize was a threat, by which they hoped to prevent the war.[21]

Up till this point, apart from his unimaginative blank cheque on 5 July, there is strong evidence that the Kaiser was genuinely trying to avert a European war. The news of Russian mobilization caused him to panic. A telegram from the British Foreign Secretary, Sir Edward Grey, at 1 pm on 30 July warned that 'if war breaks out it [would] be the greatest catastrophe that the world has ever seen'.[22] This merely convinced the Kaiser that the British too (with their large fleet) intended to attack him and that the whole chain of events was a plot by Russia, France and Britain to destroy Germany.[23]

On 31 July, the Kaiser sent an ultimatum to Russia to stop mobilizing, with a deadline of 12 noon on Saturday 1 August. At the same time, he sent an ultimatum to France demanding that she undertake not to mobilize. Neither ultimatum was, of course, accepted. Nor, at this stage, did the Germans mean them to be accepted.

The reason for this was the 'Schlieffen Plan' for avoiding Germany's nightmare – a simultaneous war on two fronts. This plan had been made by the former Chief of Staff in 1905, and regularly reviewed by General Helmut von Moltke, who had succeeded Schlieffen in 1908 and was still Chief of Staff in 1914. The essence of the plan was that Germany should, by a lightning strike similar to that in 1870, envelop and annihilate the French army within a few weeks. The bulk of the German army would then be free to move to the Eastern Front in time to meet and defeat the advancing Russians. In their staff talks with their French allies, the Russians had promised to mobilize and launch an army of 800,000 across the frontier of East Prussia on the fifteenth day of mobilization.[24] The Germans, however, were convinced that the attack would not develop for six weeks;[25] they were confident that their Eastern army could hold them until their reinforcements arrived from the Western Front after defeating the French.

Their plan therefore depended on the speed with which they could defeat the French army. In 1870, it had taken only six weeks to destroy half the French army, leaving the rest surrounded and impotent in Metz. In 1914, the Germans planned to do it faster by cutting through Belgium to outflank the French frontier fortresses and envelop the major part of the French army east of Paris. It was therefore essential for the German army to start mobilizing and moving west within a day or two of Russian mobilization, and to attack the French first.

So as soon as the Russians mobilized on 30 July, the German timetable began, with priority for the Western Front. Every 24 hours, 550 troop trains crossed the Rhine bridges. The diplomatic processes were geared to maintain the momentum. The French were given only 12 hours to reply to the ultimatum on 31 July. Had they agreed to the demands, the Germans planned to demand the surrender of the frontier fortresses at Toul and Verdun, which they knew that the French would refuse.[26]

There was a brief hiccup on 1 August, when the Kaiser suddenly lost his nerve, seeing a chance of a diplomatic denouement with France and Britain, and instructed Moltke to switch the army to the Eastern Front. Moltke was appalled. The trains were already running to capacity to the west, with horses, artillery and support units. He explained that if the entire army were now suddenly ordered to the east, 'it would not be an army ready for battle, but a disorganized mob of armed men with no arrangements for supply. Those arrangements took a whole year of intricate labour to complete and, once settled, it cannot be altered.'[27] The Kaiser made some biting comments to Moltke, but accepted his refusal. In her book *The Guns of August*,[28] however, Barbara Tuchman suggests that, on 1 August, the change could have been made, and most of the Western armies deployed to the east by the middle of August. This was also the view of General von Staab, chief of the German Railway Division, who wrote a book about it after the war. But Moltke could not bring himself to put the machine into reverse.

On 2 August, the Kaiser sent an ultimatum to Belgium, demanding free passage for his army. On the 3rd, he declared war on France (on the false pretext that French aircraft had dropped bombs on Nuremberg) and invaded Belgium. At this the British sent an ultimatum to Germany to withdraw from Belgium and, when the Germans did not do so, declared war, on the legal pretext of an international guarantee by all the main European countries of Belgium neutrality in 1839. Britain's real concern, however, was to prevent the German army (and then her navy) from reaching the Channel ports. Britain had also promised to intervene if France were attacked by Germany (though not if France were the aggressor). Many felt at the time, and many others since, that if Britain had made these intentions clear the war would not have happened, but the Kaiser's interpretation of Britain's warning of 'the greatest catastrophe' on 30 July was that Britain did intend to join in, so it is unlikely that a more specific warning would have deterred him once the Russians had mobilized.

Austria began the war to crush Serbia, with no real perception that it would spread. The Russians mobilized because they were painfully aware of the ponderousness of their army organizations, and because they believed that this would prevent the war, not start it. For the German government, however, Russian mobilization was the signal to start the war without delay or to risk losing it. Despite some nervous lurches this way and that by the Kaiser, from that moment all the actors in the tragedy were inexorably carried forward by their perceptions and by their military machines to the slaughter of 8 million people.

THE PEOPLE WHO STARTED THE WAR

Despite the impelling demands of the military mobilization machines and the ministers and generals who operated them, it was, in fact, the leaders who brought about the war and, right up to the last moment, the leaders could have stopped it. Military and logistic machinery, timescales and communications (including those affecting public opinion) have radically changed but the weaknesses of human nature and the explanations for them continue, and it is from these that there is most to learn about crisis management. The leaders will, therefore, be examined in the order in which their countries made the crucial decisions – Austria, Russia and Germany.

Parliaments had very little power in any of the three countries so they were in effect absolute monarchies. All three monarchs believed in their inherited right to exercise their power. Their ministers – the relevant ones in the case being Chancellors, Prime Ministers, Foreign and Defence Ministers – and their military Chiefs of Staff also believed in maintaining an absolute monarchy; it ensured the continuity of their appointments and their privileges and they probably feared the personal and national insecurity and the greater risk of disorder which would come from yielding power to a Parliament under a constitutional monarch or an elected President.

The **Emperor Franz Joseph** of Austro-Hungary was a pathetic figure. He was 84 in August 1914, tired, sick and soon to die. The last thing he wanted in the closing years of his life was a war. He disliked his nephew, Franz Ferdinand, and would certainly not have taken Austria to war to avenge his assassination. On the other hand, becoming Emperor at the age of 18 in the midst of the 1848 revolutions, he had presided over a chain of troubles for Austria: defeat by France and Sardinia in 1859; expulsion from Italy in the 1860s; overwhelming defeat by Prussia in 1866; constant rivalry with the Ottoman Empire and Russia about suzerainty over the Balkans and other Slav territories; and pressure for independence in those territories. Conceding universal suffrage in 1907 and ruling a country with at least eleven distinct ethnic groups (Germans, Magyars, Italians, Czechs, Slovaks, Croats, Serbs, Slovenes, Poles, Romanians and Ruthenians), he was constantly concerned about domestic disintegration. Though tired of bearing his burden after a boyhood as heir presumptive and 66 years as Emperor, he was dedicated to the survival of the Habsburg dynasty, and determined not to preside over its collapse and disinheritance.

His first reaction to the assassination was muted and he saw no reason to change his summer holiday plans. He clearly did not envisage even a local war with Serbia. After receipt of the Kaiser's promise of support on 5 July, the Austrian Chief of Staff proposed mobilization measures but Franz Joseph refused to approve them, pointing out the danger of a Russian attack. During the next three weeks, however, his strength began to fail, and he signed the documents placed before him by his Foreign Minister with a trembling hand.[29]

Count Berchtold, the Austrian Foreign Minister, displayed all the characteristics of a weak and cowardly character. Up till 5 July he vacillated; thereafter both he and the Chief of Staff, **Conrad von Hotzendorf**, set their sights firmly on a war to crush and humiliate Serbia, and drafted their intransigent ultimatum with this intent. Berchtold became nervous again on 14 July, when the French President and Premier were visiting St Petersburg, but once the visit was over he recovered his confidence that Russia would not intervene and that Austria could overwhelm Serbia, which had a population of only 5 million and an army of half a million.

Tsar Nicholas II of Russia, though in the prime of life (46 in 1914) was the weakest character in the story, yet the most jealous of his right to absolute rule. He and his Foreign Minister **Sergei Sazonov** and Minister of War **Vladimir Sukhomlinov** were all still smarting after Russia's humiliation by the Japanese in 1904–5, and the subsequent attempted revolution of 1905, in which the Tsar was forced to accept an elected Parliament. They had, in the subsequent nine years, greatly expanded both their army and their industry, and were continuing to do so. They knew that the Germans were very anxious about this expansion. The Tsar did not take the crisis very seriously, even when the Austrians sent their ultimatum, though both Sazonov and Sukhomlikov expected it to lead to a European war involving Austria, Germany and Russia. When the Austrians declared war on Serbia on 28 July the Tsar did become alarmed and initiated his direct exchanges with the Kaiser, with whom he had a warm personal friendship dating from his boyhood days, when 'Willy' had been a much admired first cousin nine years older than himself.

Though he tried somewhat petulantly to exert his authority, he was quickly swayed by his ministers. Now we know, with hindsight, that the decision which finally made a European war inevitable was the Russian decision to mobilize on 30 August. It is interesting to look at how that decision was made. Initially, the Tsar signed two ukases, one for partial and one for general mobilization, so that his ministers could act on either. When he received his first personal telegram from the Kaiser, he cancelled his ukase for general mobilization. Sukhomlikov was horrified (for timetable reasons – see p. 53), and asked Sazonov to persuade the Tsar to restore the order for general mobilization. The arguments for general or partial mobilization were equally balanced: the Tsar was having difficulty in making up his mind. Someone remarked sympathetically 'it is very hard to decide', upon which the Tsar drew himself up and said, 'I will decide: general mobilization', upon which he went out and had a swim. The decision to mobilize did not merit any mention in his diary.

Kaiser Wilhelm II had a deep inferiority complex which led him to be assertive and quick-tempered. Due to an accident when he was a baby, his left arm was withered and useless. Though he learned to ride and shoot one-handed, this disability greatly inhibited him, and he did his utmost to conceal it in public. Following the death of his illustrious grandfather, Wilhelm I, he became Emperor in his twenties, and greatly resented the power and authority of Bismarck, whom he dismissed in 1890. He then pursued the dangerously ambitious policies which provided the deeper causes of the First World War (see pp. 45–6).

He was dedicated to developing Germany's military (including naval) power, because he was convinced that this would enable him to dominate Europe without having to fight. Thus he was certain that his blank cheque to Austria on 5 July would prop up the dynasty of the Emperor (whom he despised) and deter the Russians from intervening. When a European war suddenly became likely (on 28 July – 1 August) he panicked, tried to use his influence with his cousin 'Nicky', and thereafter lurched between the military options almost as unpredictably as the Tsar, to the despair of his Chief of Staff.

His Chancellor, **Bethmann Hollweg**, was convinced of the necessity of maintaining the strength of the Austro-Hungarian Empire and it was he who encouraged the Kaiser to offer his blank cheque on 5 July. This support was reaffirmed the day after Austria sent her ultimatum on 23 July.[30] Bethmann was one of those who believed that Germany's chance of defeating Russia would decline as the years went by. He was therefore ready to risk a European war but he was hopeful that, if it could be so handled that Russia appeared to be the aggressor, Britain might keep out of it. Unlike most others, however, he did believe that a European war would be a long one, and hoped, like the Kaiser, that Germany could achieve her aims without fighting.

The German Chief of Staff, General **Helmut von Moltke**, was one of the failures in this story. He lived in the shadow of his famous uncle, who with Bismarck had won the 1870 war, and he was the Kaiser's choice. He was a courtly staff officer rather than a field commander, and had pored over the Schlieffen Plan both before and after he took over as Chief of Staff in 1908. He made what proved to be a fatal amendment in shifting the right-flanking army to turn south before reaching Paris instead of enveloping the city to the west. His execution of the plan was also indecisive, which denied Germany the quick victory on which the entire plan depended, leading to four years of bloody stalemate on the Western Front. He also shared Bethmann's belief that the war would be long and bloody. His greatest weakness, however, was his inflexibility. As a staff officer, he could not accept any change in his rigid mobilization plan to accommodate flexibility in taking diplomatic opportunities.

The greatest blame for this crisis exploding into a devastating world war must fall on the Kaiser, both for encouraging Austria to gamble to the extent of provoking Russian mobilization, and then launching the actual aggression against Russia, France and Belgium. But for this, even as late as 1 August, the war could have been restricted to a localized conflict on the Austro-Serbian border.

The Emperor Franz Joseph must be exonerated from the worst of the blame because of his age and ill-health, and he almost certainly wanted to avert the war. Full blame, however, must fall on Berchtold, who gambled under the protection of the Germans, and directly began the war by attacking the Serbians without the justification of any proof that their government had been directly involved in the assassination of Franz Ferdinand – which it was not.

Tsar Nicholas II must also take his share of the blame. Unlike Franz Joseph, he was in young middle age and good health, but he was totally inadequate as a leader, and he personally best illustrates the fatal shortcomings of a hereditary absolute monarchy. But there will always be some indecisive, vain, ambitious or malignant leaders, however they come to power, and all of those mainly to blame for failing to resolve the 1914 crisis had more than one – and the Kaiser all – of these shortcomings.

5 The Rise of Hitler

WILSON'S FOURTEEN POINTS AND THE TREATY OF VERSAILLES

After the failure of the German plan for a lightning war in 1914, both the Western and Eastern Fronts congealed into three years of static trench warfare in which most of the 8 million fatal battle casualties occurred. Attempts at a wide strategic outflanking movement by the British in attacking the Turks in Gallipoli (1915) and Mesopotamia (Iraq, 1914–17) failed. First to crack were the Russians – both cause and effect of their 1917 Revolution. The Germans, free to concentrate on the Western Front, very nearly broke it in March 1918, but the Allies counter-attacked in August, including fresh troops from the British Empire and the newly arrived expeditionary force from the USA, which was in action for the first time. The US government warned the Germans that this force was just the beginning, and that they were geared to continue the war into the 1920s. The morale of the exhausted German troops, already depressed by the failure of their spring offensive, began to collapse. The naval blockade, now also reinforced by the US navy, was causing severe shortages in Germany. Faced with the growing spectre of a Communist revolution, Field Marshal Hindenburg (Chief of the General Staff – effectively supreme commander on behalf of the Kaiser – since 1916) persuaded the Kaiser that Germany must ask for an armistice before their troops were driven back in chaos onto German soil[1]. A temporary armistice was signed in November 1918 and the Treaty of Versailles was signed on 28 June 1919 – the fifth anniversary of the Sarajevo assassination.

The United States had entered the war in April 1917; in January 1918 President Woodrow Wilson announced his Fourteen Points for a proposed peace settlement. These included the evacuation of all German-occupied territories, the return of Alsace Lorraine (ceded in 1871) to France, a free Poland and the creation of independent Baltic states; it applied the principle of self-determination, interpreted as the right of peoples of one race to have the same government if they so wished; there was to be an impartial settlement of colonial disputes, a reduction in armaments, freedom of the seas and the abolition of secret diplomacy, to be replaced by 'open covenants openly arrived at'; and the setting up of the League of Nations.[2]

The peace negotiations began on the basis of these Fourteen Points, but some of the Allied leaders were sceptical, especially the French Prime Minister, Clemenceau, who was determined to destroy Germany's power completely. He demanded an admission of guilt by Germany and of responsibility for all the damage done (i.e. for reparations) though no figure was included in the treaty. The Allies also reserved the right to maintain the maritime blockade if Germany defaulted on reparations.

None of the defeated powers – Germany, Austria-Hungary, Turkey or Bulgaria – was invited to Versailles, but all were presented with the dictated terms and given three weeks to sign them (see Map 5.1). Facing the threat of the Allies advancing into Germany, which they knew they could not stop, the Germans had no option but to sign. The terms caused bitter resentment but failed to prevent Germany re-emerging to start (and very nearly win) the Second World War 20 years later.

Nor was Russia represented at Versailles since she was still in a state of civil war and the Bolshevik government was not recognized. Moreover Italy, technically on the winning side, withdrew in protest that the Allies were cheating her out of some of the territorial concessions she claimed had been promised as an incentive to enter the war in 1915.[3]

Shortly after the signing, the US Congress refused to ratify the Treaty of Versailles or the entry of the USA to the League of Nations. President Wilson was not re-elected in 1920, and the United States turned her back on the structure he had designed to keep the peace of the world.[4]

THE FAILURE OF THE LEAGUE OF NATIONS

The League was doomed from the start. Like the UN Security Council, the League Council was intended to have five permanent members – the USA, Britain, France, Italy and Japan. The USA never joined. Japan left in 1933 when the League condemned her invasion of Manchuria, and Italy in 1937, after she invaded Abyssinia. This left only two of the permanent members

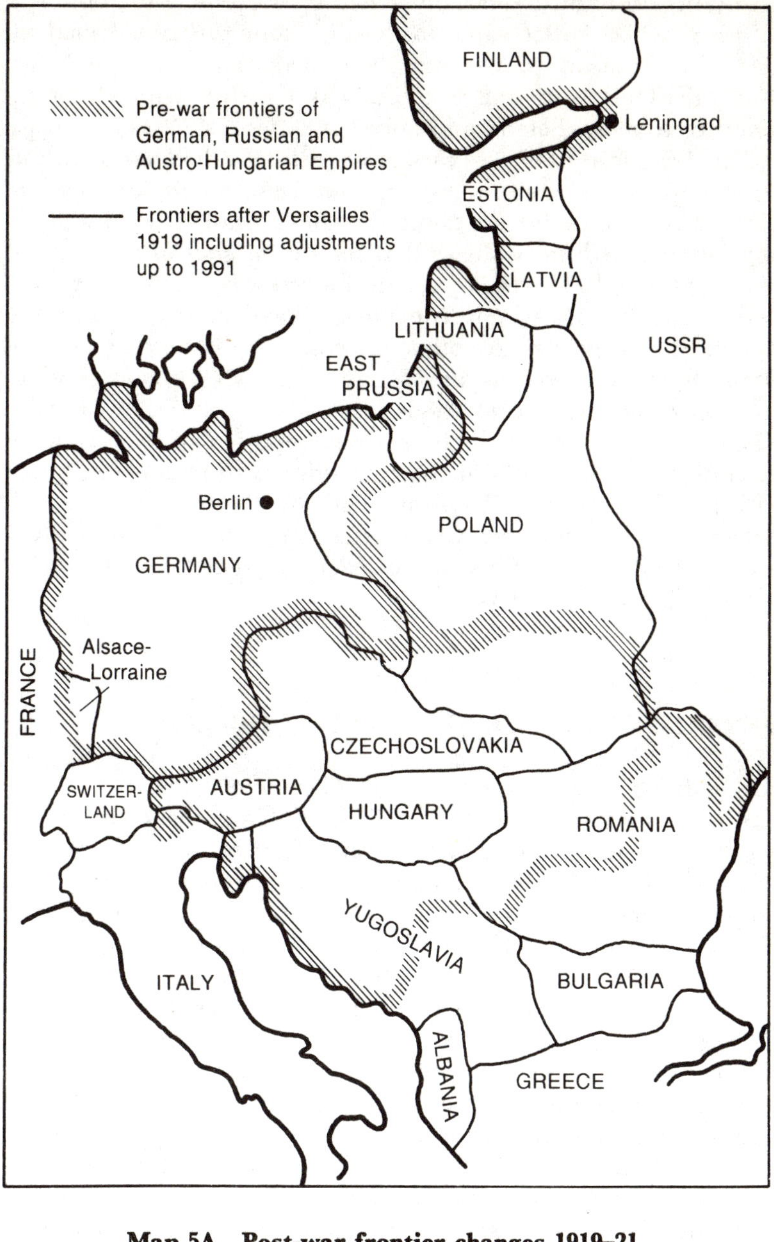

Map 5A Post-war frontier changes 1919–21

– Britain and France. Germany joined the League in 1925 but left in 1933, when Hitler came to power. Stalin's Russia joined in 1934 in reaction to Germany's rearmament, but took an ambivalent attitude, and eventually did a deal with Hitler in 1939 to carve up Poland and launch the Second World War.

The League's other weaknesses were that it had no teeth for enforcing its decisions; there was no veto, so nations had a blanket commitment to come to the aid of any victim of aggression, but history shows that no nation goes to war except in its national interest. (It can indeed be argued that no democratically elected government has any moral right to send its soldiers to die for any other purpose.) And Wilson's idea of open diplomacy was as unrealistic as it would be today to conduct diplomatic negotiations in front of a television camera. The League, not surprisingly, proved impotent in dealing with the Japanese seizure of Manchuria and further invasion of China; with Italy's invasion of Abyssinia; with the German, Italian and Soviet intervention in the Spanish Civil War; or with Germany's invasions of Austria, Czechoslovakia and Poland and the consequent Second World War.[5]

VERSAILLES AS THE CREATOR OF HITLER

Hindenburg's reputation survived Germany's defeat, and he showed considerable political skill in holding the country together when all seemed to be collapsing. In particular, he used his authority in the army to maintain its cohesion, and helped to keep the newly elected Social Democratic President of the Weimar Republic, Friedrich Ebert, in power. Hindenburg retired in June 1919 (as the Treaty of Versailles was signed) but re-emerged to be elected as President when Ebert died in 1925, until his own death in 1934. In 1933 he appointed Adolf Hitler as Chancellor, the only party leader able to attract a majority coalition in the Reichstag, and seen as the only bulwark against Communism.[6] Hitler came to power legally and legitimately. Though he quickly used this power to dismantle the feeble Weimar democratic Constitution, there is little doubt that, at the time, he had the support of the majority of the embittered German population in doing so.

The provisions of the Treaty of Versailles can be seen with hindsight to have ensured the emergence of Hitler or, had he not existed, someone else making the same nationalist appeal (see Table 5.1). The German people had been kept in the dark about the extent of their defeat; at the time of the Armistice there were

Table 5.1 The rise of Hitler, 1918–39

1918 Nov	Armistice. Hindenburg supports formation of Weimar Republic. Social Democrat government faces Communist rising. *Freikorps* (private armies) keep order on streets
1919 Jun	Versailles Treaty. Germany, Austria, Russia not represented. Germany forced to sign War Guilt and Reparation Clauses. Allied right to occupy Ruhr if reparations unpaid. German minorities (8 million) in many new states including Czechoslovakia. German army restricted to 100,000 (cadres – von Seekt)
1919 Feb	League of Nations formed, without Germany, Russia. USA rejects membership (1920)
1920 Mar	'Kapp *putsch*' (failed) supported by *Freikorps* (now 200,000)
1923 Jan	French troops occupy Ruhr. Galloping inflation
1923 Mar	Hitler's abortive Munich *putsch* (Stormtroopers formed from Freikorps)
1925	Hitler publishes *Mein Kampf* (Vols I and II)
1929–31	Wall Street Crash. World Slump. Germany 6 million unemployed
1933	Hindenburg makes Hitler Chancellor (Reichstag supports).
1933 Feb	Reichstag fire. Civil liberties suppressed (Reichstag supports)
1933 Feb	Hitler is granted dictational powers (Reichstag supports)
1933 Oct	Germany leaves League of Nations. Begins to rearm
1933 Nov	Nazis win 92% vote at general election
1935 Mar	Germany leaves Treaty of Versailles
1936	Germany reoccupies Rhineland. Allies do not react
1938 Mar	Germany annexes Austria. Referendum approves
1938 Sep	Munich. Czechoslovakia forced to cede Sudeten German areas
1939 Mar	Germany occupies remainder of Czechoslovakia
1939 Mar	British guarantee to Poland. France follows
1939 Aug	Hitler–Stalin Pact to divide up Poland
1939 Sep	Germany and USSR invade Poland. Second World War

no foreign troops on German soil and the soldiers were welcomed back as heroes who had successfully defended their fatherland against the combined might of Russia, France, Italy, Britain and her Empire and, at the end, the United States. Germany had agreed to the Armistice on the basis of President Wilson's Fourteen Points and the treaty seemed grossly unfair.

In particular the principle of self-determination was not applied to 2.8 million Sudeten Germans incorporated within the border area of the newly created Czechoslovakia in which the Germans had a two to one majority; nor to the 1 million Germans within the frontiers of the recreated Poland.[7] The German representatives who had signed the Treaty were regarded as traitors who had stabbed the German army in the back, and ordinary Germans did not realize that they had no option but to sign. The exclusion of Germany from the treaty negotiations gave plausibility to the challenge to its validity. The public odium extended both to the moderate Social Democrats who held power and to the Communists.

The War Guilt Clause especially outraged the German people, who remained convinced that the Russians had started the war, by mobilizing first and entering Germany on 19 August 1914 in support of an aggressive Serbian plot to cause a rising in the Austro-Hungarian Empire by assassinating the heir to the throne.

The reparations imposed on Germany, defined as the full cost of the damage (no figure was mentioned until after the treaty was signed) were quite impossible to meet; they precluded any hope of German economic recovery, and removed any incentive to attempt it. The treaty gave the Allies the right to send their armies into the Ruhr to seize goods to the value of unpaid reparations. This they did in 1923, resulting in total collapse of the German mark. Its value in January 1923 was 4000 to the pound sterling; in July, 84,000; in August, 1 million; in September, 24 million; in October, 6000 million; and on 1 November, 1 million million. This particularly hit the middle and lower middle classes. Rich people owned property or other assets that held their value regardless of currency; manual workers' wages went up with inflation; but the thrifty bourgeois and petty bourgeois Germans saw the savings they had built up over the years dissolve, and many, with their families, were reduced to a standard of living lower than that of the lowest paid manual workers, or complete destitution.

After a temporary stabilization under the American-backed Dawes Plan, the world financial crash of 1929 and the depression of 1930–31 brought German unemployment to 6 million, the worst in Europe, and the stock market collapse destroyed the capital of the more prosperous upper-middle class. The entire spectrum of German society – business people, white and blue collar workers – was impoverished and disillusioned and turned to the one man who offered a solution and a restoration of German pride – Adolf Hitler; Hindenburg's support removed any doubts.

Another provision of Versailles had indirectly given Hitler the physical power he needed to impose his own version of order on the streets – the Nazi Party's private army – the Stormtroopers.

The treaty restricted Germany to an army of 100,000 men. Major disturbances on the streets were fomented in 1919–20 by Communists aiming to exploit the chaos of defeat to bring about a Bolshevik revolution. An army of 100,000 was too small to maintain order. At the same time, there were hundreds of thousands more demobilized soldiers with no jobs to go to. Charismatic army officers set up freelance vigilante groups, which soon grew into organized battalions and brigades – the *Freikorps*. The Weimar government discreetly provided pay, arms and equipment for these units, as a better alternative than leaving the men idle and discontented, turning to crime or political agitation, and drawing state benefits. It seemed wiser to keep them in disciplined units, helping to reduce the chaos. The Allies – who were equally scared of the Communist revolution spreading to Germany – turned a blind eye. At one time the *Freikorps* numbered 200,000, twice the size of the army.

In March 1920, the *Freikorps* and some elements of the regular army and marines supported an attempted right-wing *putsch* by Wolfgang Kapp and General von Luttwitz. This collapsed after five days when Berlin was paralysed by a general strike. One of the leading military figures in this *putsch* was the naval Captain Ehrhardt, who later became one of the Commanders of the Nazis' private army, the *Sturmabteilung* (SA), and played an important part in Hitler's own abortive *putsch* in Munich in 1923. Hitler's only punishment was nine months of comfortable confinement, during which he enjoyed free board and lodging while he wrote *Mein Kampf* outlining his dream of expanding Germany to the east (Austria, Czechoslovakia, Ukraine) for all the world to read

– and ignore. He emerged from prison to resume his bully-boy tactics on the streets, especially to drive Jewish shopkeepers to flee – a process now called 'ethnic cleansing'. This was a prelude to his mass slaughter of Jews during the Second World War.

Hitler was at this time mistrusted by the Conservatives as his declared politics were Socialist ('Nazi' was shorthand for the National Socialist German Workers Party), but he was fast gaining the support of German nationalist voters at their expense. In the 1930 general election, the Nazis polled 6 million votes. In March 1932 Hitler stood against Hindenburg in the presidential election and took 13.4 million votes in the final ballot against Hindenburg's 19.4 million.[8] In the general election in July 1932, the Nazis gained nearly 14 million votes and 230 seats. This was short of an absolute majority (the Social Democrats won 133 seats, the Communists 89 and the Centre and other parties 90).[9] Hindenburg still shrank from inviting Hitler to be Chancellor, and reappointed the Conservative Franz von Papen. After four months a further election was called in November and to everyone's alarm the Communists' vote increased by 2 per cent to give them 100 seats. General Kurt von Schleicher became Chancellor in December for two months and tried to devise a programme that would attract majority support, which included a breakaway group of Nazis under Gregor Strasser. During these two months, Hitler and von Papen worked out a deal which Hindenburg accepted and on 30 January 1933 he appointed Hitler Chancellor with von Papen as Vice-Chancellor.[10] With the authority and legitimacy conferred by Hindenburg's support, Hitler's popularity grew rapidly and the army threw its weight behind him. The Reichstag was burned down on 22 February by a dim-witted Dutchman allegedly sponsored by the Communists (but later widely believed to have been sponsored by the Nazis). After yet another election, the new Reichstag members (excluding the Communists) met in the Berlin Opera House and passed by 441 votes to 94 an Enabling Law, giving wide powers to the government to restore order.[11] Only the Social Democrats voted against. Hitler used these powers to the full, with growing popular approval. After Hindenburg died in August 1934 Hitler, with support from the army, combined the posts of Chancellor and President, which included supreme command of the armed forces; he obtained a 90 per cent popular vote of approval for these changes in a referendum.

Hitler immediately repudiated the Treaty of Versailles and set about rearmament. He was ruthless in eliminating or intimidating any opposition, and the SA continued their persecution of trade unionists, Communists and Jews. When the ambitions of Ernst Röhm, the SA Commander, threatened to lose him the support of the army, Hitler had him and many of the other SA leaders murdered on 30 June 1934, along with other opponents including General von Schleicher and Gregor Strasser. But, for the majority of Germans, he greatly improved their lives, helped, of course, by the world's recovery from the great Depression. He brought them full employment (albeit with low wages), welfare and housing benefits, efficient public services and, above all, a restoration of German pride and sense of purpose.[12] His popularity soared and there is no doubt at all that, by 1938, when he marched into Austria and then annexed the Sudeten German areas of Czechoslovak Austria in 1938, his popular support was higher still.

GERMANY, ITALY AND JAPAN

Meanwhile Benito Mussolini had been assuming similar powers in Italy, initially, like Hitler, describing himself as a Socialist. In 1919 he formed an ex-servicemen's vigilante group in Milan, just like the German *Freikorps*. Drawing on the Roman badge of authority, the *fasces* (an axe bound by a bundle of rods), he called it the *Fascio de Combattimento*. The party grew fast, supported by industrialists and others anxious to check Communism. In 1921 the Fascists gained 35 seats in the Assembly. By 1922, with growing chaos on the streets and the democratic government falling apart, the Fascist bands were in control of most of northern Italy. On 29 October 1922, Mussolini travelled (by train) to Rome, having launched 30,000 Fascists from Milan in the 'March on Rome' to support him. He demanded that the King appoint him Prime Minister, which was agreed on the understanding that he formed a coalition government with a majority in Parliament; but to resolve the crisis situation and restore order, the King gave Mussolini dictatorial powers for a year.[13] So, like Hitler, he came to power constitutionally, and though he maintained a parliamentary façade for the next four years, he formally deprived the opposition deputies of their seats in November 1926 and Italy became a one-party Fascist state, for which Mussolini himself coined the word 'totalitarian'.[14] Like Hitler, his dictatorship improved the people's lot and 'made the trains run on time', and the Italian people responded to the nationalist call.

Until the mid-1930s, Mussolini maintained good relations with Britain and France, because one of Italy's greatest fears was that Germany would support Austria's bid to recover the areas ceded to Italy after the war, in the Tyrol and on the Adriatic. In 1935, however, he invaded Abyssinia (now Ethiopia). The League of Nations Council condemned this, but imposed only the most ineffective sanctions. France was more concerned about Germany than Italy and did not want to alienate Mussolini, and Britain had no desire to go it alone. The only effect of the sanctions was to drive Italy into the arms of Germany.

Meanwhile Japan had exploited the opportunity created by the weakening of European influences (especially Russian influence) in the Far East to extend her foothold in China, from 1915 onwards.[15] A militantly nationalist government took over in Tokyo and imposed treaties on China including the right to station Japanese troops to protect the South Manchuria Railway, of which Japan owned the lease.[16] In 1931, Japan annexed this as a pretext and as a bridgehead for invading and annexing Manchuria; thereafter she extended her control by 1939 to the whole of north eastern China including Peking and Shanghai, and most of the south-eastern ports, including Amoy, Swatow and Canton. Japan left the League of Nations in 1933, irritated but in no way deterred by the bleatings, and joined forces with Germany and Italy, which left the League in 1934 and 1937 respectively.[17]

HITLER'S WAR

While there is much argument about who should take the major share of the blame for the First World War, there is no doubt at all that Hitler began the war in 1939 and extended it in conjunction with Japan in 1941. He was quite determined to gain the objectives he set out in *Mein Kampf*, that is, German domination over Eastern Europe including the Ukraine. He hoped to gain them without fighting, especially if he could persuade France and Britain to remain neutral, but he was equally confident that he could overcome any resistance to his advance.

By October 1934 he had more than doubled the army permitted by Versailles to 240,000 (24 divisions) and in 1935 he reintroduced conscription. By September 1938, it had more than doubled again to 550,000 (48 regular and 24 reserve divisions); by the time he invaded Poland in September 1939 he had 52 regular and 50 reserve divisions and had also built up a formidable air force and navy, especially submarines.

This was an astounding achievement made possible by the German army Chief of Staff in 1920–26, General Hans von Seekt. Convinced that another war against France was inevitable, von Seekt used his permitted 100,000 strength to select and train potential leaders (officers and NCOs) who, when conscription was reintroduced in 1935, became the cadres for the mass of new battalions to be formed. Since Versailles allowed him no tanks, von Seekt established close relations with the Soviet army and arranged for them to give clandestine training to German tank crews.[18]

When rearmament began in 1934, it had a stimulating effect on the economy. The expanding army, the burgeoning tank and aircraft production, and the building of the trail-blazing autobahns or strategic roads, quickly absorbed the unemployed people and got money circulating. These things were also very popular with the German people.

The year 1936 saw the start of the progress to war. Encouraged by the weak response of the League to the Italian invasion of Abyssinia in October 1935, Hitler sent his troops in March 1936 to reoccupy the Rhineland in defiance of the treaty. His generals, conscious that the army was not nearly ready for war, advised against it and Hitler agreed that the troops should have orders to withdraw at once if Allied troops exercised their right to move in. Hitler, however, had a hunch that the Allies would not move in, and he was right.[19] In July 1936, General Franco's rebellion against the Republican government in Spain began the three-year civil war that brought Franco to power. Germany and Italy seized the chance to send 'volunteers' to support Franco. This enabled them to gain battle experience, and especially to develop and assess techniques of aerial bombardment. So too did the Soviet Union, on the other side.[20] Altogether, there were 50,000

Italian, 20,000 Portuguese and 10,000 Germans with Franco's nationalists and 500 Russians with 40,000 foreign volunteers in the International Brigades on the side of the Republicans.[21]

The Spanish Civil War brought Hitler and Mussolini together as Franco's allies. In October 1936 they formed an alliance, named by Mussolini as the Rome–Berlin Axis about which Europe was to revolve. In the same month Germany and Japan signed the Anti-Comintern Pact. So the alliances for the Second World War had taken shape: there was no doubt about where the initiative and dynamism lay.

Neville Chamberlain, who became British Prime Minister in 1937, adopted a policy of appeasement, hoping above all to prevent war, but at worst playing for time until Britain's rearmament (two years behind Germany's) would put her in a position to stand firm. French political and public opinion was split between those who wanted to prevent German rearmament and those who wanted to avoid another war at any price. Generally, the appeasement/pacifist philosophy prevailed. Hitler got his way; both he and the German people became more and more convinced that no one could or would stop him.

In March 1938, the German army marched into Austria; Hitler declared the two countries united (the *Anschluss*), and held a referendum in which he claimed 99 per cent support in both countries. Throughout the summer, he stoked the smouldering embers in the ethnic German areas which Versailles had put on the Czech side of the frontier and invasion seemed imminent. Britain began mobilization in September but Chamberlain and the French Prime Minister Daladier, still playing for time, went to Munich to meet Hitler and Mussolini and, in effect, conceded all their demands. President Benes protested in vain and left Czechoslovakia in disgust for exile. Hitler occupied the Sudeten German areas of Czechoslovakia in October, declaring (as he had after the Rhineland and Austria) that Germany had no further territorial claims (see Map 5B). The Sudeten areas contained all of Czechoslovakia's natural defences (they were the original borders between Germany and the Austro-Hungarian Empire) and also most of the coal and many other industries, accounting in all for one-third of Czechoslovakia's total exports.[22] Hitler waited only a perfunctory period of five months before grabbing the rest of Czechoslovakia, with the Skoda Works, which was second only to Krupps in armament produc-

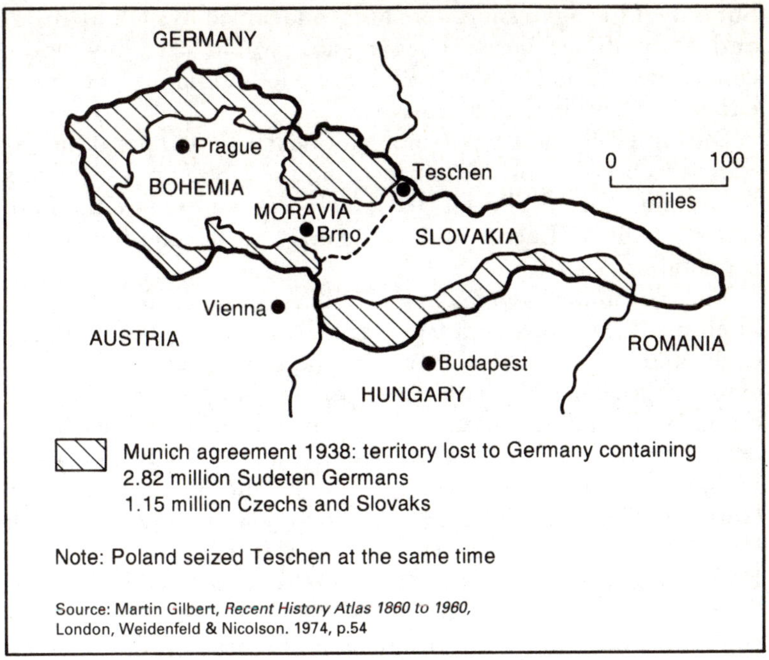

Map 5B Czechoslovakia after Munich, 1938

tion in Europe, and the large and well-equipped Czechoslovak army.

Only then (March 1939) did Chamberlain accept that war was inevitable. Poland, with its large German populations around Danzig (Gdansk) and Silesia, was clearly next on the list, so Britain and France gave a formal guarantee that any attack on Poland would be met by war. In April 1939 Mussolini jumped onto Hitler's bandwagon by occupying Albania,[23] so the same Anglo-French guarantee was extended to Romania and Greece. Britain introduced conscription, never before done in peacetime, and Hitler ordered the German army to be ready to invade Poland on 1 September.[24]

Amazingly, the USSR was not involved in any of this: she had not been invited to Munich. In 1935, under the Franco-Soviet Pact, the two sides had agreed to support each other if attacked, but only if the aggression were also condemned as such by Britain and Italy. Since German aggression would certainly not be condemned as such by Mussolini, the pact did not in fact commit either side and both sides knew it.[25]

During 1939, there were some half-hearted attempts at military staff talks between Britain, France and the USSR, but these came to nothing since Stalin insisted on the right to annex the Baltic states (Estonia, Latvia and Lithuania) as a condition of any cooperation.

The German Soviet Pact of 23 August 1939 came as a bombshell. The two countries agreed to occupy half of Poland each, and for the USSR to annex the Baltic states. This was a cynical agreement on both sides. Hitler, with his eyes still firmly on his later expansion eastwards, was convinced that, once he had occupied the western half of Poland, France and Britain would realize the futility of their guarantee, and make peace with Germany, leaving him free to prepare for his invasion of the Ukraine and Russia. He was also convinced that Britain and France would in fact welcome this, as they still probably feared Communism more than Germany. Stalin, for his part, equally cynically made sure that Britain and France would go to war with Germany in the hope that all three would exhaust themselves so that Germany's eventual and inevitable attack on the USSR would be weakened. It also gave Stalin more time to step up his tank and aircraft production in preparation for that war.

Hitler invaded Poland on 1 September; Britain and France declared war on 3 September. There was nothing they could do to help Poland, which was overrun within three weeks, despite heroic resistance on both fronts. After a winter of phoney-war, during which all sides were in full production of armaments, Hitler decided that he would have to eliminate the threat from the west before he could turn his full strength to the east (remembering the Schlieffen Plan in 1914 – see pp. 53–6). He invaded France, Belgium and Holland on 10 May 1940, knocked France out of the war by mid-July, and prepared to invade Britain. When he lost the air battle over Britain he abandoned his invasion plans, and decided to rely on his submarines to neutralize Britain, while he overran East Europe and the western USSR. Launching his invasion in June 1941, he reached the gates of Moscow before the winter bogged his army down in December.

At this point, the third member of the Anti-Comintern Pact – Japan – launched her attack on US, British, Dutch and French possessions in the Pacific and East Asia, and Hitler – astonishingly – declared war on the United States, presumably believing that they would enter the European war at some future time. With all the world against him except Japan and Italy, he began to lose ground on all fronts from the end of 1942 (the turning points being at Alamein and Stalingrad) but, thanks only to the heroism of the hopelessly outnumbered and outgunned German army, air force and navy, it took the Allies another two and a half years to drive him back and occupy the whole of Germany, leaving hardly a bridge or a factory still standing. The German dead amounted to over 4 million, excluding some 6 million Jews and Poles murdered by Hitler. Combat deaths amounted to some 20 million including 3.5 million Germans and 11 million in the Soviet armed forces – many times more than in the First World War.

WHOSE FAULT?

The primary blame for the Second World War must fall on the authors of the Treaty of Versailles, which made sure that Germany would eventually have to rebel against it in desperation against the suffering it imposed on her people; but at the same time the treaty failed to ensure that she could not gather the military strength to do so by force.

Versailles had ensured that whoever led the German recovery would have overwhelming support from the German people, but it was unlucky that Hitler was the man who emerged to do it. He combined charismatic leadership with ruthless cruelty (matched only by that of Stalin) and fanaticism. Rather than modify his aims to what was realistically achievable, he brought immense suffering to the world, and especially to the German people.

Stalin's cynical launching of the West European countries at each other's throats in August 1939 was a precipitating factor, but no more than that.

Having embarked on his mission, Hitler could not afford to turn back. It was his nerve and dynamism that cowed the other European countries, which had the misfortune to throw up some of the weakest leaders in their history in the period 1918–39. This gave Hitler his initial successes against all the odds. He became convinced that nothing could stop him.

We come back to one of the principles of crisis management enunciated in Chapter 1: if one party to a conflict is willing to fight and the other is not, the first will prevail every time. If the timid adversary does eventually decide to fight for his own survival, he will usually suffer far more than if he had been willing to fight in the first place.

Every child first learns that lesson on the school playground.

Part III

Crisis and Conflict under the Nuclear Umbrella

6 The Cold War

THE BIRTH OF THE NUCLEAR ERA AND THE COLD WAR

For most of her history, the USA had adhered to the Monroe Doctrine, isolated by the Atlantic and the Pacific, aiming to exert her influence (and retain her options) through economic power, without wasting her treasure and her people's lives in foreign wars. This philosophy worked extremely well, as it does for Japan today. In 1941, however, when both Japan and Germany declared war on her, she realized that this was a consequence of turning her back on the world in 1919. The US war effort thereafter was prodigious, both in military and financial terms, and there is no doubt at all that, without it, Hitler would have established his rule over virtually all of Europe, and Japan over east Asia, and possibly also of the Indian subcontinent.

Thinking ahead to the post war world, President Roosevelt was convinced – until the closing months of his life in 1944–45 – that world peace could be maintained with a minimum of weapons if the USA and the USSR worked together, and he put into motion the United Nations which, though imperfect, has been vastly more effective than the League. One big difference was the power of veto retained by the permanent members of the Security Council, the USA, USSR, Britain, France and China. Though frustrating at times, this has kept all the major powers in the UN. In 1990 (the Gulf Crisis) the unity of the Security Council at last enabled the UN to act as effectively as Roosevelt hoped.

In 1944, however, he did begin to realize that Stalin had no goodwill at all towards the capitalist world, and intended to gain control of the whole of Europe through fomenting internal revolutions and intervening in them when necessary,[1] and also to extend that control by similar means to as many of the capitalist world's colonies as possible.

President Truman, as Vice-President, took office on the death of Roosevelt on 12 April 1945. He saw the surrender of Germany on 8 May, and took a much more robust line with the Russians (fully in tune with Winston Churchill) at the Potsdam Conference in July. In August, he took the momentous decision to explode the world's first two nuclear weapons to force the surrender of Japan.[2] Up to the time of writing, no more of these weapons have ever been used, excepting in tests.

The anxieties of Truman and Churchill (and of Attlee, his successor, who was elected in July 1945) about Soviet ambitions soon proved justified.[3] It had already been agreed at Yalta in February 1945 (in the face of vigorous opposition from Churchill) that the East European countries, including Poland for whose freedom the world had gone to war, would remain under Soviet military occupation while they had 'free elections' (which, with the shortlived exception of Czechoslovakia, they did not have). In 1945–47 there were dangerous confrontations in Iran, Turkey, the Italo-Yugoslav border and Greece (amounting to civil war against the new government by Soviet-supported Communist guerrillas). This led to the 'Truman Doctrine', announced in a message to Congress on 12 March 1947, offering United States support to 'free people who are resisting attempted subjugation by armed minorities or by outside pressures'.[4] This was followed in June 1947 by the Marshall Plan, under which massive economic aid was offered to finance the reconstruction of all European countries ravaged by the war. It was rejected by the USSR and, on Soviet insistence, by all the East European countries still occupied by Soviet forces. Sixteen West European countries did join, forming a body to administer the Plan. It was known from April 1948 as the Organization for European Economic Cooperation (OEEC). It was widened in 1960 with the inclusion of the USA, Canada and Japan to become the Organization for Economic Cooperation and Development (OECD) and extended its activities to the developing countries.[5]

This infusion of capital enabled Germany to rebuild her totally shattered industry and to become the most prosperous country in Europe by 1970 – surely the most generous treatment of a defeated enemy in history (and, in the long term, the wisest). Britain was also a beneficiary. Having expended her massive foreign investments to finance her stand against Hitler, almost alone from 1940, Britain would have been bankrupt by 1941 without the lend-lease agreement,[6] and again if this had not been replaced by Marshall Aid in 1948–52. This also helped to underwrite her contribution to the Korean War in 1950 and the subsequent increase in the strength and modern armament of her NATO forces.[7]

STALIN AND THE PEAK OF THE COLD WAR: 1948–53

On 5 March 1946, Winston Churchill, in a speech at Fulton, Missouri, referred to the 'iron curtain' that had been drawn across Europe,[8] and, in a US congressional debate in 1947, Bernard Baruch defined what the USSR was fighting as a 'cold war',[9] a strategy of subversion, propaganda and limited use of weapons under the umbrella of restraint imposed by the fear of precipitating a nuclear war.

An outline chronology of the first years of the Cold War is in Table 6.1. It rose to its peak in 1953. Then Stalin died, whereafter it gradually subsided, though this did not become apparent until the mid-1960s.

From the time the USSR exploded an atomic bomb in 1949 through to the mid-1950s, defence planners in the West worked on the assumption that there would almost certainly be a war, conventional or nuclear, with the USSR as soon as she felt herself to be ready, and planning forecasts in 1950 put the likeliest date for this as 1957.[10]

The reason for this sombre forecast was Stalin's activity in Eastern and Western Europe. He clearly had no intention of honouring the Yalta agreement; in 1945–48 he installed Communist-dominated governments in all the occupied countries of Eastern Europe. Even before the war in Europe was over, he had treacherously arrested and eliminated the delegation from the Polish government in exile which had been invited to Poland to discuss the formation of a government. Stalin's own account of this was published verbatim by Winston Churchill in his book *The Second World War* (see note 1 to this chapter on p. 255).

Only in Czechoslovakia was a genuinely free election held, on 26 May 1946, in which the people gave the Communist Party 38.7 per cent of their votes, but the Communists merely used this as a foothold to stage a *coup d'état* in 1948, suppressing all the other parties and establishing a Stalinist state. This coup is described in Chapter 7.

The coup in Czechoslovakia sent a shock-wave through Western Europe. Italy, France, Belgium and the Netherlands

Table 6.1 Cold War chronology: Stalin 1945–53

1945 Feb	Yalta. Promise of free elections in East Europe
1945 May	Allied victory in Europe
1945 Jun	United Nations (UN) first meeting in San Francisco
1945 Aug	Two atomic bombs. End of Second World War
1945–7	Confrontations in Iran, Turkey, Yugoslavia (Trieste)
1945–8	Greek civil war
1945–53	Communist rebellion in Philippines (defeated 1953)
1946 Nov	Communist rebellion began in Indochina (succeeded 1975)
1947–8	Independence of India and Pakistan. Communal fighting
1947	Truman Doctrine (March) and Marshall Plan (June)
1948 Feb	Communist coup in Czechoslovakia (ousted 1989)
1948 May	Israel founded. First Arab–Israeli War (1948–9)
1948 Jun	Yugoslavia left Comintern
1948 Jun	Communist guerrilla war began in Malaya (defeated 1960)
1948 Aug	Berlin blockade (until May 1949)
1949	USSR series of atom bomb tests
1949 Apr	NATO founded. Started rearmament
1949 Oct	People's Republic of China declared
1950 Jun	North Korea invaded South Korea
1950 Dec	China entered Korean war
1953 Jul	Korean armistice roughly on original frontiers
1953 Mar	Death of Stalin. Diffuse leadership, with Khrushchev

all had large Communist Parties that attracted (as in Czechoslovakia) a substantial minority of popular votes, as a result of their leadership in the wartime resistance movements. The Italian Communists (PCI) and their 'Nenni Socialist' allies united as a Popular Front in the 1948 elections gaining 31 per cent of the vote. The Christian Democrats (DC) had 49 per cent of the votes but a majority of 304 of the 574 seats in the Chamber, and strengthened their position by forming a coalition with the small Centre parties;[11] but in the light of the Czechoslovak coup they were chary of the risks of forming a coalition with the Communist Party – and have never done so to this day. France, too, had a very large Communist Party from 1945 until the collapse of Communism in the 1990s, and French governments were very much aware of the risk of them trying to take over as they had in Czechoslovakia.

US and West European countries had a further shock when Stalin suddenly imposed a total land blockade of the Western sectors of Berlin (administered by four occupation forces since 1945, provided by the USSR, USA, Britain and France). He shrank from closing the air corridors that were demarcated in the treaty, because he realized that the mass casualties resulting from shooting down a civilian aircraft would almost certainly lead to a military response, by the superior US Air Force, and possibly with nuclear weapons, of which the USA still had a monopoly. The Allies maintained Berlin by airlift from 4 August 1948 until the blockade was lifted on 12 May 1949. This crisis and its resolution are discussed in Chapter 7.

The Berlin blockade had been precipitated by the decision in March 1948 to extend Marshall Aid to West Germany and to put in motion the formation of the Federal Republic of Germany, which was formally recognized on 21 September 1949. The Soviet government thereupon proclaimed the formation of the German Democratic Republic in the Soviet-occupied zone, with its capital in the Soviet sector of Berlin. Germany remained divided until 1990; at the time of writing (1993) the four military garrisons remain in Berlin, which will in due course become once again the capital of a united Germany.

The Soviet Union successfully tested an atom bomb in 1949, thanks both to the intense concentration of effort on the specific project at the expense of all else, which was Stalin's greatest strength, and to the power of Marxist–Leninist ideology which led a number of American, British and Canadian scientists to pass on their secrets to the USSR. Some of the German scientists and engineers captured by the Russians also continued with the research they were doing for Hitler. Suddenly the nuclear monopoly, which had seemed the best guarantee of peace, became a nuclear arms race, to the lasting detriment of the world's economies.[12]

This, and the events in Czechoslovakia and Berlin, led to the US initiative in forming the North Atlantic Treaty Organization (NATO). NATO was built upon the West European Union, formed in March 1948 by Britain, France and the Benelux countries. NATO quickly expanded to include 15 countries, each of which undertook to regard an attack on one as an attack on all, and to go to the aid of the party attacked. In 1955, the USSR responded by signing the Warsaw Pact with its East

European allies, and NATO expanded to 16 countries with the inclusion of West Germany.

The most immediate task was to strengthen the armed forces of the member countries, and the USA began a massive aid programme, financing and generally manufacturing the armaments most urgently needed. A Supreme Headquarters Allied Powers in Europe (SHAPE) was set up with an American as Supreme Allied Commander in Europe (SACEUR), a British Deputy and a multinational staff. Though never tested in battle, this was the most comprehensive military alliance ever attempted. It relied ultimately on US nuclear weapons (though the British and French developed a small nuclear capability in the 1950s) and some 400,000 US troops were stationed in Germany. The armies of occupation then became allied armies, and West Germany contributed a large army contingent from 1955 onwards.

Also in 1949, Mao Zedong completed the conquest of mainland China, with huge numbers of men under arms, so the world regarded with some anxiety a 'Sino-Soviet bloc' with awe-inspiring potential military manpower. Though the USSR and China fell out in 1960, Western policy for the next four decades was to maintain a technological superiority in weapons sufficient to deter the deployment of these massive resources of manpower for either global or local aggression. In this respect it has been remarkably successful. There have been many regional conflicts accumulating millions of casualties, but there have been no wars between major powers for the longest period in modern history.

One of the most dangerous regional conflicts was the Korean War in 1953, in which China, the USA, Britain and France were involved, but not the USSR.

The Koreans are a distinctive people with their own culture, and Korea was more or less united under its own monarchy for nearly 1000 years from AD 918. The rulers were forced to accept Japanese hegemony in the nineteenth century, and Japan formally annexed Korea in 1910. In 1945 it was agreed that the USSR would accept the Japanese surrender in the northern half of the country and the USA in the south, with the 38th Parallel as the boundary. Both sides agreed to 'free elections', but it became clear that the USSR – as in Europe – had no intention of honouring this and would accept nothing but a Communist government. In 1948, a Communist state was established in the north, and a parliamentary democracy south of the 38th Parallel. In 1949, Soviet and US forces were withdrawn, apart from military advisory teams, but the USSR had equipped and trained a large army in North Korea, which invaded South Korea on 25 June 1950.

This invasion could not have taken place without Soviet sponsorship. It is most unlikely that Mao Zedong in China would have wished to start a new war on his borders less than a year after the conclusion of nearly 20 years of continuous warfare against the Japanese and Chiang Kai-shek. The invasion appears to have taken the US government by surprise. An American division was rushed over from the occupation army in Japan to help delay the advance and hold a tiny bridgehead around the port of Pusan on the southern tip of Korea.

Soviet motives are uncertain, but the circumstances suggest that it was a calculated attempt to prove the impotence of the USA in her self-appointed role of checking Communist expansion worldwide. At the time of the invasion, the USSR was boycotting the Security Council in protest at the refusal to replace the defeated Chiang Kai-shek government's representative with that of the People's Republic of China (this did not happen for 21 years – in 1971). The USA called an emergency meeting with the intention of getting UN Security Council authority to deploy a UN force to drive back the invasion, and the US delegate specifically informed his Soviet opposite number of this intention in advance, giving him time to get his own government's authority to return to the council to veto the resolution if they so wished. The Soviet failure to do this could conceivably have arisen from themselves being taken by surprise by the timing of the invasion, or from the ponderousness of bureaucratic consultation with Moscow. Neither of these, however, seems at all likely. It is therefore fair to assume that the USSR actually wanted the UN to intervene and be seen to fail – as they very nearly did.

As it turned out, the US and South Korean armies, supported by a British brigade hastily flown from Hong Kong, just held on to Pusan and were able to mount a decisive counter-attack on 15 September, including an amphibious landing at Inchon in rear of the North Korean army which, pounded by naval and air bombardment all along the coast, was driven back in confusion, to the 38th Parallel. By this time the US General MacArthur had been appointed UN Commander, and had been authorized to proceed beyond the 38th Parallel to destroy the North Korean army and unite the country so that free elections could be held – provided that there was no sign of Soviet or Chinese intervention.[13]

On 1 October, South Korean forces crossed the 38th Parallel and on 3 October India passed on a warning that China would not tolerate US forces entering North Korea. Since the Soviet representative had by then returned to the Security Council, the USA put forward a resolution to the General Assembly recommending that 'all appropriate steps' be taken towards a unified government in Korea which, in the terms of the debate, was generally understood as sanctioning the occupation of the North.[14]

MacArthur then continued his offensive and his forces overran most of North Korea, reaching the border of China (the Yalu River) by 27 October. Here they clashed with Chinese 'volunteers'. After a lull, and some barren diplomatic activity, the Chinese launched a full-scale offensive on 26 November and within a month they had driven the UN forces out of North Korea and captured the South Korean capital Seoul. Early in 1951 the UN forces counter-attacked, recaptured Seoul and advanced up to and in places beyond the 38th Parallel. Here the Front stabilized, and a two-mile demilitarized zone was established, with a cease-fire in March 1952. Argument continued, however, mainly about whether prisoners should be handed back to their armies or allowed to choose where to go, which was eventually agreed – but not until after the death of Stalin. The armistice was signed on 27 July 1953. Three-quarters (14,000) of the Chinese prisoners and 35,000 North Korean prisoners chose to remain in South Korea or go to Taiwan rather than be repatriated.[15]

One lesson of this war was that poorly armed footsoldiers, *en masse*, could still overwhelm a modern army if they were prepared to accept heavy casualties. The number of Chinese troops reached 12 million in 1952.[16] Allied soldiers compared their ordeal with using tanks and machine-guns to mow down a mass demonstration. Chinese soldiers in the rear sometimes carried no weapons, picking up guns from those who had fallen, and the survivors pressed on to engulf the tanks and gun positions. (The collapse of Saddam Hussein's Iraqi soldiers in 1991 would probably not have happened if they had been Chinese.)

The other valuable learning process that came from the Korean War was in the working of the United Nations: the absence of the Soviet veto when the Security Council launched the UN force; and the emergence of the General Assembly's 'Uniting for Peace' procedure provided at least a partial answer to the blocking of Security Council action by a veto. One bizarre effect of this sequence of events is that the UN force still remains in Korea 42 years on, with an American commander and a large contingent of US troops but flying the UN flag, because a resolution to remove it could be vetoed by the USA. Although a Uniting for Peace resolution could recommend its withdrawal, it would not be able to enforce it.

In January 1953 a Republican, Eisenhower, became President of the United States, committed to ending the war.[17] In March 1953 Stalin died. Whether or not this affected the rapid resolution of the armistice talks in Korea, it certainly changed the nature of the Cold War, though this did not become apparent until after 1956.

THE KHRUSHCHEV ERA: 1953–64

Stalin had tried to ensure that, in his lifetime, no individual had sufficient power to attempt a coup. He was temporarily succeeded by a rather colourless technocrat, G. M. Malenkov, as Chairman of the Council of Ministers, later redefined as Premier. The party machinery continued to function and on 17 June an attempted rising in East Berlin was ruthlessly suppressed. On 6 July one of the leading contenders for power, L. P. Beria (Interior Minister and head of the KGB) was arrested and later shot; on 6 September 1953 Nikita Khrushchev was appointed to the key position of First Secretary of the Communist Party. Khrushchev dominated Soviet policy from 1954 to 1964, though he had to share power with Malenkov until 1955 and then Bulganin until 1958, when he assumed the combined posts of First Secretary and Chairman (see Table 6.2).

On 1 March 1954 the USA successfully tested an H-bomb.[18] Within a few years, Britain, France and the USSR had also developed theirs, with a power up to 250 times greater than that of the 1945 atom bomb. Whereas the Hiroshima bomb equated to 20,000 tons (20 kilotons) of high explosive (HE), or a raid by

Table 6.2 Cold War chronology: Khrushchev 1953–64

1953 Mar	Diffuse Soviet leadership. Khrushchev's power grew steadily
1954 Mar	USA exploded H-bomb
1954 May	French defeated in North Vietnam
1955 Jan	US advisers began replacing French in South Vietnam
1955 Mar	USSR and Czechoslovakia signed arms deal with Egypt
1955 May	Warsaw Treaty signed (USSR and seven others)
1955 Jul	Geneva conference partitioned Vietnam. French withdrew
1956 Feb	Khrushchev denounced Stalin at twentieth Party Congress
1956 Jun	USA withdrew financial support for Aswan Dam (Egypt)
1956 Jul	Egypt nationalized Suez Canal
1956 Oct	Second Arab–Israeli War
1956 Nov	USSR invaded Hungary to crush reformist government
1957 Mar	Treaty of Rome, founding the EEC (six countries)
1957 Oct	Soviet 'Sputnik', first satellite launched into space
1958 Mar	Khrushchev gained supreme power in USSR
1959 Feb	Castro seized power in Cuba
1960	Sino-Soviet split. USSR withdrew aid
1960–5	UN intervened in civil war in Congo (Zaire)
1961 Apr	Bay of Pigs invasion failed in Cuba
1961 Apr	First man in space (Yuri Gagarin, USSR)
1961 Jul	Iraqi invasion of Kuwait prevented by British intervention
1961 Aug	Berlin Wall built
1962 Oct	Cuban Missile Crisis
1963 Nov	President Kennedy of USA assassinated
1963	15,000 US military advisers in South Vietnam
1964 Oct	China exploded atom bomb
1964 Oct	Brezhnev ousted Khrushchev in USSR

2000 heavy bombers in a single burst, the H-bombs often equated to 5 million tons (5 megatons) of HE. Statesmen had shrunk from detonating or seriously threatening to detonate an atom bomb, and it was almost inconceivable that anyone would fire an H-bomb. This fact accelerated the policy of *détente* that developed on all sides during the Khrushchev era.

On 7 May 1954, the French regular army in Indo-China was defeated at Dien Bien Phu by a mass of North Vietnamese footsoldiers who had hauled heavy weapons through the jungle, underlining some of the lessons of the Korean War. With other insurgencies in the Far East in a critical stage (including Malaya and the Philippines), some senior voices in the USA were urging President Eisenhower to use or at least threaten to use nuclear weapons to stop the rot, but he was not persuaded. The five major powers (USA, USSR, Britain, France and China) held a summit meeting at Geneva in July 1954 in which agreement was reached on Vietnam, which was partitioned (at the 17th Parallel) with the now familiar formula of a Communist regime in the North and a Westernized democratic regime in the South, with the pious hope expressed that they would be united with 'free elections' which, as always, never came about. In 1955, Ngo Dinh Diem became President of the new Republic of South Vietnam. The French withdrew, and were replaced by a small number of American advisers.

This set in motion the tragedy of the US involvement in Vietnam, which unfolded inexorably towards total defeat in 1975. Though Soviet-supplied arms played a big part, and there was always a possibility of the USSR or conceivably China being drawn in, these were not the reasons. For the only time in her history the United States lost a war, and it was due to a lack of political will to see through what she had begun. The story of Vietnam from 1955 to 1975 will be briefly told in Chapter 11.

In February 1956, Khrushchev astonished the twentieth Party Congress in Moscow by denouncing Stalin's 'one-man rule, intolerance, brutality and abuse of power'. He exposed the wrongful convictions in the Great Purge of the 1930s; as a result, thousands of political prisoners were released.[19] An attempt by the old guard to oust him led to the dismissal of Molotov and Malenkov from the Party Presidium in 1957. All of this 'revisionism' caused unease in China, leading inexorably to a rapid decline in the Sino-Soviet alliance.

Khrushchev and Bulganin, travelling as a pair, began a series of goodwill visits around the world in the hope of relieving tension. Though they tolerated more flexibility in interpreting Communism in some of the East European countries, they imposed firm limits on how far this could go. In October 1956, Hungary attempted to liberalize its administration and to leave the Warsaw Pact. Soviet intervention led to mass demonstrations, and these were ruthlessly suppressed by Soviet tanks. This caused serious splits in Communist Parties worldwide, driving many of their more idealistic members to resign.

The world reaction to the invasion of Hungary in 1956 was, however, smothered by the simultaneous invasion of Egypt by Israel, Britain and France in the same month. The Suez crisis had begun in 1952, with a military coup in Egypt, fronted by a respected general, Mahammad Neguib, but masterminded by Colonel Gamal Abdel Nasser, who assumed full power in 1954. In 1955, Nasser turned to the East for arms, which were provided by Czechoslovakia but financed by the USSR. As a result of this, the USA in June 1956 withdrew a previous offer to finance the Aswan High Dam, a key project in the economic development of Egypt. The USSR happily took over this project but Nasser also used his need for funds as a pretext for nationalizing the Anglo-French owned Suez Canal on 26 July 1956. After three months of fruitless diplomacy – including a UN Resolution vetoed by the USSR – France and Britain connived with Israel in a military seizure of the Canal from 30 October to 7 November, diverting attention from the invasion of Budapest by Soviet tanks on 4 November. The USA and the USSR joined forces in the UN Security Council to force the British, French and Israelis to withdraw and hand over the Suez Canal and Sinai Peninsula to a UN peacekeeping force.

In 1957 the USSR astonished the world by launching the first vehicle into space, the Sputnik I. Its orbit was close enough to the earth for it to be seen as a small bright 'planet' moving steadily across the sky each night; the effect on the USA's reputation as the leading technological power was shattering, especially in the Third World. This effect was further enhanced with the launching of the first man into space (Yuri Gagarin) in 1961.

The immediate military implications of these events were not significant, since the USA was years ahead in development and manufacture of missiles, but it undoubtedly had an effect in 1962 on Khrushchev's decision to position offensive missiles on Cuba, capable of delivering nuclear warheads over a wide area of the eastern United States.

Until the 1962 crisis, the handling of Cuba by successive US governments had been inept. Fidel Castro had seized power from the corrupt Fascist Batista regime in 1959, a move which was initially given a guarded welcome. Castro certainly cooperated with the Cuban Communist Party in this revolution, but there is still doubt about whether he was originally an ideological Marxist himself. When he began to nationalize US businesses in Cuba in

1960, the USA tried to strangle his economy. Since Cuba had up till then been economically dependent on the USA, Castro turned to Khrushchev, who gleefully stepped in, offering to buy all Cuba's sugar crop and to supply oil and other commodities at very low prices. This gave Khrushchev a heaven-sent opportunity to establish a base for political activity in Latin America, and a military base close to the USA, to match some of those provided by the USA's allies all around the Soviet borders from Norway through Turkey to Pakistan.

President Kennedy took office in January 1961. He inherited a plan prepared by Cuban *émigrés* to invade Cuba with US assistance, with the aim of providing a focus for the supposedly seething Cuban majority to rise against Castro. This plan was well advanced under the Eisenhower administration, and was strongly supported by the Central Intelligence Agency (CIA). Cuban volunteers had been trained to make the landing, supported by US naval and air forces. Kennedy was extremely unhappy about this plan but, having almost lost the election in November 1960 as a result of accusations of being "soft on Communism", he was under immense pressure to let the invasion go ahead. He did so only when assured by the CIA that it would succeed without the use of US naval and air forces, provided that ships and aircraft were 'leased' to the Cubans to be operated by themselves.

The compromise was fatal. The invasion was a total fiasco, all the 1400 invading troops being rounded up on the beaches of the 'Bay of Pigs' within five days.[20] It made a disastrous start to Kennedy's presidency.

Khrushchev pressed home his advantage at his first summit meeting with Kennedy in Vienna in June 1961. Khrushchev needed a foreign policy success to counter the effect of the Sino-Soviet split, which had become public and seemingly irrevocable in 1960. He demanded from Kennedy an end to the Allied occupation of West Berlin, and made this public. Kennedy, equally under internal pressure, declared in a broadcast on 25 July that the freedom of West Berlin was not negotiable, called up over 100,000 reservists and put military preparations in motion. The fear of a Soviet clamp-down accelerated the drain of East Germany to the West, which became a torrent of 22,000 in the first 12 days of August.[21] On 13 August the East Germans erected the wall across Berlin to keep them in, in flagrant contravention of the four-power occupation agreements. There was much diplomatic activity. The USA reinforced her Berlin garrison with an additional battle group, but took no decisive action. Khrushchev, though he made a show of some harassment of air traffic to Berlin, was content that his domination continued, and he did not attempt to repeat the 1948 blockade.

Throughout the summer of 1962, there was a Soviet military build-up in Cuba, to continue the pressure on Kennedy. This included missiles, which surveillance at first identified as air-defence weapons. In September, however, there was evidence of offensive surface-to-surface missiles and Kennedy decided in October to publish the evidence and demand their removal. This built up into perhaps the most serious crisis of the Cold War. Kennedy was undoubtedly prepared to fight: this time Khrushchev knew it and removed the missiles. The 1962 Cuban Missile Crisis is examined in more detail in Chapter 8.

The crisis established Kennedy's reputation and destroyed Khrushchev's. Kennedy, however, was assassinated in November 1963 and was succeeded by Lyndon Johnson; Khrushchev was ousted from power by the Politburo in October 1964.

Khrushchev in his long career played an ambivalent role. A lifetime Communist, loyal to Stalin through the 1938 purge, he had become a Politburo member in 1939, and rose steadily to power through Communist Party channels. His denunciation of Stalin in 1956 was the hinge in Communist Party history, prompted by his realization that Stalinism, both socially and economically, would lead inexorably to the failure and collapse of the USSR. In 1959 he coined the phrase 'peaceful coexistence', disowning the cardinal Communist precept that the war with capitalism was in the end inevitable. He was convinced that, in the Cold War, Communism as he interpreted it could be made to prevail in open competition, both economically and in attracting the allegiance of the Third World. He continued, however, to support 'wars of national liberation', and did not hesitate to crack the Soviet whip in Hungary in 1956.

Khrushchev was ousted as First Secretary by his Second Secretary, Leonid Brezhnev, with Alexei Kosygin as Premier. In the same month (October 1964) the Chinese exploded their first atomic bomb. Once again there was a change of gear in the Cold War.

BREZHNEV AND THE ARRIVAL OF GORBACHEV: 1964–85

Brezhnev and Kosygin were aware that the USSR was far behind in the arms race, and could never afford to catch up, so they continued to pursue Khrushchev's policies of peaceful coexistence and *détente*; but they also continued the policy of supporting 'wars of national liberation' in the Third World and this included Vietnam, where the war was going wonderfully well for them (see Chapter 11). Following the assassination of President Diem in November 1963, there was a series of military coups in Vietnam leading to chaotic instability throughout 1964. The Soviet leadership felt that, if they could bring about another Geneva conference (as in 1954), the North Vietnamese and the Viet Cong would get everything they wanted. Kosygin led a powerful delegation to Hanoi in February 1965, and found the government split. The hawks were being encouraged by China to fight on to victory while the doves were anxious to achieve the same by negotiation. With a poor sense of timing, the USA bombed Hanoi during Kosygin's visit (see Table 6.3), and this decided the issue. In the competition to maximize influence over revolutionaries throughout the Third World, the USSR could not risk being sneered at by China for wanting to make a deal with the USA.[22] Having gone to Hanoi to urge negotiation, Kosygin had no option but to throw the weight of the Soviet Union behind the hawks.

Thereafter the war escalated rapidly, with growing involvement by North Vietnam, and it was clear that the South was losing. Having thus far sent only advisers, President Johnson took the fatal step of committing US combat units. In 1965, both the US and North Vietnamese armies deployed in increasing strength, the US involvement rising to half a million men by 1967.[23]

The US public became disillusioned with the war in 1968, and prolonged peace talks began. By 1973, all US combat troops had disengaged and the North Vietnamese army was poised to make a full-scale invasion of the South, which they did in 1975. The Vietnam war is analysed briefly in Chapter 11.

Reverting to 1965, the Soviet Premier Kosygin appeared in an unusual role when war broke out between India and Pakistan on

Table 6.3 Cold War chronology: Brezhnev and after 1964–85

1964 Aug	Naval incident in Tongking Gulf. US aircraft bombed North Vietnam
1965 Mar	US combat troops deployed in Vietnam
1965 Apr	Indo-Pakistan war
1966 Mar	French forces withdrew from NATO command
1967 Jun	Third Arab–Israeli war
1967–70	Nigerian civil war
1968 Feb	North Vietnamese Tet Offensive (Feb) led to peace talks
1968 Aug	Soviet invasion of Czechoslovakia
1969 Jul	First two men on the moon (from USA)
1969 Sep	Colonel Gadafi seized power in Libya
1970–75	Cambodian Civil war. Pol Pot massacres
1972	US combat troops disengage in Vietnam
1973 Jan	Peace in Vietnam left North poised for victory
1973 Oct	Fourth Arab–Israeli War
1974 Jul	Cyprus: Greek coup; Turkish invasion
1974 Sep	Communist revolution in Ethiopia (ousted 1991)
1975 Apr	South Vietnam overrun by North. Communist government
1976 Sep	Mao Zedong dies. Deng Xiaoping starts reforms
1977 Nov	Sadat (Egypt) and Begin (Israel) peace talks
1979 Feb	China–Vietnam Border War
1979 Jul	Guerrilla rising in El Salvador (ended 1992)
1979 Jul	Sandinista revolution in Nicaragua
1979 Dec	USSR invaded Afghanistan (withdrew 1988)
1980 May	*Sendero Luminoso* (SL) rising in Peru. 25,000 killed by 1992
1980 Sep	Iraq invaded Iran (war ended 1988)
1980 Aug	Anti-communist trade union in Poland (Solidarity)
1982 Apr	Argentina seized Falkland Islands. British recaptured (May–June)
1982 Nov	Brezhnev died; Andropov succeeded him (grooming Gorbachev)
1984 Feb	Andropov died; Chernenko succeeded him
1985 Feb	Chernenko died; Gorbachev succeeded him
1985–92	Liberalization and disintegration of Warsaw Pact and USSR

three sectors of their frontier, the most sensitive being in the partitioned territory of Kashmir. China, which had inflicted a humiliating defeat on India in a frontier dispute in 1962, threatened to intervene again in 1965. After the failure of the United Nations, the USA and Britain to resolve the crisis, a Soviet offer of mediation was accepted. President Ayub Khan of Pakistan and Prime Minister Shastri of India met with Kosygin as Chairman in Tashkent in January 1966, when the crisis was resolved with a remarkable display of conciliation on all sides.

In 1966, President de Gaulle, who harboured a deep personal dislike of the USA, withdrew all French forces from the NATO military command, though France, somewhat illogically, remained a member of NATO and continued to send representatives to its supreme political body, the NATO Council.

In 1967, the Soviet position in the Indian Ocean was greatly strengthened when Britain withdrew from Aden, making way for a Communist government of South Yemen, which thereafter provided a base for the Soviet navy. In the same year, in the Third Arab–Israeli War (the 'Six Day War'), Israel took the Sinai Peninsula and Gaza strip from Egypt, the West Bank from Jordan and the Golan Heights from Syria. This war is discussed in Chapter 9.

In 1968 a remarkable wave of student unrest got into its stride, with student protest and riots in the universities and in public demonstrations in the USA. These spread in May to France, where violent riots, combined with industrial strikes, came within sight of overturning the government; but President de Gaulle's firm handling reassured the alarmed majority and led to a massive swing to the right when he called an election. Student protest also spread to Germany, Britain, Italy and Japan.

Its origins were primarily in the USA, where student opposition to the Vietnam War had been growing. A major impetus came from the Military Selective Service Act of 1967, whereby all men between 18 and 26 were required to register, with the expectation of being sent to Vietnam. The numbers required, however, were limited, so there were many ways of gaining exemption. In particular university students were exempted if they wished to complete their degrees (i.e. for up to four years, and sometimes more to follow for graduate studies). There were many other ways in which the sons of prosperous parents could avoid the draft. The result was that a large percentage of those drafted to Vietnam were 'the poor and the black'. As well as their ideological objections and their genuine disgust at US military technology being used to slaughter Vietnamese peasants, the feeling of guilt amongst radical middle-class students that the working classes were taking their places – and up to 500 a week being killed – was probably as strong a motivation for militant opposition to the war as any other.

This movement, labelled the New Left, was Trotskyist in philosophy, and scathingly hostile to Soviet Communism. This hostility was intensified in 1968 when Soviet and other Warsaw Pact tanks crushed the brief attempt of Alexander Dubcek in Czechoslovakia to respond to the growing demand of students and intellectuals for greater freedom of speech and assembly.

In France, Germany, Italy, Britain and Japan, the New Left owed a great deal to the large number of American students at their universities, bringing stirring tales of triumphs at Berkeley and elsewhere. There was, however, a great deal of frustration with their own inability to get any response either from their own industrial workers or from their political systems. De Gaulle bestrode France, and in Germany from 1967 to 1969 there was a unique coalition between the two main parties – the Christian Democrats and the Social Democrats. In Italy the Christian Democrats and in Japan the Liberal Democrats were permanently in power, and the Italian Communist Party (PCI) seemed to be playing the despised 'bourgeois parliamentary game'. So did the British Labour Party.

As a result of this frustration, small fringes of New Left militants formed terrorist movements. Two of these, the Red Army Faction (RAF) in Germany and the Red Brigades (BR) in Italy, between them selectively killed about 100 people during the next 15 years, which was in retrospect little more than an irritant, but did provoke a substantial reaction. Much more damaging were the Palestinian terrorists who, frustrated by the loss of all their frontier access to Israel in the 1967 war, switched to the international stage, mainly by bombing and hijacking of aircraft, for the next 20 years.

The Soviet Union did not directly sponsor these movements, though the Palestinians did largely use Soviet weapons obtained through Arab governments whose armed forces were being supplied by the USSR. This became easier after 1969, when Colonel Gadafi seized power in Libya, and became a major supplier of arms, not only to the Palestinians, but also to other terrorist movements, including the Irish Republican Army (IRA) which began a major terrorist campaign in 1970 resulting in over

3000 deaths in the next 22 years. Brezhnev, while publicly dissociating himself from terrorism, must have watched the discomfiture of the West with some satisfaction.

In 1969, the USA recovered the psychological lead in space technology which she had lost 12 years earlier with the launch of the Sputnik satellite, by landing men on the moon.

In 1971, India intervened in the attempt of East Pakistan to break away from West Pakistan, resulting in the creation of the independent state of Bangladesh. Although this was a small war with no great international repercussions, it did teach some interesting lessons in crisis management: it is the subject of a brief case study in Chapter 12.

In 1973, the Fourth Arab–Israeli War resulted in the end of Soviet influence in Egypt, its replacement by massive US economic aid and the beginnings of a process of conciliation which resulted in a Peace Treaty with Israel in 1978. This war and its consequences are discussed in Chapter 10.

In July 1974, President Makarios was overthrown in a military coup by an extreme Greek Cypriot Nationalist, Nicos Sampson, who attempted to use the National Guard (officered mainly by professional army officers from mainland Greece) to dismantle the precarious power-sharing Greek/Turkish Cypriot government. The government of Turkey decided to come to the rescue of the Turkish minority (20 per cent) and invaded the island, occupying the whole of the northern half. This brought down not only the government of Cyprus but also the military government of Greece, which had been in power since a *coup d'état* in 1967. This crisis is examined in Chapter 12.

In 1974, Brezhnev was showing increasing interest in Africa, resulting in a series of Communist revolutions, first in 1974 in Ethiopia and then in 1975 in Mozambique and Angola, with the assistance of large numbers of Cuban military and technical advisers (later totalling some 20,000) financed by the USSR. Elsewhere, the Communist tide also flowed strongly in the completion of the conquest of South Vietnam (1975 – see Chapter 11), a Communist revolution in Nicaragua (1978) and the launching of a major guerrilla rising in El Salvador. However, these adventures and the immense cost of the arms race with the USA were fatally overstretching the Soviet economy; Brezhnev's decision to launch a large Soviet army into Afghanistan in 1978 got the USSR into a protracted war as unpopular with his own people as the Vietnam War had become in the USA.

In 1976, Mao Zedong died. There was then a period of rivalry between puritanical Marxists (led by Mao's widow and her 'Gang of Four') and pragmatists (led by Deng Xiaoping). By 1978, Deng was in full control, and for the next ten years the economy, especially in the rural areas which predominate in China, was liberalized, with incentives for enterprise, to an extent never approached by the USSR in the Gorbachev era (see Chapter 13). Political reforms were more cautious, and were severely set back by the burgeoning and ruthless repression of the pro-democracy movement in Tiananmen Square in Beijing in 1989 (see Chapter 13).

In 1979, the Shah of Iran was toppled by the Ayatollah Khomeini, who introduced a militant and ruthless Islamic Fundamentalist regime, as hostile to the USSR as it was to the USA. In November 1979, a crowd of extremist Islamic students (or ex-students) broke into the US Embassy and kidnapped the entire staff, holding more than 50 of them (having released women, blacks and some others) for 444 days with Khomeini's connivance. President Carter was uncertain and indecisive in dealing with this crisis, and launched a military rescue attempt in April 1980 which ended in disaster, adding to the humiliation and loss of confidence that had already resulted from the US abandonment of Vietnam. This fiasco was one of the main causes of Carter's failure to be re-elected as President. His last months in office after losing the election were devoted to intensive negotiation, using Algeria as an intermediary, which ended with the release of the hostages on the day that President Reagan was inaugurated – 20 January 1981.

In September 1980, Iraq invaded Iran, starting an eight-year war which is estimated to have cost more than 1 million lives. This war can now be seen as a first stage in Saddam Hussein's plan to gain control of all the oil in the Gulf which, containing as it does the majority of the world's oil reserves, would virtually have made Iraq a superpower, and certainly the unassailable leader of the Arab world.

As a pretext for the invasion, Saddam resurrected the ancient dispute between the Ottoman Empire and Persia, especially over the Shatt al-Arab, the common waterway which provides the only access to the Iranian oil port of Abadan and the Iraqi port of

Basra – or indeed up the Tigris to Baghdad. In the Tehran Treaty of 1937 it had been agreed that the frontier should lie along the low water mark on the Iranian side except for an enclave stretching out to the Thalweg (mid-channel) opposite Abadan.[24] In the Algiers accord of 6 March 1975, it was agreed that the frontier should henceforth follow the Thalweg; this had been signed by the Shah of Iran and Saddam Hussein himself.[25]

In 1979, following Khomeini's accession to power in Iran, Saddam initiated proposals to negotiate a revision of the 1975 accord, to restore the river frontier to the low water mark as in 1937, that is, to give Iraq sovereignty over the whole navigable waterway except for the Abadan enclave.

Iran was not prepared to negotiate on this basis and on 21 September 1980, Iraqi forces invaded Iran, quickly seizing most of the Iranian bank of the Shatt al-Arab and advancing inland. Another pretext for the attack was the alleged persecution of the Arab population in that province of Iran, known to the Iranians as Khuzestan and to the Arabs as Arabistan.

There was no 'cold war' aspect to this conflict so it will not be discussed in detail, either here or in the case studies that follow this chapter. Other aspects of it were, however, relevant to the background of the Gulf War of 1990–91: these will be examined in Chapter 14.

The cracks in the Soviet Empire began to appear in 1980 with the establishment of a free trade union in Poland, led by Lech Walesa. Initially the Polish government tried to live with it but in December 1981 they declared martial law. Attempts at repression, however, were half-hearted, and seemed to be no more than the new President, General Jaruzelski, judged to be the minimum necessary to avert military intervention by the USSR. Poland led the way to the collapse of Communism in Eastern Europe in 1989 and in the Soviet Union herself in 1991. This story will be told in Chapter 13.

The crisis management of the Falklands conflict in 1982 also has some interesting aspects: it is considered as a case study in Chapter 12.

Leonid Brezhnev died shortly after the Falklands War in November 1982. He was succeeded by Yuri Andropov, who had been head of the KGB and was regarded by the world as a hardliner. It transpired, however, that in the closing years of his life, Andropov had realized that the Soviet economy was heading for collapse under the strain of the continuing and ever more sophisticated arms race, and that, as well as continuing the policy of *détente*, it was essential to liberalize the economy and give some scope and incentive to the initiative of the Soviet people. Mikhail Gorbachev had been one of Andropov's protégés in the KGB, and he appointed him to the task of revolutionizing the economy, giving also the strong impression that he would be groomed as his successor. Gorbachev began to visit Western countries to discuss economic problems and made an excellent impression on both political leaders and the public. In February 1984, Andropov died and was succeeded by the ailing Konstantin Chernenko, who himself died a year later in February 1985. Gorbachev took over and it soon became clear that he was intending to pursue a radical policy of liberalization both of the economy and of the social and political structure, and to press ahead with disarmament and encouragement of capital investment. Within four years, the Warsaw Treaty had disintegrated, and all the former satellite members of it had introduced some form of parliamentary democracy. Within six years, the Soviet Union had disintegrated into fifteen independent democratic states, its Communist Party largely disappeared (through some of its hardline members strove to perpetuate its policies under new labels), and Gorbachev himself, having no longer either a country or a party to lead, retired from public life.

These dramatic events, probably the most widespread and far-reaching series of revolutions in the world's history, will be examined in Chapter 13, after the case studies of conflicts and crisis management in the Cold War era.

7 Czechoslovakia and Berlin 1948

THE COMMUNIST COUP IN CZECHOSLOVAKIA

President Benes returned to Prague on 18 May 1945, nine days after its liberation by the Soviet army.[1] In view of his betrayal at Munich in 1938, Benes was understandably more inclined to trust the USSR than the West. Stalin invited him to form a government, so he nominated a Provisional National Assembly which elected him President, pending a general election. This was duly held on 26 May 1946, and the Communists won 2,695,293 votes (38.7 per cent of the total). As this made them the largest single party, Benes appointed the Communist leader, Klement Gottwald, as Premier of a Coalition government from all the six parties which had stood in the election. The other parties accepted this with confidence because, provided that they stuck together, they held a commanding majority (61.3 per cent). The Communists were in a similar minority in the Cabinet. Gottwald, however, put Communists or their fellow travellers in all the key ministries, including Interior, Defence, Information, Agriculture and Finance.[2]

In February 1948 the Communists seized power in a political *coup d'état*. This crisis initially developed from Gottwald's refusal (on Stalin's orders) to accept the vote of the majority of the Coalition Cabinet to accept Marshall Aid from the USA in 1947. It came to a head on 13 February 1948 when the democratic majority at a Cabinet meeting adopted a resolution instructing the Communist Minister of the Interior to stop the practice of packing the police force with Communists. Gottwald supported the minister in refusing to carry out this resolution. The non-Communist ministers then made a tactical error in resigning *en bloc*, assuming that this would force President Benes to call a general election. Gottwald, however, immediately put Communists in place of the resigning ministers, and seized all their party headquarters. The Communists issued arms to workers loyal to the Party and led them in mass columns on the streets of Prague.

Communist 'action committees' were set up in Prague and in the provinces and local authorities ordered to cooperate with them. Benes bowed to the inevitable. Most of the former non-Communist ministers fled the country. In March, the Foreign Minister, Jan Masaryk, was found dead in the street under a window of the Foreign Office. Masaryk had been one of Czechoslovakia's nationalist heroes before and during the war, and was one of the few members of the wartime government-in-exile in the Cabinet. He had been persuaded by Benes to remain in Gottwald's new Cabinet after the coup, rather than resign with the other non-Communist ministers. There was much conjecture about whether he had committed suicide or had been murdered.

Gottwald promulgated a new Constitution on the Soviet model on 9 May 1948. President Benes refused to approve it and resigned (he died three months later). On 30 May, a 'general election' was held with only a single list of Communist-approved candidates; Gottwald was duly elected President of what had now become a totalitarian Communist state.

Sadly, the Communist realization of the depth of the Czechoslovak people's yearning for democracy resulted in them being subjected to one of the most repressive of all the East European regimes. The gallant attempt in 1968 by a reformist Communist, Alexander Dubcek, to relax this repression and allow freedom of speech was ruthlessly snuffed out by tanks from the USSR and – to their shame – from their Warsaw Pact neighbours, whose Communist leaders feared the risk of contagion (see p. 96). The Czechoslovak people had to wait 21 years until the general collapse of Communism in Eastern Europe in 1989 (see Chapter 13).

THE BERLIN BLOCKADE

In September 1944, the USA, Britain and the USSR had agreed on temporary three-power occupation of Germany (later four, with France). Stalin never envisaged this as other than a transition to a single united Communist Germany, to remove his main fear, a resurgence of a German military threat to the USSR.[3] Berlin was to be occupied by four Allied contingents under a *Kommandatura* of the four generals. Access across the 260 km from the West (British) zone was by single road and rail routes, supplemented by three air corridors through which Western aircraft had overflying rights without notice. These routes were not agreed in writing; the Allies preferred to keep them vague because they did not wish to prejudice their claim of unlimited access throughout occupied Germany.[4]

Initially the USSR, who got there first, installed a city administration in Berlin for the German Communist Party but, in view of the Allied presence, they had to accept the process of a democratic local election on 26 October 1926, in which the Communists did unexpectedly badly. An anti-Communist Socialist, Ernst Reuter, was elected Mayor.[5] Thereafter, four-power administration became a fiction and a struggle developed on two levels, 'that of inter-Allied relations, which centred on the *Kommandatura*, and that of Allied relations with the city population, which centred in the party political battle'.[6]

Marshall Aid (introduced in June 1947) was extended to the Allied zones of West Germany in March 1948, but vetoed in the Soviet zone, where officials began to harass and obstruct transit by road and rail from the West to Berlin. The West began a limited airlift, mainly for personnel. In June, the Soviet commander walked out of the Berlin *Kommandatura*. On 20 June, the Allies introduced a reformed currency (the Deutschmark replacing the Reichsmark at one for ten) in the Western zones but not, at this stage, in Berlin. The USSR responded on 23 June by introducing a separate currency into the Eastern Zone of Germany including Berlin. Next day the Allies made the Deutschmark available in Berlin also (there was, of course, no 'Berlin Wall' at this time) and the USSR blocked all military traffic by road and rail. In July the Allies considered but rejected a plan to send an armed convoy along the autobahn.[7] By 4 August the road and rail blockade was complete, against all civilian as well as military traffic.

Throughout August, talks with Molotov and twice personally with Stalin failed to resolve the crisis and the West began an airlift for freight as well as personnel into Berlin. They also imposed a counter-blockade on goods going by rail into East Germany.[8]

On 29 September 1948 a UN Security Council Resolution to resolve the crisis was vetoed by the USSR. The fear of the situation developing into war reached a peak and part of the US long-range bomber force was moved to bases in Britain.[9]

The Allies established a Task Force for the airlift. Through the winter they flew in 5000 tons per day into West Berlin. In the spring of 1949 this was raised to 8000 tons per day, which had been the normal daily freight by land. The highest in one day exceeded 12,000 tons. The massive US and British air force transport fleets, reactivated on a wartime scale, were landing two aircraft every minute. It was a brilliant feat of organization of all-weather flying and air traffic control, inevitably involving some accidents but mercifully few. In all, more than 1 million tons were flown into West Berlin.[10]

Secret talks between the US and Soviet representatives at the UN, Dr Philip Jessup and Jacob Malik, had begun in January, and initially Jessup said that he thought these were merely being used as an excuse to prolong the blockade. In April 1949, NATO was formed, guaranteeing a binding US military presence and commitment in Europe and massive rearming of its Allies. Perhaps alarmed by this, the Soviets became more conciliatory: Malik suggested that the Berlin blockade might be lifted if the counter-blockade was raised and if the establishment of a West German government was postponed pending a meeting of the Council of Foreign Ministers. No mention was made of currency – the original pretext for the blockade;[11] the Deutschmark remained the sole legal currency in West Berlin, and the Ostmark in the East. The blockade ended on 12 May 1949 after 318 days.[12]

Following approval by the Allies of the Basic Law drawn up by the West German Parliamentary Council in May, the Federal Republic of Germany was established on 21 September, leaving the status of Berlin unchanged. On 7 October, the USSR proclaimed the German Democratic Republic in East Germany.

From 1949 to 1961, there was a continuous flow of refugees from East Germany into West Berlin and thence into West Germany. This consisted primarily of the more skilled and successful people whom the East Germans could ill afford to lose, so in August 1961 they built the Berlin Wall. In 1989, with refugees again becoming a flood, through Austria, Hungary and Czechoslovakia, the wall was demolished; in 1990, Germany was reunified (see Chapter 13).

The Berlin blockade was the Soviets' most direct challenge to the West. Their concern about the resurgence of Germany, only three years after the war, was understandable. They saw (correctly)that the Marshall Plan would result in an economic division into a rich capitalist and poor Communist part and would remove forever the chance of a united Communist Germany as part of their empire in East Europe.

No one would have expected the Allies to be able to maintain delivery for eight months of the necessary 8000 tons a day, including such bulk supplies as coal, by military air transport. Stalin realized, however, that shooting down a transport aircraft would involve a very high probability of war, and at this time the USA had a monopoly of the atomic bomb. The corresponding restraint of the Allies in not sending an armed convoy down the autobahn was presumably based on the realization that Western public opinion was not ready to resume the war, and that the USSR would soon also have an atomic bomb (the first one was exploded in 1949). Apart from the risk of launching a general war, the US government was probably concerned not to create a precedent by threatening a nuclear attack to get their way.

Both sides were wise enough throughout the crisis to look through the eyes of their adversary, to gauge how each would react to every possible course of action. In the event, neither went too far, and the diplomatic dialogue, albeit barren and sometimes aggressive, continued. From the Allied viewpoint, the confrontation established their ascendancy, which was further enhanced in Cuba in 1962 and culminated triumphantly in 1989.

8 Cuba 1962

KRUSHCHEV'S GAMBLE

In June 1962, Khrushchev saw an opportunity to exploit what he perceived to be Kennedy's weakness, based on the humiliation of the Bay of Pigs disaster, their Vienna summit meeting in June 1961 and Kennedy's inability to prevent the building of the Berlin Wall in August (see pp. 91–2). He believed that he would be able to redress his disadvantage in global missile deployment by installing Medium and Intermediate Range Ballistic Missiles (MRBMs and IRBMs) in Cuba and that Kennedy would be powerless to prevent it (the range of the MRBM was 1000 and of the IRBM 2000 miles.)[1]

This was important to him because the USA had missiles stationed all round the periphery of the USSR within range of her major cities (in Western Europe, Turkey, Pakistan and South Korea), while the USSR had none within range of the US heartland at all. The Inter Continental Ballistic Missile (ICBM)[2] was still in the development stage and, with current technology, IRBMs and MRBMs could for the first time reach Washington or New York if they were based in Cuba.

Khrushchev, despite his confidence that he could psychologically dominate Kennedy, was conscious of weaknesses in his own position at home: he was blamed for the failure of his agricultural policy; some Politburo members distrusted his policy of peaceful coexistence, and despised and were ashamed of his often undignified behaviour at international conferences. He badly needed a foreign policy success. On the other hand, as a realist, he dared not risk going over the brink to war, in view of the powerful military advantage of the USA.

Kennedy also badly needed a foreign policy success, because his own internal position was weak too. Unlike Khrushchev, however, he *was* prepared to carry a confrontation to the brink of war, because he was convinced that Khrushchev would in the end have to give way. His confidence was greatly reinforced by the presence of a spy at the heart of the Soviet intelligence organization, Colonel Penkovsky. Penkovsky was handled by the British intelligence service (through a not very professional contact who regularly visited the USSR on business – Greville Wynn). Penkovsky's most immediate information was about the design and capability of various types of Soviet missiles, and of the dimensions and layout of their storage and launching facilities. This proved immensely valuable in identifying the types of missiles and likely dates of readiness from high altitude air photos of construction sites. Equally important, however, were the hard facts about the Politburo's realization of the extent of the US military superiority, such that they would almost certainly back off if the risk of war were imminent. This awareness gave Kennedy a huge negotiating advantage.

ANATOMY OF THE CRISIS

The secret preparation of Soviet missile sites in Cuba probably began in June 1962,[3] and photos from high-flying U2 reconnaissance aircraft began to arouse suspicion. It had always been anticipated that the USSR would provide air defence, that is, surface-to-air missiles (SAMs), to Cuba. US intelligence confirmed that some of these had been spotted, and that there were 3500 Soviet technicians in Cuba. Kennedy announced this publicly on 4 September and warned that 'the gravest issues would arise' if any offensive, that is, surface-to-surface missiles (SSMs), appeared in Cuba.[4] He repeated this warning on 13 September.

On 15 October, the US Department of State repeated a previous warning that the USA would *not* agree to any proposal for a bargain that if the USSR withdrew from Cuba, the USA would withdraw from Berlin.

Also on 15 October, analysis of air photographs from U2 flights on 14 October and earlier, showed conclusively (based on Penkovsky's dimensions and layouts) that IRBM and MRBM sites were under construction. On 16 October, Kennedy decided that some US reaction to this was essential and formed an Executive Committee (ExCom) headed by the Attorney-General (his brother Robert Kennedy) with the Secretaries of State (Dean Rusk)and Defence (Robert McNamara), the Chairman of the Joint Chiefs of Staff (General Maxwell Taylor) and others.[5] One of the aims of this was to enable the President to continue his public engagements (which were considerable in the run up to mid-term congressional elections due in November) lest his sudden or repeated absence might give rise to a crisis atmosphere which at this stage he wished to avoid. ExCom, however, could and did meet frequently without attracting attention, and referred their analyses and recommended decisions to the President informally. This organization, established early in the crisis, proved extremely successful, due partly to the high degree of mutual understanding between the Kennedy brothers, Rusk and McNamara, and the professional competence of Maxwell Taylor.

ExCom considered the following options

1 No action other than diplomatic (public through the UN or private through the Soviet Foreign Secretary Gromyko, who was in Washington at the time)
2 A blockade
3 Pinpoint bombing of missile sites
4 Invasion of Cuba (carrying the risk of nuclear war).[6]

On 18 October, Kennedy kept a long-standing engagement to meet Gromyko. Kennedy drew attention to his warnings of 4 and 13 September and Gromyko stated emphatically that no offensive capability was being provided for Cuba. Kennedy shrewdly did not challenge this undertaking, because, if he had indicated that he had *knowledge* of the installations in progress, Gromyko might deduce that the USA intended to confine their response to words, and not action.[7]

On 19 October, ExCom decided on a limited naval blockade (ie checking ships incoming to Cuba and turning away only certain specified cargoes) which they termed a 'quarantine'. President Kennedy agreed to this on 20 October, but preparations were also made for the air strikes and for an invasion. Assembly of a full-scale invasion force at southern US ports and airfields was begun and nuclear deterrent forces were placed at maximum alert.[8]

On 22 October, President Kennedy announced the quarantine, and the reason for it, in a nationwide (and thus immediately worldwide) television broadcast. He was impressively relaxed and confident.[9]

Throughout the crisis, Kennedy had kept his European NATO Allies informed. He had a particularly warm relationship with the British Prime Minister, Harold Macmillan, and the British had also wisely posted a long-standing friend and contemporary of Kennedy's, David Ormsby-Gore, as Ambassador to the USA. Kennedy spoke to Macmillan by telephone almost every day and discussed his dilemmas with Ormsby-Gore, repeatedly, on a personal basis. Kennedy also went to great trouble to keep the Latin American nations informed through the Organization of American States (OAS), which met at 9 am on 23 October and unanimously supported the quarantine,[10] for they had no desire to see offensive nuclear missiles based in Cuba.

On 24 October the quarantine came into force and early on the 25th the first Soviet ship, the oil tanker *Bucharest*, was stopped: it was allowed to proceed as petroleum was not one of the quarantined cargoes. Of 25 Soviet ships approaching Cuba, air reconnaissance revealed that 12 had turned away – presumably those with incriminating cargoes. This report prompted the now famous comment by Dean Rusk at ExCom: 'We're eyeball to eyeball, and I think the other guy just blinked'.[11]

Also on the 25th, the UN Security Council met and, live on television, the US Ambassador to the UN (former presidential candidate Adlai Stevenson) challenged Soviet Ambassador Zorin to answer yes or no to whether the USSR was placing MRBMs and IRBMs in Cuba and, when Zorin declined to reply, Stevenson displayed the incriminating air photographs on the screen.[12]

On 24 October, the UN Secretary-General U Thant had appealed to Khrushchev to suspend arms shipments to Cuba and to Kennedy to lift the quarantine. Khrushchev at once agreed, no doubt welcoming the excuse to turn his ships away without seeming to be giving way to the US Navy. Kennedy, however, replied that the threat was created by offensive weapons already secretly landed in Cuba, and that the crisis could be resolved only by removing these weapons. The intensive US air reconnaissance now revealed that construction work on the missile sites was proceeding at full speed.[13]

On the 25th U Thant sent a second message, appealing to both to avoid direct confrontation at sea. Again Khrushchev agreed and so too did Kennedy, on condition that the USSR also did so, that is, not attempt to run the blockade.[14] On 26 October a ship flying the Lebanese flag under charter to the USSR, the *Marucla*, was stopped and boarded by the US Navy and allowed to continue.[15]

On the same day, the White House issued detailed reports of continued and intensive construction activity at both MRBM and IRBM sites, obviously trying to achieve 'full operational capacitity as soon as possible'.[16]

Meanwhile intensive diplomatic activity, direct and indirect, was proceeding in Washington. Alexander Fomin, Counsellor at the Soviet Embassy, met television reporter John Scali for lunch on 26 October, and indicated that Khrushchev might be ready to withdraw the missiles if the USA lifted the blockade and undertook not to invade Cuba. Scali checked with Rusk (and through him Kennedy) and was authorized to tell Fomin that the US government would be interested in this proposal.[17] Later that night (9 pm 26 October Washington time and 4 am 27 October Moscow time) a personal letter from Khrushchev (No 1) was received by cable at the State Department, putting this same proposal in emotional terms, and making no other conditions.

Next morning (27th), a second letter from Khrushchev (No 2) was received. This was written in a stiffly official tone, much more aggressive than No 1, specifically demanding a direct *quid pro quo*, the removal of Soviet missiles from Cuba in exchange for removal of US missiles from Turkey. This arrived while ExCom were drafting a reply accepting the proposals in the first letter. They had to decide whether the official letter, No 2, was overriding No 1. They guessed, however, that No 2 was in fact drafted first, at a Politburo meeting on the 26th and that Khrushchev, unhappy about its tone, had gone home and written his letter (No 1) personally to Kennedy in a desperate attempt to avoid the drift to war; and that he then had it transmitted directly on the wire around midnight Moscow time, without passing through the bureaucratic channels as No 2 did later on the 27th.[18] Indeed No 2 was dated the 27th and No 1 the 26th. ExCom therefore decided to ignore letter No 2 completely and answer No 1, accepting Khruschev's proposal (i.e. that if the missiles were withdrawn they would lift the quarantine and undertake not to invade Cuba) and making no reference to missiles in Turkey. This reply was sent on the evening of 27 October. Robert Kennedy gave a copy of the letter to the Soviet Ambassador, adding a verbal hint that the missiles in Turkey were now obsolete and would in any case be gone before long.[19]

Two other events on 27 October indicated the determination of both sides not to allow the resolution of the crisis to be blown off course. A U2 reconnaissance aircraft was shot down over Cuba, clearly indicating that the SAMs were now operational, and Fidel Castro crowed triumphantly, shouting his defiance of the USA. Kennedy confirmed that air reconnaissance would continue, and called up US Air Force reserves, but did not threaten to bomb the SAM sites. One the same day, another U2 strayed over Siberian territory. Soviet fighters were scrambled but thc U2 was not attacked. Khrushchev later complained in modest terms and Kennedy apologized.[20]

At 9 am on 28 October (4 pm Moscow time) Moscow radio announced that Khrushchev had accepted Kennedy's reply to his letter (No 1). In the written version wired to Washington, Khrushchev said that he had ordered work on the missile sites to be stopped, and for the missiles to be shipped back to Moscow. He promised that the UN would be permitted to verify the dismantling.[21] In the event, the Soviet ships removed the covers and made the missiles clearly visible on the decks of the cargo ships for US reconnaissance aircraft flying overhead to photograph. By mid-November, all the missiles had gone, but some Ilyushin bombers capable of carrying nuclear bombs were still there. Khrushchev said that these could not be withdrawn as they were a gift to Castro, but Kennedy warned that he would destroy them by air attack and they were quickly withdrawn. The quarantine was lifted on 20 November.

CRISIS MANAGEMENT

The Cuban Missile Crisis was the hinge of the Cold War. In the 1950s, it seemed to political, intelligence and military leaders on both sides that war between NATO and the Warsaw Pact was eventually certain to come – just as certain as it seemed in the 1930s that a war with Hitler was inevitable. The handling of the 1962 crisis had an effect as far reaching as if Britain and France had in 1935 made it clear that they would fight if Hitler continued to rearm and expand his army in breach of the Treaty of Versailles. But for this to be effective it would have been essential for Britain and France to be *genuinely* ready and willing to fight. In fact, Hitler was confident that they would seek 'peace at any price'. Kennedy definitely was prepared to fight. Khrushchev realized this and backed off.

The phrase 'crisis management' (credited to Robert McNamara) was coined – or at least became common currency – during this crisis. The successful resolution gave rise to a large number of books and articles on crisis management during the next few years. These remain generally the best that there are,[22] because much of the more recent writing on the subject has become too complicated and theoretical, and confuses rather than enlightens the practitioners (political, intelligence or military) who are trying to apply themselves to resolving anticipated or current crises. Nigel Forward (a serving British diplomat) in his book did bring theory and practice together, and for academic purposes his is probably the best source.

The most professional and concise was Harlan Cleveland's article 'Crisis Diplomacy', in *Foreign Affairs* in July 1973. Cleveland was in the US Foreign Service at the time and personally involved. He summarizes the principles followed by President Kennedy as follows:

Keep your objectives limited Kennedy aimed to get the missiles out of Cuba, not to oust Castro or Khrushchev. He was sensible enough to realize that wider dividends would follow in any case.

Decide how far you would go Kennedy was prepared to go right through to invasion, with the risk of nuclear war, envisaging that Khrushchev would realize this and that when he did he would back off. This is, however, a high-risk strategy (as 1914 proved) and depends above all on good intelligence.

Creep up carefully on the use of force Kennedy insisted that the navy did enough to ensure that Khrushchev realized that his ships would be stopped, but was careful to avoid inflicting intolerable humiliation or to leave him no practicable way out.

Widen the community of the concerned Kennedy was assiduous in keeping his Allies in NATO and the OAS informed, and ensuring their support.

The law you make may be your own Kennedy avoided any action which would have given Khrushchev a plausible excuse to do the same to Kennedy's disadvantage on some future occasion.

There were two other important principles which Kennedy observed, though Harlan Cleveland did not mention them:

Keep your own options open Coupled with 'creeping up carefully on the use of force', Kennedy ensured that his armed forces were in fact fully prepared for the higher options, such as air strikes or invasion. This was a major factor in ensuring that Khrushchev did know for certain that Kennedy was prepared to use these options, since the massive concentration of an invasion force at ports and airfields on a war footing could not possibly escape detection by the efficient and pervasive Soviet intelligence system.

Ensure that your adversary has some tolerable option other than to fight Kennedy certainly did this. Khrushchev was able to claim that he had not come away empty-handed; Kennedy gave a public undertaking not to invade Cuba; and he indicated (privately through his brother) that the obsolete US missiles would shortly be removed from Turkey.

Though hardly a principle, **good intelligence** is a decisive element in crisis management. Technical intelligence, especially using modern surveillance techniques, is invaluable but almost always the best intelligence of all comes from human sources, from people in or with means of observing the actions and (by deduction therefrom) the intentions of the adversary. Penkovsky's information was worth morc than all the rest.

Finally, as mentioned in Chapter 1 (p. 8), **signals** can be an important crisis management tool. Signals are actions which may transmit the messages more convincingly than public pronouncements or formal communications.

Amongst the effective signals used, and almost certainly reported were the following:

21 October	Movement of troops in readiness for invasion Evacuation of non-essential personnel from the US base in Guandanamo, Cuba Invasion rehearsals on an island off Puerto Rico

22 October	Nuclear forces alerted 180 US Navy ships moved to the Caribbean Kennedy's TV announcement of the quarantine.

And, in moving towards a settlement, also:

26 October	Scali-Fomin meeting
27 October	Robert Kennedy's verbal hint to the Soviet Ambassador about forthcoming redundancy of US missiles in Turkey Restrained reaction by Kennedy and Khrushchev to U2 incidents.

Those on 21 and 22 October clearly indicated that Kennedy's readiness to fight was serious; those on 26 and 27 October indicated that he was anxious to settle, within clear limits, provided that the missiles were removed.

Potentially this was the most dangerous crisis of the Cold War and both sides deserve some of the credit for its peaceful resolution. Kennedy, though he wanted to avoid war, realized that willingness to fight was an essential ingredient for resolving the crisis successfully, and for preventing worse crises in the future that would have followed if he had accepted an unsatisfactory settlement.

9 The First Arab–Israeli Wars 1948–67

THE FOUNDATION OF ISRAEL

There were about 700,000 Jews and 800,000 Arabs in Israel when it was created by the UN in 1948. By 1992 there were about 3 million Jews and 400,000 Arabs within Israel's legal borders, and another 1 million Arabs in the additional territories occupied by Israel in 1967; there were about 1.5 million Palestinian refugees, of whom just under 1 million were (or were descended from) Arabs driven from their homes in what was to become Israel during the months before partition in May 1948. The terror that drove them out was mainly perpetrated by two small Jewish terrorist movements in one of the earliest and most ruthless manifestations of 'ethnic cleansing'.[1] These Palestinian Arabs and their descendants demanded the right to reoccupy the land within Israel's legal (1949) borders, from which they were evicted. Their personal suffering at the time was comparable with that of a rather larger number of refugees displaced in Bosnia and Croatia in 1992 (see Chapter 15). Yet the Arab–Israeli conflict has had a malign influence on the world's international relations for nearly half a century, out of all proportion to the populations involved and seems likely to continue to do so.

The purpose of the next two chapters is first to summarize in a few pages why this conflict is so deep-rooted and why the adversaries are so intransigent, and second, to draw lessons from the crisis management of two of the most violent explosions of this conflict into war in 1967 and 1973.

'Two dogs, one bone' is the short answer. The strip of coastal plain which legally constitutes Israel (only nine miles across at its narrowest point) is one of the most fertile in the whole of the Middle East (see Map 9A). Both the Jews and the Arabs are totally convinced of their right to possess it, leading from

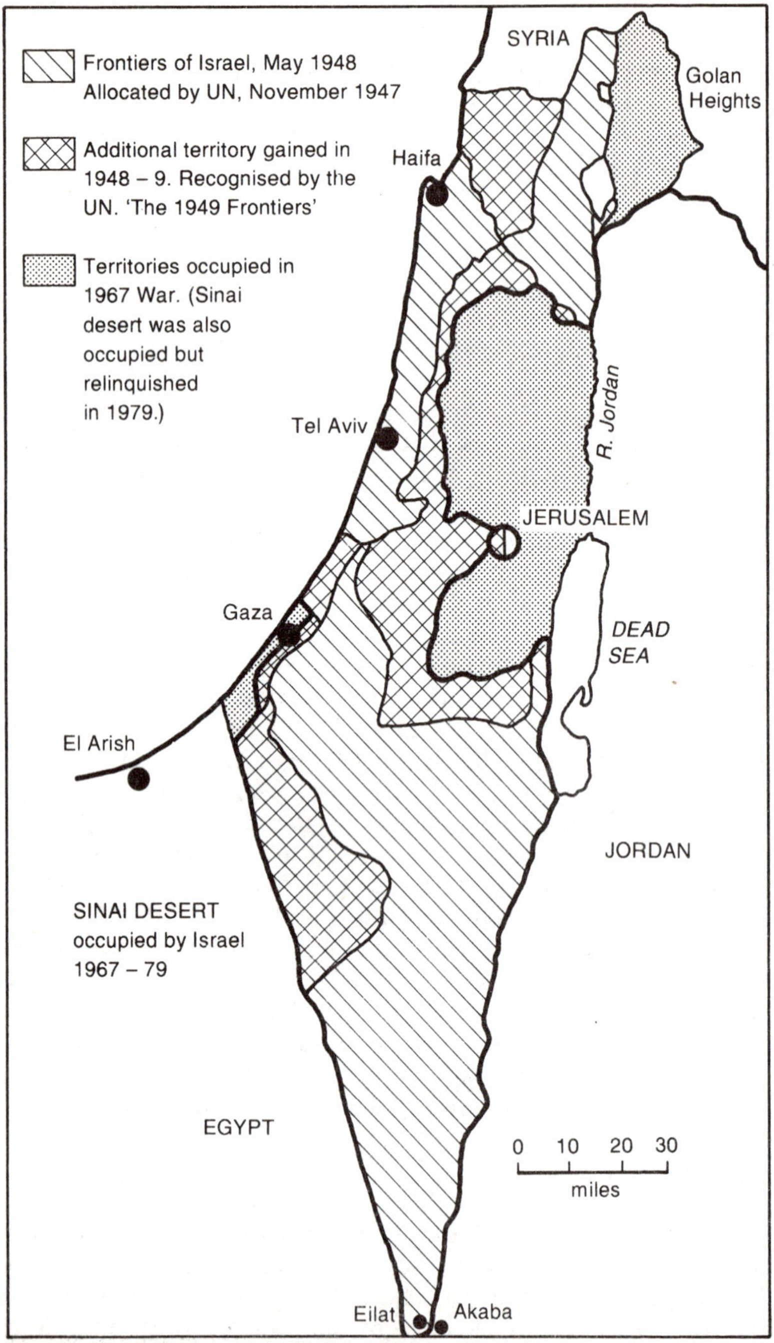

Map 9A Israel 1948 – 92

historical and religious reasons. The Jews possessed it (latterly under Roman occupation) until AD 70, and their religion teaches them that it was given to them by God – though ironically the 'Land of Israel' was Judea and Samaria, now the occupied West Bank territory, while the coastal plan was the 'Land of the Philistines' – their greatest enemies. In AD 650, Muhammad's immediate successors occupied the whole region, which continued, as part of the Muslim Ottoman Empire until 1917, with an almost entirely Arab population.

The Jews, since AD 70 dispersed all over the world, maintained their identity and to a great extent their ethnicity, largely by resisting intermarriage with gentiles. Their long-held aspiration to return to their biblical homeland was specifically declared at the First Zionist Conference in Basel in 1897. Jewish immigrants to Palestine formed their first *Kibbutz*, and their first Jewish town (Tel Aviv), in 1909.

The British army drove out the Turks in 1917, allied with Arab irregulars for whom T. E. Lawrence was a military adviser. The League of Nations then mandated Britain to remain in occupation (a mandate only reluctantly accepted by the British government). From 1924 to 1939, with refugee pressure mounting due to Nazi persecution in Germany, controlled immigration brought the number of Jewish settlers to 29 per cent and they bought, irrigated and developed large areas of land from the Arabs. They also built up their commerce and industry in the towns. Arab resentment eventually exploded in the Arab revolt of 1936–8.

In 1947, amid rising communal violence, the British announced that in 1948 they would terminate the mandate and invited the UN, as successors to the League, to take responsibility. A UN Special Commission on Palestine (UNSCOP) produced a partition plan based on borders incorporating as closely as possible the land at that stage owned by Jews, individually or through the Jewish Agency, which in May 1948 became the government of Israel. Egypt, Jordan and Syria at once invaded the infant state which, to the world's astonishment, drove the vastly stronger Arab armies back. During the fighting, anomalies in the borders (e.g. the 1947 UN plan had allocated three separate areas to Israel connected only by an isolated crossing point – see Map 9A) became clear; in April 1949 the UN brokered an armistice based on revised frontiers which, by a UN majority vote, became the legal borders of Israel ('the 1949 frontiers').

Egypt, Jordan and Syria, however, did not accept them or any other borders and remained in a state of war with Israel: Egypt until 1977 and Jordan and Syria to the present time.

THE SUEZ WAR OF 1956

In July 1952, a group of young officers led by Colonel Gamal Abdel Nasser, then aged 34, organized a *coup d'état* that ousted King Farouk of Egypt. He initially made the respected General Neguib Prime Minister (and later President), rightly believing that this would make the regime more acceptable to the world. In 1954, they successfully negotiated the termination of the Anglo-Egyptian Treaty of 1936, under which Britain maintained an army garrison on the Suez Canal, and the last British troops withdrew in June 1955 (see Table 9.1). By that time, Nasser had elbowed Neguib aside and become President. Also in 1955, he negotiated a deal to obtain arms from Czechoslovakia (funded by the USSR). This was a major coup for the USSR, since it aligned them squarely with the Arabs against the Israelis, who were armed and financed by the USA. The Arab–Israeli dispute thus became an extension of the Cold War, with many Soviet military bases and advisers in Egypt. Among other things, this maintained a continuous injection of poison into US–Soviet relations (until Nasser's successor, Anwar Sadat, expelled the Soviet bases and advisers in 1972).

In 1956, Nasser nationalized the Suez Canal, formerly owned and operated jointly by Britain and France. He also encouraged raids by *fedayeen* (armed guerrillas, mainly Palestinian) into Israel. After long and fruitless negotiation, France and Britain decided to cooperate with Israel in a surprise attack on Egypt, with the British and French invading the Suez Canal. The Israeli army rapidly encircled and captured almost the entire Egyptian army in the Sinai Desert. The UN General Assembly called for a cease-fire and withdrawal of the invading forces, and Britain and France said that they would welcome a UN garrison taking over the Suez Canal area. A UN Emergency Force (UNEF) of 30,000 men from six countries took over on the ground from the Anglo-French troops and, as the Israelis withdrew, established posts in the Sinai Desert on the Israeli border with the task of observing and deterring any repeat of the Israeli invasion. As was normal

Table 9.1 The Arab–Israeli conflict, 1948–67

1920	League of Nations mandate to Britain in Palestine
1936–38	Arab rebellion against Jewish immigration
1947	Britain gave notice to end mandate – UN Partition Plan
1947–48	'Ethnic cleansing' operations by Jewish terrorists
1948 15 May	Israel independent. Arabs invaded from all sides
1944 Jan	Armistice signed. UN recognized '1949 borders'
1954	British withdrew garrison from Suez Canal
1955	Soviet–Czech arms deal with Egypt
1956 July	Egypt nationalized Suez Canal
1956 Oct	Israel, Britain and France invaded Sinai and Suez
1956 Nov	Cease-fire. UNEF took over Sinai and Suez
1965–67	Intensified Arab guerrilla attacks on Israel
1967 15 May	Egypt moved 100,000 troops into Sinai
1967 15 May	Egypt asked UNEF to withdraw from Sinai
1967 18 May	Egypt occupied Sharm el Sheikh
1967 22 May	Egypt closed Straits of Tiran
1967 26 May	Nasser declared intention of destroying Israel
1967 30 May	Egypt, Syria, Jordan defence pact
1967 31 May	Iraqi troops entered Jordan in support
1967 1 Jun	Cabinet crisis in Israel. Decision to attack
1967 3 Jun	Nasser order of the day 'Holy War'
1967 5 Jun	Surprise attack decimated Egyptian Air Force. Israeli army advanced on all fronts
1967 7 Jun	Jordan accepted cease-fire on Jordan River
1967 8 Jun	Egypt accepted cease-fire on Suez Canal
1967 11 Jun	Syria accepted cease-fire on Golan Heights
1967 22 Nov	UN Resolution 242 (never carried out)

with UN peacekeeping forces, it was agreed that the UNEF would withdraw at once if requested to do so by the host government (Egypt). UNEF, however, did not appear to take any action to prevent continued *fedayeen* raids into Israel.

THE SIX DAY WAR OF 1967

Nasser's prestige, both in Egypt and throughout the Arab world, was enormous. He had nationalized the Suez Canal with impunity and was given unfounded credit for the ejection of the combined forces of Israel, Britain and France in 1956. It is surprising that, notwithstanding his triumphant rhetoric after that war, he had not, as a soldier, taken a realistic note of the two overwhelming tactical defeats which the Israelis had inflicted on vastly superior Egyptian forces in the Sinai Desert in 1948 and 1956. In 1967, however, he was supremely confident, because he had stitched together an alliance of Egypt, Syria and Jordan and was convinced that, with a simultaneous war on three fronts, Israel was certain to be defeated.

On paper there were grounds for this confidence. Egypt, Syria and Jordan had between them 340,000 troops, 1800 tanks and 610 aircraft compared with the Israelis' 264,000, 800 and 300.[2] Added to that, five other Arab states, including Iraq – and Saudi Arabia – had promised to provide troops, and some were moved up to the frontiers through Jordan, so that potentially the Israelis were outnumbered by about three to one in infantry and by more than that in tanks.

Nasser never made any secret of his intentions regarding Israel, either before or during the 1967 crisis, when he precipitated the crisis by closing the Straits of Tiran on 22 May, as will be described. He frankly declared that 'the Arab people is firmly resolved to wipe Israel off the map' (22 May), and that 'our basic objective will be the destruction of Israel' (27 May).

In October and November 1966 *fedayeen* raids into Israel intensified, both from Egypt and Jordan. These were mainly by members of the Palestine Liberation Organization (PLO), into which previously fragmented guerrilla groups had been united in 1964. Israel replied with a reprisal raid into Jordan. In April 1967, Syrian artillery bombarded the Israeli agricultural settlements laid out before them in the plain below the Golan Heights. This resulted in military clashes on land and in the air and six Syrian MIG fighters were shot down on 7 April.[3] On 10 May, the Israeli Chief of Staff threatened to attack Damascus if Syrian attacks continued. The Egyptians reported a build-up of Israeli troops on the Syrian border. Nasser said later that on 13 May the Soviet government had warned that an Israeli attack was likely on 17 May, and had urged him to take action to relieve the pressure on Syria. On 15 May, he moved 100,000 troops and 800 tanks up to the Israeli frontier in the Sinai Desert. On 16 May, the Egyptian Chief of Staff sent a personal message to the Commander of the UNEF asking him to withdraw. This was followed by a formal communication to that effect addressed to the UN Secretary-General.[4]

This was entirely within the rights of the Egyptian government. Nasser was sensitive to the jibes of fellow Arabs that he was 'sheltering behind the UNEF'. The timing, however, was such as to leave no doubt that his purpose was to avoid hampering or revealing the deployment of his troops. The UNEF detachments and observation posts were harassed and hustled. Ominously a strong Egyptian force gave the 32 Yugoslav blue-beret troops 15 minutes to evacuate Sharm el Sheikh, on the southern tip of the Sinai Peninsula. Sharm el Sheikh controls the ten-mile-wide Straits of Tiran, which are the entrance to the Gulf of Akaba, an international waterway leading to the Israeli port of Eilat. This was Israel's only sea access to the sea south of the Suez Canal, which was already closed to Israeli cargoes.

On 22 May, Nasser announced the closure of the Straits of Tiran to all Israeli ships and cargoes. Israel interpreted this as a declaration of war, a view that the government-controlled Cairo radio reinforced:

> with the closing of the Gulf of Akaba, Israel is faced with two alternatives, either of which will destroy it; it will either be strangled to death by the Arab military and economic boycott, or it will perish by the fire of the Arab forces encompassing it from the South, from the North and from the East.[5]

Led by the USA and Britain, a number of maritime powers attempted to organize a multinational naval escort to ensure the free international passage of the Straits, but this was still being discussed when overtaken by the war.

Both the US and Soviet governments were doing their best to restrain Israel and Egypt. The Israeli Foreign Minister, Abba Eban, visited the USA on 25 and 26 May, but failed to get President Johnson to agree to regard an attack on Israel as an attack on the United States.

On Sunday 28th, the Israeli Prime Minister, Levi Eshkol, made a restrained broadcast, saying that aggression would be opposed at the time if used, but that decisions about the Straits of Tiran had been taken so that it would not be necessary to take military action for self-defence. This caused a furore amongst the hawks in his Cabinet and especially amongst the generals. General Bull, the Chief of Staff of the UN Truce Supervision Organization (UNTSO) later commented: 'I don't think Eshkol wanted a war. The military establishment, however, certainly wanted a showdown with their Arab neighbours.'[6]

This precipitated an Israeli Cabinet crisis, further fuelled by the Egyptian declaration on 30 May of a defence pact with Jordan, whereby the Jordanian army came under Egyptian command, and on 31 May by an Iraqi commitment to provide troops, who moved into Jordan.

Eshkol gave way on 1 June to an overwhelming demand from his Cabinet, the army and the public to appoint General Moshe Dayan, a hero of the 1956 war, as Minister of Defence, and to bring in opposition parties to form a Coalition government. Dayan told them that, given a decision on Sunday 4th, he could launch an attack in the early morning of 5 June and that the war would be over in three to five days.

On 3 June Nasser issued an Order of the Day to his army, announcing that they were to take part in a Holy War. On the weekend 3–4 June, as an act of deception, large numbers of Israeli troops were seen swimming and relaxing on the beach, which was widely reported by the international press.

At 8.45 am Cairo time on Monday 5 June, the Israeli Air Force, flying first down the Mediterranean and then coming into Egypt from the west, achieved total surprise and destroyed 309 of Egypt's 340 combat aircraft on the ground. With air superiority, the Israelis then overran the Arab part of Jerusalem and the West Bank down to the Jordan River by 7 June. They sliced up and encircled the Egyptian army, forcing the remnants to accept a cease-fire on the Suez Canal on the 8th, and drove the Syrians off the Golan Heights, ending with a cease-fire on the 11th.

ASSESSMENT

This was a brilliant campaign for which the Israelis were fully prepared. The trigger was the deployment of the Egyptian army in the Sinai Desert, where the Israelis already knew how to defeat them.

The war was probably inevitable, since both sides were convinced that they could win. Nasser had achieved a rare degree of Arab unity and intended to seize this chance to destroy Israel; no other explanation of his actions, with or without his rhetoric, is feasible. Israel's military establishment were in no doubt that the war was coming, and believed it was better to fight early rather than late. Crisis management on both sides was aimed, not to prevent the war, but to get the world to blame the other side, and to achieve tactical surprise.

Could Nasser have handled it better? Although he had the legal right to do it, his expulsion of the UNEF revealed his intentions and, by its arrogance, alienated world opinion. His closing of the Straits of Tiran was no doubt intended to provoke Israel to mobilize and attack, since he believed that his troops were ready, but it contributed nothing else, further alienating world opinion and alarming the USSR, who gave him no further encouragement at all.

Could the UN, the USA or the USSR have prevented the war? Probably not, since both sides were fully equipped, willing to fight and anxious not to be pre-empted.

In such crises, Israel has a particular problem. Her armed forces have a small professional cadre and a large and highly trained reserve which, on mobilization, engulfs almost the entire male and much of the female population of military age. The economy and the social life of the country therefore comes to an almost total halt. It is imperative not to mobilize too early, and urgent thereafter to get the war over quickly, but they must also keep the war out of their own tiny country because they have no room for depth to manouevre within it; they must therefore not leave their mobilization too late.

Because of this factor, Israel has stubbornly refused to give up the territory she has gained; also because her own people, resentful at losing the 'arm's length' they had won in 1956, would have thrown over any government that allowed it to happen again. Eventually, they and the UN settled for UN Resolution 242 of 22 November 1967, calling for *inter alia* (numbers referring to subparagraphs in the Resolution)

1(i) withdrawal of Israeli armed forces from territories occupied in the recent conflict

1(ii) termination of all claims or states of belligerency and respect for and acknowledgement of the sovereignty, territorial integrity and political independence of every state in the

> area and their right to live in peace within secure and recognized boundaries free from threats or acts of force

and affirming further the necessity

2(a) for guaranteeing freedom of navigation through international waterways in the area
2(b) for achieving a just settlement of the refugee problem
2(c) for guaranteeing the territorial inviolability and political independence of every state in the area, through measures including the establishment of demilitarized zones.

There was much discussion, in formal sessions and in the corridors of the wording of 1(i) '. . . withdrawal . . . from territories occupied . . .'. Britain, which drafted the Resolution, wanted it to be '. . . from *the* territories . . .' and so, of course did the Arabs and the USSR. Israel and the USA, however, insisted that some flexibility was essential, officially to allow for minor adjustments,[7] and also, presumably, because Israel would never have committed herself to withdraw from East Jerusalem or from that part of the Golan Heights overlooking the Jordan Valley.

Resolution 242 was accepted at the time by Israel, Egypt and Jordan, but rejected by Syria (until 1973) and the PLO (until 1988).[8] Generally, for the next 25 years it was the basis for all peace talks, and Israel did in 1979–80 withdraw from Sinai in exchange for peace with Egypt. Otherwise each side claims non-compliance by the other. Syria and Jordan remained in a state of war with Israel into 1993; Israel still occupied the West Bank, Gaza and (with some realignment in 1974) the Golan Heights.

10 The Arab–Israeli War of 1973

SADAT'S INITIATIVE FOR PEACE

In 1967, the UN appointed a Swedish diplomat, Gunnar Jarring, highly respected by all sides, as Special Representative to implement Resolution 242. It soon became apparent that the Israelis were not prepared to begin even a limited withdrawal until the state of war was ended and their right to exist was recognized, while the Arabs were not prepared to talk without an Israeli commitment to withdraw to the 1949 frontiers. In March 1969, frustrated with lack of progress, the Egyptians began a War of Attrition, bombardment and counter-bombardment across the Canal (see Table 10.1).[1] Meanwhile the USSR was building up a series of sophisticated surface-to-air missile sites (SAM 2) some 25 miles back from the Canal. By the end of 1969 there were 22 SAM 2 sites operated by Soviet soldiers, of whom about 40 had been killed or wounded in Israeli attacks by that time. In February 1970, the more modern SAM 3s were being added, and Soviet pilots were also flying MIG 21J fighters, with strict orders not to fly within 30 miles of the Canal. By July 1970, there were 10,000 Soviet personnel in Egypt; the Soviets had taken over 5 major air bases, and had the use of about 20 others; they had also sealed off a large area of Alexandria as a Soviet naval base.[2]

On 7 August 1970, a US-sponsored cease-fire was accepted by both sides. Four or five Soviet-piloted aircraft had by then been shot down, and both the US and Soviet governments were alarmed at the prospect of the superpowers being drawn into the conflict.[3]

On 28 September 1970, Nasser died suddenly from a heart attack, and his Vice-President, Anwar Sadat, took over. Sadat was one of the young colonels involved in Nasser's coup; he was a very able politician and administrator, but he lacked Nasser's charisma. He therefore wasted no time in trying to make his mark, both in Egypt and in the world.

Table 10.1 The Arab–Israeli War of 1973

1969 Mar	Egypt began 'War of Attrition' across Canal (artillery exchanges)
1970 Jul	Air defences (missiles and fighters) with 10,000 Soviet crew
Aug	Cease-fire
Sep 28	Nasser died. Sadat President of Egypt
1971 May	Soviet–Egyptian Treaty. Soviet bases, advisers, air defence
1972 Jul	Sadat renounced treaty. Soviet bases began run down Soviet crew remained with air defences. Others left
Nov	Egyptians began planning attack across Canal
1973 Jan	Egypt and Syria agreed joint action without Jordan
Jun	Objectives agreed: restore 1949 borders; not destroy Israel
Summer	Deception plan. Reservists mobilized 22 times
Sep 21	Egyptian troops again concentrated 'for manoeuvres'; US intelligence said this was 'for real'; Israelis disbelieved it
Oct 1	Israelis on Golan reported Syrian deployment 'defensive'. Israeli intelligence officer saw through Egyptian deception but could not convince his chief
Oct 5	Israelis decided *not* to mobilize. Risk of attack assessed as low
Oct 6	4.30 am Israelis got firm evidence of attack that day. 10 am Cabinet rejected pre-emptive strike but ordered mobilization. 2 pm Egyptians crossed canal. Bridgehead 50 miles wide. Egyptians kept within 5 miles of Canal (range of air defences)
Oct 9	USSR began equipment airlift to Egypt, USA to Israel
Oct 15	General Sharon counter-attacked across Canal, splitting Egyptian army. Syrians driven back 10 miles into Syria
Oct 24	Cease-fire leaving Egyptians with bridgehead. Israelis withdrew leaving UN buffer zone between armies
	Arabs quadrupled world oil price by 1974, resulting in world recession

In December 1970, Sadat launched his 'Initiative for Peace', in which he proposed a phased Israeli withdrawal from Sinai and the Gaza Strip, in exchange for which he would commit himself to a peace agreement with Israel. 'If Israel agrees to withdraw to international borders, I am ready to negotiate the details of the final permanent peace.' Jarring put this to Israel on 17 February

1991, but received a total rejection, stating that Israel would definitely not withdraw to the 1949 armistice lines. Even the US government was astonished at the arrogant tone of the Israeli reply.[4]

This rejection convinced Sadat that he would have to fight another war to break the deadlock. On 27 May 1971, he signed a fifteen-year treaty with the Soviet Union. On 11 October, he went to Moscow with a shopping list of offensive weapons. Though the joint communiqué spoke of measures 'further to strengthen Egypt's military might', it became clear to Sadat that the USSR was prepared to provide weapons only for defence, because the Soviets were sceptical (understandably in the light of 1956 and 1967) of Egypt's ability to use their weapons effectively, and because their greater concern was not to prejudice *détente* with the USA. Further visits in February and April 1972 convinced him that they were determined to restrain him from offensive action. Their own strong military presence in Egypt meant that they could, in effect, veto his plans. In June 1972 they had 5000 advisers with the Egyptian forces and 10,000–15,000 other personnel, manning 50 SAM 2 and SAM 3 sites, and including 200 pilots for their fighter aircraft. There were large Soviet naval contingents at four ports and they virtually controlled seven airfields.[5]

SADAT PREPARES FOR WAR

On 8 July, Sadat instructed the Soviet Ambassador in Cairo to notify his government officially that he had decided to dispense with the service of all Soviet military experts: the Soviet equipment in Egypt should either be sold to Egypt or taken back to the USSR, and that all this should be carried out within one week.[6]

To the world's surprise, the Soviet government raised no objection and began their withdrawal on 17 July. This suggests that they too were disillusioned with the relationship and glad to be out of it. The withdrawal, of course, took some time, and the last Soviet advisers left in some haste as the war was about to begin in October 1973.

Sadat began in October 1972 to plan the war with his service chiefs. He decided that, rather than try to deny it, he should make regular rhetorical references to his intention to fight to evict the Israelis from Egyptian territory. In March 1973 he gave an interview to *Newsweek* in which he referred to the rejection of his 'Initiative for Peace' by the Israelis, despite the avowed approval of his proposal by the USA, and concluded that there would be no movement without another war. He continued to make regular references to the forthcoming war, and called up reservists repeatedly for manoeuvres near the Canal, visible to the Israeli observation posts and reconnaissance aircraft. During the summer of 1973, reservists were called up and demobilized 22 times; when they were recalled yet again on 27 September, neither they nor the Israelis saw any reason to believe that this time it would be the real thing.[7]

The Egyptians decided to attack in the evening so that they could build up their troops in the bridgehead in darkness for a decisive tank battle next day, within the range of their missile sites west of the Canal. They chose the evening of Saturday 6 October, which was a solemn Jewish religious holiday (Yom Kippur, the Day of Atonement). It would also be the tenth day of Ramadan, and they judged that the Israelis would not believe that a Muslim country would start a war when its troops would be weakened by the Ramadan fast. On that night, the moon and the current in the Canal would be right for them. And Israel would be concentrating on the general election due in October.

In May, they began planning with the Syrians for them to make a simultaneous attack to recover the Golan Heights.[8] In Syria, too, there was an elaborate deception plan. Because the Israelis had a view from the Golan Heights of the entire Syrian plain as far as Damascus, the Syrians built up their force in defensive formation, that is, with the tanks deployed hull down in defensive fire positions and the artillery well back so that it could cover their own front, but troops advancing onto the Golan Heights would be well beyond its range. This was duly noted by the Israeli observation posts. The Syrians did not redeploy their tanks and artillery in readiness to advance until the eve of the attack.[9]

On 28 September there was an incident which may or may not have been a calculated element in the deception plan. Two Arab terrorists from the Syrian controlled Sa'iqa group kidnapped five Russian Jewish immigrants transiting through Austria, together with an Austrian customs official; they demanded the closure of the Schonau Transit Camp through which the considerable flow of immigrants bound for Israel was processed. The Austrian Chancellor, Bruno Kreisky, agreed to the demand and let the terrorists go. The Israelis were furious. The Prime Minister, Mrs Golda Meir, personally visited Vienna and the Council of Europe in Strasbourg to try to get the Austrian decision reversed. The Schonau story dominated both the Cabinet meetings and the Israeli media, right up to the morning before the Arab attack. Discussion of the military build-up on the Canal and in Syria was elbowed to the sidelines. Furthermore, the extremely belligerent threats being made in Israel gave the Arabs the excuse to say that they were strengthening their deployment facing the Canal and the Golan Heights in readiness to meet an Israeli attack.[10]

ISRAELI INTELLIGENCE

Through the first five days of October, Israeli intelligence stubbornly clung to their conviction that the Arabs were not going to attack, because their rhetoric and repeated provocative manoeuvres suggested bluff; also for the reasons anticipated by Sadat in choosing his date (see p. 128). A young officer in the intelligence branch of the Israeli army's Southern Command, Lieutenant Benjamin Siman-Tov, did interpret the Egyptian movements correctly, and submitted detailed and reasoned reports on 1 and 3 October but, because they did not follow the line being put by his branch, these reports were stifled and not passed upwards. The Agranat Commission of Inquiry after the war found these reports 'penetrating' and considered the action of his superior officers 'particularly grave'.[11]

Even as late as 5 October, in the face of air photographs taken on the 4th and analysed through the night, showing bridging equipment being moved up to the Canal, Israeli intelligence chiefs still reported the probability of attack to be 'low, even lower than low' On the strength of this, the Israeli Cabinet decided unanimously not to mobilize.

At 4.30 am on Saturday 6 October (Yom Kippur) the Israeli government intelligence agency, Mossad, reported that they had finally obtained the Arab plan. The Egyptians and Syrians were going to attack simultaneously at 6 pm. The military intelligence chief, the Chief of Staff (Elazar), the Defence Minister (Dayan) and the Prime Minister (Golda Meir) were in turn roused and informed. Elazar wanted to fly pre-emptive air-strikes at once and to order general mobilization by public broadcast. Dayan opposed this, particularly the air-strike, as this would give the Arabs immediate justification for launching their attack. Mrs Meir supported Dayan. At 8 am she summoned the US Ambassador and told him the news. The Ambassador warned her not to make a pre-emptive strike, saying that if the Arabs were proved irrefutably to be the aggressors, the USA would feel morally obliged to help.[12] Elazar was allowed to order general mobilization at 10 am. The Arabs in fact began their attack at 2 pm, a change they had made three days earlier in response to a Syrian request.

The Israeli defences on the 50-mile east bank of the Suez Canal were based on the Bar-Lev line – a line of 31 heavily fortified bunkers, overlooking the Canal, each normally garrisoned by about 30 men. These were between one and two miles apart, and designed for prolonged all-round defence. The area between them was patrolled by tanks and armoured personnel carriers (APCs). Some miles back was another line of 20 bunkers, with a reserve of tanks and APCs for counter-attack. Behind these were the three passes over the Sinai Central Ridge – Khatmia, Gidi and Mitla – a little over 10 miles from the Canal. The Israeli plan was, if possible, to destroy Egyptian troops on the Bar-Lev line before they could get a secure bridgehead but, failing that, to destroy them in a tank battle amongst the bunkers in the 10-mile zone between the Canal and the passes. In this zone, the Israelis had some 240 tanks, 50 of them in the forward Bar-Lev line and the remainder ready to counter-attack.

On 6 October 1973, the Bar-Lev bunkers were manned by only 600 men in all, mainly older recruits recalled for their annual month's call up; they were below strength because about 25 per cent had been allowed home on leave for Yom Kippur.[13] These reservists, many with the experience of the 1956 and 1967 wars behind them, fought stubbornly, and some held out for a week or more after they were surrounded.

ATTACK AND COUNTER-ATTACK

The Egyptian attack was brilliantly and meticulously prepared, and they gained a foothold much more quickly than the Israelis expected. The Israelis thought that it would take several hours to get tanks across the river, largely due to the steep 60-foot bank of soft sand on both sides of the Canal, which tanks could not climb. The Egyptian engineers used over 100 mobile fire-pumps to blast gaps in these sand banks. Meanwhile, modern Soviet pontoon bridging equipment could assemble bridges within half an hour. Within 9 hours, they had blasted 60 gaps and established 10 bridges and 50 ferries. By dawn on Sunday 7 October, 16 hours after the assault, they had 8000 infantry and at least 400 tanks across the Canal. The infantry carried a large number of hand-held anti-tank missiles, some of them being wire-guided Soviet Sagger missiles. By the fifth day, 10 October, the Egyptian bridgeheads had linked up and covered the whole of the East Bank up to three or four miles from the Canal.

At this point, the Egyptians, with greatly superior strength, could have advanced and seized the Gidi and Mitla passes, but they preferred to consolidate their bridgehead, still within range of their SAM air defences west of the Canal, in the hope of attrition of Israeli tanks and aircraft in counter-attack. In view of the proven Israeli tactical superiority in open warfare, this was probably wise.

On 9 October, the USSR began to fly military equipment to both Syria and Egypt, and during the next three weeks, had delivered equipment and supplies to the value of $3500 million. During the same period, the USA flew $2200 million worth of military aid to Israel.[14] There is in fact evidence that the aim of both the US and Soviet governments was to stablize the situation with a view to a cease-fire, not to encourage a major victory by either side. Neither Egypt nor Israel, however, was ready to consider a cease-fire at this stage.[15]

On 15 October the battle took a sudden turn. Major-General Arik Sharon, commanding the centre division, crossed to the West Bank, between the Egyptian 2nd and 3rd Armies. The plan was simply to establish a bridgehead from which to disrupt Egyptian communications and air defences by raids into their rear areas along the Canal. After some fierce but brief resistance (the Egyptians had left few combat troops on the West Bank), Sharon pushed south, destroying the Soviet/Egyptian SAM sites and advancing to within a few miles of the southern tip of the Canal, poised to cut off the entire Egyptian 3rd Army.

Meanwhile, things had gone even worse for the Syrians. After gaining some ground in the first five days they had been driven back, in places ten miles into Syrian territory.[16]

At this point the Arab world, led by Saudi Arabia, exploded its long-planned bombshell of the oil weapon. They cut off all supplies to the USA and raised the price of oil over the next few months by more than four times, from $2.50 to $11.30 a barrel. This was to have a devastating effect on the whole of the world's economy.[17]

CEASE-FIRE AND DISENGAGEMENT

By now there was intense pressure for a cease-fire by both the USA and the USSR. The USSR had no confidence in either the Egyptian or the Syrian armies' ability to withstand Israeli counter-attacks; the USA was alarmed at the possible effects of another total Arab disaster on the prospects of future peace.

The UN Security Council called for a cease-fire on Monday 22 October and both the Israeli and Egyptian governments accepted it, the Israelis only under intense pressure from the US government. Sharon's tanks, however, in the guise of 'mopping up' continued to advance south, captured Suez and completed the encirclement of the 3rd Army. UN observers were on their way, but Sadat requested that both superpowers should send troops to enforce the cease-fire. The USSR agreed, and announced that, in default of US agreement, she would unilaterally send troops to enforce it. A highly dangerous situation developed: on 24 October both the USA and the USSR placed airborne and naval forces at instant readiness and nuclear forces on full alert. In alarm at this situation, the US and Soviet governments cooperated in almost frantic diplomatic pressure to enforce the cease-fire and get the UN observers onto the ground.[18]

The Israeli intransigence and apparent double-dealing in these final days, and the intensity of the superpower crisis that it provoked, caused great resentment in the USA. As a result, they also cooperated with the USSR in working out and enforcing a disengagement agreement advantageous to Sadat. The Israeli troops west of the Canal had to be withdrawn. The Egyptian army was left in possession of the whole of its original bridgehead along the Canal; indeed it was deepened to about five miles. The Israelis were required to withdraw to the east of the Gidi and Mitla passes, which were garrisoned by a UN observation force that also patrolled a demilitarized zone between the two armies.[19]

On the Golan Heights, the Israelis did a little better. There was a demilitarized zone on the eastern slopes, but the Israelis were left in occupation of the western slopes overlooking their Jordan Valley settlements. This occupation also incorporated all the 17 major settlements that the Israelis had established in the Golan Heights since 1967.[20]

ASSESSMENT

Thanks to the success of their counter-attacks and the almost certain destruction of a large part of the Egyptian army if these had been allowed to take their course, the Israelis can claim to have won the battle militarily on both the Sinai and Golan fronts. They also inflicted many more casualties than they suffered (see Table 10.2).

Table 10.2 Losses in the war of 1973

	Killed[21]	*Tanks lost*[22]	*Aircraft lost*[23]
Egypt and Syria	22000	2000	400
Israel	2404	800	115

On the other hand, Israel, with a Jewish population of 3 million, could not afford such casualties as easily as Egypt with its population of 35 million. The disengagement settlement, however, especially in Sinai, could certainly be claimed as an Arab victory.

For Sadat, it definitely was a victory. He had destroyed the legend of invincibility of the Israeli armed forces and he had driven Israel back from the Canal. His handling of the run-up to the war had been masterly. His 'Initiative for Peace' in December 1970, with the support of almost the whole world including the USA, and its intransigent rejection by Israel, gave him the moral justification to use force. His termination of the Soviet–Egyptian Treaty gave him freedom of action, without losing the essential support he needed in the 1973 war. His launching of the war itself, and particularly the success of his deception plan, will remain a model of politico-military strategy.

As a result of Sadat's performance, he attracted massive US aid and support far more valuable than any the Soviet Union could offer. This began immediately after the 1973 war.

In 1977 he pursued his original 1970 'Initiative for Peace' by negotiating a bilateral peace settlement with the new (and otherwise hardline) Israeli Prime Minister Menachem Begin, which earned them both the Nobel Peace Prize. As a result, he recovered (in 1979 and 1980) the whole of the Sinai Desert. Peace with Egypt suited the Israelis too, because it was most unlikely that Syria would attack them other than in concert with Egypt. A cynic might add that, if there were another war, it was better that the Egyptian army should be in the Sinai Desert, where the Israelis had twice proved that they could quickly destroy it, rather than on the Canal.

11 The Vietnam War

THE MAO ZEDONG PATTERN

Ho Chi Minh's Viet Minh campaign against the French in 1946–59[1] was a classic demonstration of the Mao Zedong strategy for rural revolution, more so even than Mao's own fifteen-year campaign against Chiang Kai-shek in China, which was obscured by the intervention of Japan and the impact of the Second World War. There was no such interference in the Viet Minh's war of liberation in North Vietnam in 1946–54.

Mao Zedong's pattern is in four phases: organization, terror, guerrilla war and mobile war. In the first phase, which may take several years, clandestine 'agit-prop' teams arouse the people in rural areas about their grievances and organize them into cadres to develop their political activity, and to be ready to support terrorist and guerrilla groups which in due course are formed from their ranks. In the terror phase, they pick out and murder collaborators and especially local government officials, so that their replacements either discreetly 'live and let live' with the revolutionaries or suffer the same fate. In the third stage, the guerrillas, using hit-and-run tactics, make it impossible for local officials and isolated police posts to function, so that 'no go areas' are created in which the guerrilla groups reform and train as companies and battalions which can hold ground and fight and defeat regular troops in the fourth phase, mobile warfare. The Viet Minh did this in 1946–54, first liberating the remote areas, then gaining control of the agricultural countryside so that the French were confined to fortress towns and escorted convoys on the roads between them. Finally, Ho Chi Minh built up an army big enough to surround, attack and defeat a regular French garrison several thousand strong at Dien Bien Phu in 1954.

Up till 1954, the Viet Minh campaign had been mainly in the North, and Vietnam was partitioned in 1955. About 1 million refugees, mainly Catholic, moved to the South and Ho Chi Minh amongst them sent cadres to set up agit-prop teams around the villages. This was the start of the Viet Cong organization that fought for the next 20 years in South Vietnam.

The primary aspiration of the Vietnamese peasants was to get title to land. The Viet Cong agit-prop teams[2] pointed out that Ho Chi Minh had distributed most of the land in the North and given it to the peasants, and that he had started doing the same in the South before partition. After partition, most of the land in the South had been handed back to the landlords, and very little was now being distributed. The fact that the North Vietnamese distribution had been merely a prelude to collectivization had not at this time sunk in.[3] Consequently, it was the prospect of land reform that drew so many to the Viet Cong cadres.

The organization phase took about two more years in South Vietnam, and the terror phase was getting into its stride by 1957. Nearly all the victims were civilians, as is the way with 'people's wars'; most of them were local government officials or those who cooperated with them in their villages. In 1957, the Viet Cong killed about 500 civilians; in 1958, 1000; in 1959, 2000; and in 1960 over 3000. In 1959 their armed guerrilla strength was about 5000 with some 100,000 supporters (just under 1 per cent of the population).[4]

US MILITARY ADVISERS

South Vietnam had gained its independence from France in September 1954. The new government of President Diem asked for US military assistance, and in January 1955, a number of US officers joined for a handover period until April 1956, when the last French advisers left. At this time there were 685 US military advisers.[5]

The killing continued to rise in 1960–61; when President Kennedy came to power in January 1961, there were just under 1000 US advisers. Kennedy's response was to increase the number of advisers, to 1300 by the end of 1961 and to 15,000 by the time he was assassinated in November 1963. President Johnson continued this policy and there were 20,000 by the end of 1964. These were at every level in the South Vietnamese army, each usually being one rank below the officer he was advising, down to a US lieutenant with each company and a sergeant with each platoon.

Kennedy in 1961 switched the US army's priority to training for counter-insurgency: this was successful at lower levels from, say, major or colonel downwards. He did not succeed, however, in changing the ideas of his generals who, one by one, handled Vietnam in quite the wrong way. They organized the Vietnamese army to fight battles at company and battalion strength against enemies they could see. What was needed was to protect the villages against raids and infiltration, and also to support the local police so that they could maintain this protection day and night. As it was, local officials and policemen did not stay overnight in the villages at all, but in fortified compounds outside. So the villagers did not dare to cooperate with government (e.g. to give information) for fear of being murdered by the Viet Cong during the night. The Viet Cong therefore in effect controlled those villages. Junior US officers knew this very well, but they were never given the chance to build up confidence in the villages because their senior officers (US and Vietnamese) repeatedly ordered the companies and battalions to abandon the villages in order to take part in futile large scale 'search and destroy' operations in the jungle, against a nimble enemy who had already got out of the way.[6]

THE DEPLOYMENT OF US COMBAT TROOPS

On 2 November 1963 President Diem, who had become increasingly unpopular in Vietnam and had also lost the confidence of the US government, was assassinated in the course of a military *coup d'état*. This was followed by eight changes of government in 1964 alone, mostly by more military coups. The war was going from bad to worse, and there was increasing evidence of North Vietnamese involvement, including sophisticated rocket attacks on US bases and, in August 1964, an attack by torpedo boats on two US destroyers in the Gulf of Tongking. The USA responded by bombing North Vietnam and (as described in Chapter 6) this led to increased Soviet support. In March 1965, 3500 US Marines landed in Da Nang; in the same month US intelligence identified a North Vietnamese regular army battalion, 500 strong in South Vietnam. By the end of 1965 there were 14,000 regular North Vietnamese troops in South Vietnam, and 200,000 US troops,[7] rising to more than 500,000 by 1967, including large numbers of conscripted soldiers. At the peak in November 1967, over 500 US soldiers were being killed each week, and this caused growing public protest, since many felt that no US vital interests were involved; others objected to Americans killing Vietnamese in a war in which they doubted that the USA had any moral right to interfere. The protests reached a peak after the North Vietnamese and the Viet Cong made a series of coordinated attacks in rural areas and in Saigon, the South Vietnamese capital, at the time of the Chinese New Year (the 'Tet Offensive' of February 1968). Their aim was to precipitate a general rising against the government, but this did not materialize. The risings were quickly crushed by the South Vietnamese and US armies, and such as remained of the Viet Cong village cadres and 'popular forces' (local guerrillas) were decimated. Nevertheless, the propaganda and moral effect of the rising, plus the continuing toll of US army casualties, tipped the scale of US public opinion, which thereafter showed a majority against the war in the public opinion polls.

A very revealing conversation took place between a US Marine Corps major and an old friend of his, then with the North Vietnamese army, soon after the Marines landed in 1965. The major discovered from intelligence sources that the local North Vietnamese commander in his area was an officer who had earlier been in the French colonial army and had attended a course in USA at the Marine Corps School. The two had become friends: we shall call them 'Tom' and 'Nguyen'. Tom found a roundabout means by which he could get a personal message to Nguyen suggesting a clandestine meeting. Both trusted that neither would double-cross his old friend and they duly met. Tom said: 'It is crazy to go on fighting now that the USA have committed troop units, because there is no limit to the equipment and manpower we can deploy. You know you cannot win'. Nguyen replied: 'On the contrary, Tom, we know that now we cannot lose. Even if you overrun most of our country, we will still be in the jungle. Our strategy, both here and if you invade North Vietnam, will be to inflict such casualities on your soldiers that your public will not accept them. This war will not be won or lost in Da Nang or Quang Ngai. It will be won by us in Los Angeles, Chicago and New York'.[8]

This was a remarkably far-sighted prediction to make early in 1965, but it proved to be right.

The US forces lost 47,000 killed in battle in Vietnam, nearly as many as in the First World War (53,000) and more than in

Korea.[9] The worst week was in November 1967, when 517 Americans were killed.[10] On 31 March 1968 President Johnson announced that he would not stand for re-election in order that he could have a free hand in opening peace negotiations. Nixon took office in January 1969, elected on a platform of getting the US troops home. By 1972, US combat troops had been disengaged, leaving 65,000 mainly supporting and logistic forces. The USA also maintained a strong air force and naval presence, including aircraft carriers, providing support to a South Vietnamese army of 492,000.[11]

In March 1972, the North Vietnamese attempted a conventional invasion, launching 150,000 troops across the partition line (the 17th Parallel) with tanks, infantry, MIG 21 aircraft, and radar-guided and heat-seeking missiles provided by the USSR.[12] They also launched thrusts from Laos and Cambodia into the Central Highlands to keep the South Vietnamese army stretched down the full length of the country, for example besieging An Loc 70 miles from Saigon and 400 miles south of the 17th Parallel. The North Vietnamese captured the northern town of Hue 50 miles south of the border, but by June they had been driven back with heavy losses. This was a moment of opportunity for which the South Vietnamese army had been trained – far better than it had been trained for guerrilla warfare. But it would have meant responding to the invasion (as in Korea in 1950) with a counter-invasion into North Vietnam. This would have involved US support, certainly from the sea and air, and possibly also on land, especially if the USSR or China threatened to intervene. The US public and their elected leaders were in no mood to provide this support or to face these risks. They wanted to get out, and threw away the opportunity they had at last created by 17 years' involvement at a cost of 47,000 Americans killed.

VICTORY AND MISERY IN VIETNAM

In 1973, a Peace Treaty was signed, handing over possession of much of the highland spine of South Vietnam to the North Vietnamese army, so that the South Vietnamese army had to be stretched out to defend the 1000-mile length of the country, hemmed into a coastal strip mainly less than 50 miles deep with no room for manoeuvre. The North Vietnamese government then worked intensively to build up their clandestine shadow administration in readiness to provide a working Communist Party bureaucracy. It was now quite easy for them to recruit volunteers amongst the South Vietnamese, who could see clearly who was going to win. When they were ready, in 1975, North Vietnam launched its army in several concentrated thrusts to the coast. The demoralized South Vietnamese army was quickly cut into isolated slices and rounded up. The war ended with the last Americans clambering aboard their helicopters on the roof of the US Embassy, with South Vietnamese who had remained loyal to the government frantically fighting for any spare seats.

Twenty years on, the tragedy continues. Hundreds of thousands of miserable 'boat people' have faced untold hazards and uncertainties to escape from the bleak Communist society for which the Viet Cong fought so hard, with an economy even less successful than in the other Communist countries that collapsed in 1989: the Americans have, not surprisingly, offered them no aid or trade.

12 Bangladesh, Cyprus and the Falkland Islands

This chapter briefly examines three small conflicts which teach valuable lessons, especially in crisis management.

BANGLADESH 1971

Bangladesh is intensely cultivated, mainly with jute and rice, but, having the highest rural population density in the world, its 75 million inhabitants are very poor. The Ganges Delta, which contains 90 per cent of the country and most of the population, is only six feet above sea level at its highest point: it is extremely vulnerable to floods, storms and tidal waves.

Its people are predominantly Muslim. In British India it was East Bengal, and became East Pakistan on Independence in 1947, when the predominantly Hindu West Bengal (Calcutta) became part of India. From 1947 to 1971, East Pakistan was separated from West Pakistan by 1000 miles of Indian territory. The only things that held them together were their common Muslim religion and their common fear of India. Although East Pakistan had a larger population than West Pakistan, the dominant races of the west, Punjabis and Pathans, held most of the top jobs in both west and east: senior officials, business people and managers. Bengalis felt themselves to be a subject race in their own country, and from the time of independence there was a growing demand for autonomy. These aspirations were eloquently voiced by Sheikh Mujib-ur Rahman (Mujib) who was Secretary-General of the Awami League. They were set out in 1966 in the 'six points' in the Awami League's manifesto. These proposed a federation of Pakistan in which the federal government would be responsible only for defence and foreign policy. East Pakistan would have its own currency and fiscal policy, power to negotiate foreign trade and aid, and its own militia or paramilitary force.[1]

In 1969 Pakistan had a military government resulting from a coup led by General Ayub Khan in 1958. From 1968 onwards there had been growing demonstrations in both West and East Pakistan demanding democratic government. Ayub retired in March 1969, handing over to General Yahya Khan. Yahya banned strikes, marches, public meetings and political activity, but announced in November that a general election would be held on 5 October 1970. In the event, due to floods in East Pakistan in August, the election was postponed until 7 December. But then, on 11 November, a cyclone and tidal wave hit East Pakistan, killing 200,000 people. Yahya faced wide condemnation for the dilatory response by the 'West Pakistani bureaucrats'.[2]

Despite the cyclone, the election was held on 7 December 1970, Pakistan's first general election since Independence. Mujib's Awami League won 167 of the 169 seats in East Pakistan. Zulfikar Ali Bhutto's Pakistan People's Party (PPP) won 85 out of 144 in West Pakistan.[3]

Yahya clearly intended to allow the result of the election to take its course; he sent a telegram of congratulations to Mujib (who replied insisting on a new Constitution incorporating the Awami League's six points). On 13 February 1971 Yahya announced that the National Assembly would meet in Dhaka (the capital of East Pakistan) on 3 March. Bhutto said that PPP would boycott it and called a general strike. Under intense pressure from the Punjabi establishment, Yahya announced on 1 March that the National Assembly due on 3 March would be postponed *sine die*, and appointed military officers to replace provincial governors.[4]

Mujib launched a non-cooperation movement and there was an explosion of East Bengali nationalism, ruthlessly suppressed by the army, whose officers were almost all West Pakistanis, under the new Military Governor of East Pakistan, General Tikka Khan. There was much violence on both sides. As well as the hated West Pakistani officials and business people, the Bengali rioters had three other target groups, all of whom had a vested interest in the survival of West Pakistani control: the so-called 'Kulaks', prosperous farmers who had taken over land from Hindus who fled in 1947, and feared that an Awami League government would take that land away; the 'Biharis', Muslim refugees who had poured in from India, again in 1947, and whose presence the Bengalis resented; and, of course, the substantial Hindu minority.

Despite some promising talks between Yahya and Mujib (who was essentially a moderate man, but had to be militant enough to retain the leadership of his party) the situation deteriorated rapidly. On 25 March, Bengali policemen and soldiers in East Pakistan regiments mutinied against their West Pakistani officers. West Pakistani regiments (already deployed in East Pakistan to a strength of 40,000) intervened.[5] The Awami League was banned and Mujib arrested.

By the end of June, after many casualties on both sides, the revolt had been suppressed. Some 4 million refugees had fled to India. So had a large number of Bengali soldiers, who formed guerrilla units, again many of them crossing to India.

Just as the rest of the world was to be shocked by the actions of the Serbs in Bosnia in 1992–93 (see Chapter 15), it was equally appalled in 1971 at what was happening in East Pakistan. Britain and the USA suspended aid to Pakistan, which had sympathy only from China (because India was an ally of the USSR).

Mrs Gandhi, the Indian Prime Minister, was particularly outspoken. She expressed her support for Mujib, and drew attention to the horrific strain on India caused by the flood of refugees. On 1 June, cholera was reported in the refugee camps and by 4 June 2500 had died from it.

It is probable that, in about July, Mrs Gandhi began to make plans for Indian military intevention. Clearly she saw it as in India's interest to split Pakistan into two, so that the constant threat of a war on two fronts would be removed. And the need to end the repression, the plight of the millions of refugees, both Hindu and Muslim, and the strain they imposed on India will also have been factors in her decision.

East Pakistan was surrounded on three sides by Indian territory. Indian strategy was to draw the Pakistan army to the borders, where it would be easier to defeat than if it were concentrated around Dhaka. The best way to do this would be to launch guerrilla attacks across the border from India. Amongst the refugees (including former East Pakistani soldiers and policemen) about 5000 were trained by the Indians as guerrillas. Some conducted cross-border operations to draw the Pakistan army; others went back to lie low in the villages, ready to cooperate with advancing Indian troops when the time came, for example by giving information, seizing bridges intact (Bangladesh is a maze of rivers and dykes) or harassing Pakistani troops. The guerrillas were known as Mukti Bahini.

The date picked for the invasion was 4 December. A large-scale invasion takes a long time to plan, and it showed remarkable coolness that Mrs Gandhi spent three weeks touring Western capitals from 24 October to 13 November, explaining India's policy in a series of official meetings, public lectures and broadcasts. By that time, the number of refugees in India had risen to about 10 million, so she had a convincing case. While she did not specifically say that India would invade, she left little doubt that she would be ready to do so. By staying away until 13 November, only three weeks before D-Day, she may well have deceived Yahya into believing that India would not attack so soon. She must have had great confidence in her ministers and generals.

Skirmishes in fact began on 21 November, when Indian tanks crossed the border near Bayra, allegedly in response to a Pakistani attack on Mukti Bahini positions on the Indian side, the Indians penetrated about 8 miles and destroyed 13 Pakistani tanks. Mrs Gandhi gave an account of this to the Indian Parliament on 24 November, and declared that Indian troops had been authorized to cross the border if necessary to repel Pakistani attacks.[6] Two more incidents followed, one by Indian troops and the other by Mukti Bahini. This was no doubt part of the strategy of drawing the Pakistani army away from the centre.

On 3 December, the Pakistani air force made a number of pre-emptive attacks on Indian airfields, and army units made raids into India from West Pakistan and in Kashmir.[7] They presumably hoped to exploit the fact that India would have denuded her Western border of troops, but the raids were quite futile, and gave India more excuse to attack.

On 4 December, the Indians attacked East Pakistan from all three sides – west, north and east. The Pakistani garrison comprised four divisions (95,000 men) and the Indians deployed seven divisions, with air superiority. The war was over in two weeks and most of the world approved. The state of Bangladesh was established and Mujib returned from captivity to be its President. The Indians announced that they had no intention of staying once the situation was secure, and they kept their word. All Indian troops were withdrawn by March 1972.

Yahya Khan's crisis management throughout was disastrous. His intention to restore democracy was undoubtedly sincere but, since there were 169 seats in East Pakistan and only 144 in the West, the result was predictable. He showed that he was willing to accept Mujib as Prime Minister, but he lacked the political strength to convince the West Pakistani establishment that they must accept this too. Before he ever called the election, he should have warned them that the alternative would be disintegration and the loss of East Pakistan, leaving West Pakistan without the power to stand up to India. His strongest card in persuading them should have been that Mujib did not want to do this (presumably for the same reason), provided that he had autonomy within a federal Pakistan.

Yahya's handling of Mujib was equally inept. Until the army crackdown on 25 March 1991, Mujib had no intention of breaking up Pakistan, but there was a more extreme fringe whom he had to carry with him. Yahya should have helped him to do this, and should have stamped more firmly on Bhutto and others in the establishment who would not see this.

Finally, once it became clear that India was going to intervene, Yahya should have realized that armed resistance would lead to disaster, swallowed his pride and settled for the best he could get. But that would have meant ignominious dismissal as President.

Mrs Gandhi's crisis management, however, was confident and pragmatic. Her efforts for the welfare of the 10 million refugees were admirable. Her handling of the Mukti Bahini was far sighted and successful. She realized the importance of world opinion, and showed wisdom and courage in devoting three weeks to it at a time when planning for the war must have been at its peak.

Both came out of it with some honour but, while Yahya Khan was initially well-meaning, his leadership was weak; Mrs Gandhi's showed sure judgement and flair.

CYPRUS 1974

Cyprus is 40 miles from Turkey and 500 miles from Greece, but the population is 80 per cent Greek and 20 per cent Turkish. Cyprus was part of the Ottoman Empire for 300 years, until handed over for administration by Britain as a Mediterranean base in 1878 in exchange for British help against Russia. When Turkey became an enemy in 1914, Britain annexed Cyprus and offered the island to Greece as an inducement to join the Allies in the war but Greece declined the deal. So Cyprus became a Crown Colony in 1931.

There has always been a strong movement in Cyprus for union with Greece (*enosis*) but Turkey, historically an enemy of Greece, has always opposed it. The demand for *enosis* reached a peak in the 1950s but Britain was reluctant to agree for fear of offending Turkey, a valuable NATO ally. An *enosis* movement (EOKA) lead by a former Greek regular army officer, Colonel Grivas, began terrorist attacks on British targets and Cypriots who collaborated with the British, not, as he explained, to destroy the British army but to sicken the British government and people of the task of governing Cyprus. (The philosophy was to be seized upon and made its own by the Provisional IRA in the 1970s for their campaign to drive the British from Northern Ireland.)

In February 1959, the London Agreement was signed by the British, Greek and Turkish governments, and by the Greek and Turkish Cypriot leaders, Archbishop Makarios and Dr Kutchuk. Under this agreement, Cyprus was to become independent apart from two NATO military bases at Episkopi and Dhekelia, which remained under British sovereignty. The Cyprus Constitution stipulated a Greek President and Turkish Vice-President, each with the power of veto, and there were strict rules on the percentage of Greeks and Turks not only in a Council of Ministers, House of Representatives, Civil Service and police (70/30), but also in the army (60/40), which was limited to 2000 men.

There was a unique Treaty of Guarantee, under which three powers, Britain, Greece and Turkey, had the right to act singly or collectively to maintain the status of Cyprus (i.e. to prevent either *enosis*, annexation or partition). The Greek and Turkish governments were authorized to maintain garrisons of 950 Greek and 650 Turkish regular troops on the island.[8] Their official task was to train the Cypriot army, but the real purpose, understood by all sides, was to provide each government with a force on the spot with which they could initiate military action to prevent or reverse any breach of the Constitution (for the British, of course, the two sovereign base areas covered this contingency).

Like Bosnia in 1992 (see Chapter 15), Cyprus was not tidily divided into homogeneous Greek and Turkish areas. Nicosia was split into a predominantly Greek modern city and a Turkish walled 'old city' (reminiscent of Jerusalem). Other cities were similarly mixed, with Greeks preponderant in commercial activities and Turks providing a large number of the rural and urban manual workers. Villages had generally shaken down as Greek or Turkish, but were dotted about in no particular pattern. Most villages ran their own vigilantes or home guards, and sprouted Greek blue and white or Turkish red and white flags in profusion, especially if the next village in sight was of the opposite colour.

This Constitution came into force on 16 August 1960 and worked surprisingly well, with Archbishop Makarios as President until 1974. There were, however, repeated clashes between the rival vigilantes in the towns and villages; many of these were clandestinely prompted by EOKA, still active and again under the leadership of Grivas from 1964 until his death in 1974. It was therefore agreed by the Cyprus, British, Greek and Turkish governments in 1964 that there should be a 6000-strong UN peacekeeping force on the island. Typically, this was deployed in small observation posts on hilltops between opposing villages, each with call on a battalion reserve. The officers of the UN battalions spent their days trying to persuade village vigilantes to avoid provocative activities.[9]

On 15 July 1974, the Cyprus National Guard, which was largely commanded by Greek regular army officers, staged a *coup d'état*, and a former leader of EOKA, Nicos Sampson, became President. Makarios escaped from Nicosia and called for help from a British helicopter to take him to sanctuary.

The Turkish government reacted exactly as had been allowed for in the Constitution, exercising the right to act unilaterally to uphold it. The 650 regular Turkish troops were located in an enclave in which Turkish villages predominated in the hills between Nicosia and the (predominantly Greek) port of Kyrenia, on the north coast. In accordance with a long-rehearsed plan, these 650 soldiers came down the hill and seized the port of Kyrenia and the beaches around it. Five days later, 6000 troops crossed the 40 miles from Turkey and expanded the bridgehead. They were followed by further waves of troops totalling 60,000, which rapidly fanned out to occupy the whole of the northern part of the island.

The Greek National Guard was overwhelmed, and the Greek regular army contingent attempted only to hold Nicosia and its environs, while the UN peacekeeping force managed to keep the two sides apart, especially keeping them off the airfield, of which occupation by either side would have provoked an attack by the other.

The military government in Athens had seized power in the 'Colonels' coup' in 1967. Some of its members may have connived in Sampson's coup, but Greece was clearly unable to match the Turkish military response from 500 miles away and made no attempt to do so. The Greek government was dismissed by its own President, who recalled the exiled Konstantinos Karamanlis to form a new government, and democracy was restored to Greece.

After several unsuccessful attempts, a cease-fire eventually became effective on 16 August, 32 days after the Sampson coup, leaving the Turkish army in possession of the northern third of the island. This has been administered as a Turkish Cypriot state ever since and, though lip-service is given by all sides to the intention to reunify the island, no proposal on terms to do so have ever looked likely to be agreed by both sides.

The signatories of the London Agreement in 1959 had to accept the fact that Turkey would never have signed the agreement without some means by which she was satisfied that she could ensure that the rights of the Turkish Cypriot minority could be maintained. They will have had no confidence in the will of the Greek government to do this, and, on the island itself, the Greek community was in a position to have its way unless there were some countervailing Turkish intervention. The enclave held by the 650 regular Turkish soldiers, despite its official role of 'training the Cypriot army', can have had no real purpose but this. Makarios certainly realized that, which was why he was ousted, but it is astonishing that the EOKA plotters did not – especially as the Turkish coast is visible from Cyprus on a clear day. It should have been clear to any intelligent Greek politician that tearing up the Constitution would be suicidal.

Though the Turks can be criticized for seizing more of the island than the Cypriot Turkish population justified, and then for holding onto it for the next 18 years, they cannot be condemned for exercising their right to unilateral action when the Constitution was so flagrantly flouted; nor for being careful to ensure that any reunification contains safeguards at least as effective as those enshrined in the 1960 Constitution.

The problem of securing the rights of minorities in mixed populations is likely to be a recurring one in the post Cold War World (see Chapter 15). The experience of Serbian behaviour in Croatia and Bosnia in 1991–92 has given rise to discussion as to what military action could be effective in preventing or overcoming it. Some of the lessons from Cyprus in 1974 may prove to be relevant.

THE FALKLAND ISLANDS 1982

The Falklands War in 1982 occurred because neither Mrs Thatcher of Britain nor President Galtieri of Argentina believed that the other one would do what he or she actually did. This was due to bad intelligence and bad judgement.

The Falklands[10] comprise two islands of roughly equal size amounting together to 4700 square miles, about half the size of Wales. For most of their history they have been uninhabited except for a large penguin population. The first recorded landing was in 1690 from a British ship, whose captain named them after Viscount Falkland, Treasurer of the Royal Navy. Early in the eighteenth century, French seal hunters from St Malo named the islands *Isles Malouines*, a name later corrupted to the Spanish *Malvinas*. In 1765 the British established a settlement and declared possession of West Falkland in the name of King George III, to discover a year later that the French had established a settlement in 1764 on East Falkland, but had since sold it to the Spanish. In 1770 a powerful Spanish naval force ordered the British to withdraw their settlement, but the Spanish government later apologized and the British returned. They abandoned it three years later but retained their claim to sovereignty. The Spanish abandoned their post on East Falkland in 1811, and the islands were empty again until the newly independent Argentina set up a small settlement in 1826. They, however, seized some US ships in a fishing dispute; the USS *Lexington* destroyed the settlement and deported the settlers in 1831. An Argentine attempt to establish a convict settlement failed when the settlers mutinied. Britain decided to reassert her sovereignty in 1833. An Argentine ship was found there, with 50 men on shore, who left quite amicably when requested to do so.

Thereafter British settlers came to the Falkland Islands to farm sheep, and Britain used them as a naval station in the First and Second World Wars. By 1982 the population was 1800 (with 658,000 sheep – 365 for every inhabitant). All were British except for 17 Argentine gas workers under contract, and an Argentine Airlines representative.

The idea that the Falkland Islands should be Argentine was first seriously propounded by the populist President Peron in 1946, in order to arouse patriotic sentiment. Subsequent Presidents also found this useful. In 1965, the UN invited Argentina and Britain to negotiate to resolve the dispute. This they did sporadically for the next 15 years. By 1972 relations were good, with Argentine Airlines and ships regularly bringing tourists to the Islands, and Falkland children taking scholarships at Argentine schools.[11] There was a brief threat in 1977 which prompted the British government to send a submarine and two escort vessels to the South Atlantic on an 'exercise', upon which the threat dissolved.[12]

By 1980, it seemed that the Islands were of negative economic value and no strategic value to Britain, but were an embarrassment in relations with Spain and Latin America. On the other hand – as with Gibraltar – the population almost unanimously desired to remain British, and the government felt that it could not hand them over against their will. Mrs Thatcher's Foreign Office Minister, Nicholas Ridley, proposed a 'lease-back' arrangement, whereby sovereignty would be transferred to Argentina but leased to Britain for, say, 99 years. This was rejected by the islanders and provoked a debate in parliament which produced a flood of jingoistic rhetoric from both sides of the House, which could have come out of the mouth of President Peron at his worst. The proposal was not pressed, but was interpreted by the Argentines as evidence that the British government had no firm commitment to the Falklands.

In July 1981, the British Defence Minister, John Nott, announced that the only remaining Royal Navy ship in the South Atlantic, the lightly armed survey ship *Endurance*, was to be withdrawn during 1982. This was taken as a further indication of declining British determination to hold onto the Islands.

Meanwhile, the military junta in Buenos Aires, facing serious economic difficulties, was preparing to restore Argentina to an elected presidency. To forestall this, General Leopoldo Galtieri ousted the newly appointed President of the junta, General Viola, in March 1981. Faced with rising discontent amongst the strongly unionized workers and resentment amongst the middle class wanting a restoration of democracy, Galtieri decided to exploit what he perceived to be British weakness and play the strongest populist card of all – the recovery of the *Malvinas*.

In February 1982, UN-sponsored Anglo-Argentine negotiations in New York were cordial but made no progress. Whether this cordiality was deceptive or just due to the good manners which come naturally to most Argentines, is uncertain, but as soon as the talks were over, the Argentine government became increasingly belligerent.

The South Atlantic crisis began in a bizarre way. Three years previously a commercial contract had been signed with an Argentine contractor, Constantino Davidoff, to dismantle an abandoned whaling station at Leith on the British island of South Georgia, 800 miles east of the Falklands. This was used by Argentina as a pretext for a naval transport vessel on 19 March 1982 to deliver Davidoff and 41 men to Leith, where they raised the Argentine flag. Leith itself was unoccupied, but there was a British Antarctic Survey Team in Grytviken, five miles away. The commander of the Survey Team, Steven Martin (age 29), who also had the power of magistrate and administrator of South Georgia, trekked over to tell the Argentines, politely, that their presence without notification was illegal and so was the raising of their flag. The ship left, leaving a small group behind, but on 27 March two corvettes and a naval patrol vessel arrived to protect them. The Argentines had, in effect, annexed South Georgia.

On 29 March, the rest of the Argentine fleet sailed out for well-publicized naval manoeuvres with large numbers of Marines on board. There was much belligerent talk by ministers and in the Argentine press, but the British authorities had been hearing this for years and paid little attention. Whether British intelligence failed to read the signs, or whether their interpretation of them was disbelieved, is uncertain. (A similar situation in Israel in the days before the Egyptian invasion across the Suez Canal in 1973 was described in Chapter 10.) At all events, it was not until 1 April that Mrs Thatcher received firm information that the Argentine fleet was on course for the Falklands and that an invasion was inevitable.

Up till 4.30 pm (Falklands time) on Thursday 1 April, the Governor, Rex Hunt, had been told to expect only a token landing, probably from a submarine on a similar scale to that on South Georgia. The Islands were defended by a detachment of 40 Royal Marines but fortuitously there were 80 there on 1 April as a routine relief was in progress (which happened every 12 months). So, themselves a token force, the Royal Marines stood by to repel or round up another token force. But suddenly they learned that an Argentine naval force of twelve warships (including a carrier, several cruisers, destroyers, corvettes, and three landing ships assumed to be carrying several thousand men) would reach the Islands at dawn next morning.

The Governor broadcast to the Islands at 9.30 pm, and later declared a State of Emergency. He broadcast several times more during the night and at 6 am on Friday 2 April he announced that 16 amphibious armoured personnel carriers carrying Argentine troops were entering the Narrows off Port Stanley. At 6.30 am, a combined helicopter and amphibious assault took place and within a short time there were 2000 Argentine troops on shore. The 80 Royal Marines defended Government House for about three hours before the Governor accepted the inevitable and decided to surrender. He and the Royal Marines were then flown to Uruguay and released. The Argentines built up the garrison to 10,500, confident that this, with their navy and air force, would be enough to deter a British response.

It was not until 6 pm London time (2 pm in the Falklands) that the British government called a press conference, announced that the Islands had been seized and the Governor captured, that the Royal Navy would send a task force to recapture them, but that since the Islands were 8000 miles away, it would take them at least two weeks to get there.

For the next seven weeks there was intense diplomatic activity. As soon as it had become clear on 1 April that the Argentine force was approaching the Islands, the UN Security Council met and called upon both sides to refrain from the use or threat of force. On 3 April, it passed Resolution 502, drafted by Sir Anthony Parsons, the British Ambassador to the UN, calling on the Argentines to withdraw from the Islands. Thanks to skilful lobbying by Parsons, this was passed without veto, with ten affirmative votes, four abstentions and only one negative (Panama). The British interpreted this as endorsing their use of force for their 'inherent right of self-defence' under Article 51 of the UN Charter.

From 7 April onwards, there were three phases in the attempts at mediation: by US Secretary of State Alexander Haig, who shuttled between Buenos Aires, London and the UN in New York; by the Peruvian government; and by Perez de Cuellar, the UN Secretary-General, himself a Peruvian. None came to anything, because the Argentines regarded the Islands as their territory and refused to withdraw, and the British were not prepared to negotiate until Argentina had acceded to Resolution 502 and withdrawn from the Islands.[13]

The British naval task force sailed on 5 April. This was a remarkable achievement in organization, bearing in mind that the government had not taken the threat of invasion seriously until 1 April. The heart of it was an *Arctic* task force designed to operate as part of NATO, supported by land-based aircraft in Norway, Denmark and Iceland, as well as the huge US Navy. In three days it was reconstituted to go to the *Antarctic*, 8000 miles away, with no possibility of land-based air support, and no allies within range. It was supplemented by requisitioned ships, including two large ocean liners. In all it comprised 20 fighting ships (including 2 aircraft carriers and 4 nuclear-powered submarines), 12 fleet auxiliaries (tankers, logistic ships, etc.) and 28 requisitioned merchant ships. Between them these carried three brigades: the 3rd Commando Brigade Royal Marines, the Parachute Brigade and later the 5th Infantry Brigade (which followed up, complete, in the ocean liner *Queen Elizabeth II*).[14]

As he approached the islands, the Task Force Commander, Admiral Woodward, was most concerned about two threats: from land-based Argentine aircraft, and from Exocet missiles fired either from aircraft or from naval ships. Especially, he kept his two aircraft carriers, *Hermes* and *Invincible*, beyond the range of land-based aircraft, since he relied for air support entirely on the Sea Harrier fighters which took off from their decks. In order to deter the Argentine Navy from coming close enough to threaten them, he was determined to sink one of the two Argentine 'big ships' – the aircraft carrier *Vientecinco de Mayo* or the heavy cruiser *General Belgrano*. On 2 May, the British submarine *Conqueror* was shadowing the *General Belgrano* and was authorized to attack. The *General Belgrano* was sunk with the loss of 368 lives,[15] more than twice the total number of British fatal casualties in the entire campaign.

This sinking was widely criticized on two grounds: first, the *General Belgrano* was 240 miles from the Islands and therefore outside the 200-mile 'exclusion zone' declared by the British, and second, the Peruvian peace plan was still under discussion. The incident was interpreted by some as proof that Mrs Thatcher wanted war for domestic political reasons and was determined to sabotage any settlement. In fact, the sinking was purely for operational reasons: ten years later, in anniversary celebrations, the Captain of the *General Belgrano* said that the sinking was entirely justified and that he would have done the same.[16] It certainly had the desired effect, since the Argentine Navy at once withdrew into its 12-mile territorial waters and never emerged again.

The British Commando and Parachute Brigades landed on 21 May in San Carlos Bay, in the Straits between West and East Falkland. On 14 June, Port Stanley was captured and the Argentine army surrendered.

President Galtieri resigned on 17 June and democratic government was restored to Argentina.

Who really did rightfully own the Falkland Islands? The British, French, Spanish, Argentines and British (again) all declared sovereignty over small settlements (usually under 50) on the coast of one or other of the Falkland Islands between 1690 and 1833. The French sold theirs to Spain, but the others all ousted each other's settlements on various occasions. The British made the first recorded landing in 1640 and first named the Islands. They too were the first and last to claim sovereignty. The justification of these claims, however, is not what the war was about.

Argentina's case is based on proximity: the Islands are 400 miles from Argentina and more than 1000 from any other country. On that basis, however, the USA could claim Cuba (90 miles), Malaysia could claim Singapore (1 mile) and India could claim Sri Lanka. There would be no end to this.

Britain's case is based on self-determination, which is the most generally accepted of all international principles. No one questions that none of the 1800 inhabitants (except for the Argentinine contract gas workers and airline officials) wished to be transferred to Argentina.

The Islands have a negative economic and strategic value to Britain. Indeed, Britain was actively seeking an acceptable formula for handing them over (the 'lease-back') in 1980. Mrs Thatcher was not, however, prepared to allow anyone to hijack 1800 British islanders against their will, whether on an island or in a ship.

Did Mrs Thatcher really do it for domestic political reasons? She certainly benefited; before the war she was trailing badly in the polls; after it (in 1983) she was re-elected by a landslide. But the evidence against this theory is that it was her government which (against almost unanimous parliamentary opinion) proposed the lease-back; she did not think an invasion was coming; and she was patently unprepared for it up till the day before it.

General Galtieri definitely did need a foreign policy success. Beset by a militant and vociferous opposition, he knew that recovering the *Malvinas* would rally the people behind him. It did, but he fell all the harder when he failed.

As in Israel in 1973 (Chapter 10), the most striking feature of the crisis was the failure of intelligence. Because of this, and of bad psychological judgement, Mrs Thatcher did not believe that Galtieri would be so foolhardy as to invade the Islands, and he did not believe that she would be so foolhardy as to try to take them back. Both got it wrong.

Part IV
After the Cold War

13 The European Revolutions of 1989–92

MIKHAIL GORBACHEV

In March 1985 Mikhail Gorbachev was installed as General Secretary of the Soviet Communist Party and thus leader of the USSR (see Chapter 6). Having been groomed for the job by Yuri Andropov, under whom he had already made the beginnings of economic reform, he had a flying start, with the party and especially the KGB behind him. In just under six years in office, he ended the Cold War and unleashed the series of revolutions which were to transform the USSR and East Europe in 1989–92. Though their long-term effect cannot yet be finally assessed, the social, political and economic changes were deeper and more genuinely revolutionary than in any of the three most famous revolutionary landmarks in European history – in 1789 (France), 1848 (most of Europe) and 1917 (Russia).

In visits to the West in 1984, Gorbachev had already displayed a totally new style of Soviet foreign relations, being constructive, frank and flexible.[1] Once in power in 1985 he adopted a policy of 'openness' (*glasnost*) and lifted controls on freedom of speech and of the press. He launched a drive against corruption and excessive drinking of alcohol. He relaxed the restraints on emigration and a number of celebrated dissidents were allowed to leave (e.g. Anatoly Sharansky to Israel). He set about 'restructuring' (*perestroika*) of the political and industrial establishment to unshackle the initiative of the Soviet people. He began reduction of Soviet troops in Afghanistan, and completed their withdrawal by 1988. Both to save money and to foster international cooperation, he took the initiative in accelerating arms reduction talks with the USA and, though those suffered a set-back at the summit meeting with President Reagan in Reykjavik in October 1986, the progress exceeded the wildest of expectations of a year or two previously.

He established an excellent personal relationship and trust with President Reagan (blossoming further with President Bush) and with Mrs Thatcher; he became one of the most popular of all foreign statesmen visiting the West.

His initial popularity in the USSR, however, soon began to wane. The lifting of controls and reduction of subsidies did not produce more food and consumer goods, but instead increased the black market, since powerful dealers (including some party officials) held back supplies to create shortages and raise prices. Indeed, party officials at all levels not only were concerned at the loss of their privileges, but also were genuinely alarmed about the decline of the order and discipline they had known all their lives, on which they blamed both the shortages and the increase in crime.

Gorbachev faced one particularly pervasive dilemma. Though he was anxious to relax the inhibition of popular initiative and enterprise by the Communist Party, public administration at almost every level overlapped the activities of party officials. Many local government offices were in the same building as the local party headquarters, and most of the officials were also active party members; indeed, it was difficult to get on the list for selection for important posts (the *nomenklatura*) without being a party member. These officials had great privileges, enjoying a better lifestyle than the public at large, and were certainly not keen to give it up. Without the party structure, and without the cooperation of the party officials, *glasnost* and *perestroika* were unlikely to succeed; this was a major cause of the limited success of the domestic economic reforms, and of the growing decline in Gorbachev's popularity.

Nor could he afford to alienate the Politburo, because they had the power to oust him, as they had ousted Khrushchev 20 years earlier.

At the top level, these tensions came to a head in November 1987, in a clash between Boris Yeltsin and Yegor Ligachev. Yeltsin, Mayor of Moscow, was urging faster economic reforms, and Ligachev, a hardliner, was trying to block them. Eventually Gorbachev, under pressure from the Politburo, dismissed Yeltsin as Moscow party chief.

By 1989, Gorbachev's popularity in the West had reached a peak, but in the USSR it had sunk very low. It was at this point that the Warsaw Pact began to crumble, and it crumbled very fast.

PEOPLE POWER

Violent demonstrations on the streets have overthrown governments a great deal less frequently than is generally imagined. Much more often, they result in growing alarm at the prospect of collapse of order, employment and supplies of food, water and fuel, so that the public rallies to whoever in the existing system can offer the best hope of restoring order. This may be an authoritarian politician (the 'strong man') or, more often, the army, as the only visible body with an organizational hierarchy in being, and the means to maintain law and order. If real revolutionary change does take place, the result is usually an even more tyrannical regime, as in Russia in 1917 and Iran in 1979. Public disorder has in practice seldom led to greater freedom and democracy.

It did occur, however, in 1986, when Mrs Coryzon Aquino was hoisted to power by mass street demonstrations. This was because President Marcos had relied on US support and the USA pulled the rug from under him, forcing him to hold an election and disowning him when he tried to falsify its result.

An attempt to force the government of the People's Republic of China to accept democratic reform was ruthlessly suppressed in Tiananmen Square, Beijing, in June 1989. This was a tragedy in every way, not least because it brought the quite remarkable progress in liberalization of China to a halt. Since he became firmly established in power in 1987, Deng Xiaoping had taken China further down the road to a market economy than has been achieved (even to this day) in the former Soviet Union, and without the shortages and price rises which have so damaged *perestroika*. Political liberalization, however, has been much slower in China, and this too was completely stifled by the events in Tiananmen Square. The tragedy was that the students and intellectuals in Beijing in 1989 tried to push their government too fast, and inflicted a public loss of face on the country, during Gorbachev's very important visit, aimed to restore relations between the USSR and China, from 15 to 18 May. The demonstrators were in occupation of Tiananmen Square for six weeks in all, from 22 April to 4 June. During this time, Prime Minister Zhao Ziyang made repeated efforts to conciliate and negotiate. The troops sent to persuade them to clear the square went in unarmed, and were jostled by the demonstrators and

Table 13.1 Disintegration of the Warsaw Pact and the USSR

	Poland
1980 Aug	Lech Walesa formed democratic trade union (Solidarity)
1981–82	Martial Law. Jaruzelski President. Solidarity banned
1989 Apr	Solidarity legalized. Plan for partly elected Assembly
Jun	Solidarity won 161 of 162 seats contested (35% of Assembly)
Jul/Aug	Jaruzelski (Communist) President; Mazowiecki (Solidarity) PM
Sep 12	Coalition Cabinet (Solidarity-Communist) got 100% vote of confidence
1990 Jan	'Big Bang' change to convertible currency, market economy
1991 Oct	Free elections: 20 parties, 460 seats. None won more than 51
	Hungary
1987	Karoly Grosz(reformist) replaced President Kadar
1989 10 Sep	Austrian borders opened. 6000 East Germans crossed to West
27 Sep	Parliamentary elections announced for Spring 1990
1990 Mar /Apr	Democratic coalition won 229 of 386 seats
	East Germany
1989 Sep	22,000 emigrated to West Germany via Hungary
1–4 Oct	15,500 emigrated after squatting in Czech Embassy
18 Oct	Honneker handed over to Egon Krenz (reformist Communist)
23–4 Oct	40,000 demonstrated demanding free elections
6 Nov	Cabinet and Politburo resigned. Krenz remained President
9 Nov	Berlin Wall opened. 3 million visited West Berlin
21 Nov	100,000 demonstrated in Leipzig
6 Dec	Krenz resigned. Free elections announced for March
1990 Mar	Christian Democrats/Social Democrats won 280 out of 400 seats
Jul	Monetary union
Oct	Reunification
Dec	Pan German election won by Christian Democrats
	Bulgaria
1989 10 Nov	President Zhikov ousted
1990 1 Feb	Reformist coalition government. Election planned for June
Jun	Socialists (former Communists) won 211 of 400 seats

1991 Oct	Anti-Communists won 134 of 250 seats (including 23 Turkish)

Czechoslovakia

1989 14 Nov	German frontier opened (after Berlin Wall opened 9 Nov)
20 Nov	Prague. Demonstrations 100,000–200,000.Vaclav Havel formed Civic Forum (12 parties)
21 Nov	Adamec (reformist Prime Minister) talks with opposition
27 Nov	Two hour general strike (noon). Massive turnout
28 Nov	New Constitution. Communist Party (CP) 'leading role' to end
3 Dec	Adamec proposed coalition Cabinet 16 CP, 5 others
5 Dec	Havel ultimatum. Adamec resigns. New cabinet 10 CP, 11 others
20 Dec	Havel elected President (unanimous Cabinet vote)
1990 Jun	Free elections. Civic Forum won 87 of 150 seats

Romania

1989 24 Nov	CP unanimously re-elected President Ceauşescu
17 Dec	Army fired on 5–10,000 demonstrators in Timisoara
18–20 Dec	Ceauşescu 3-day visit to Iran. More demonstrations
21 Dec	Ceauşescu booed by crowd. Securitate fired (20 killed?)
22 Dec	Army changed sides and fired on Securitate. Ceauşescu and wife fled. Caught by army and shot (25th). Ion Iliescu and National Salvation Front (NSF) took power
1990 20 May	Free election. NSF won 233 of 396 seats

Soviet Union

1985	Gorbachev came to power. *Glasnost* and *perestroika*
1990 Mar	Lithuania declared independence after multiparty election
May	Latvia and Estonia declared independence
1991 Mar	Referendum, when 76% voted for federation of sovereign states (boycotted by Baltic states and by Armenia, Georgia and Moldova)
19 Aug	Attempted coup by Gorbachev's senior ministers. Boris Yeltsin led resistance with massive popular support. Army refused to fire. Coup collapsed. Conspirators arrested
23 Aug	Yeltsin dissolved Russian (not Soviet) CP. Gorbachev called for retention of CP. Lost public support
Dec	Soviet Union disintegrated into 15 republics
1992	Yeltsin led creation of Commonwealth of Independent States (CIS) (11 members: Baltic states and Georgia opted out). Ethnic conflicts including Azerbaijan, Georgia, Moldova and Tadjikistan

publicly humiliated in front of the world's television cameras. There is little doubt that a large proportion of China's rural population, who have much pride in their soldiers and little sympathy for intellectuals, welcomed the deployment of troops from rural areas to take ruthless action to 'give these city slickers what they deserved'. But the whole event set back the previously encouraging progress in China by at least three years.

In Eastern Europe, in 1989–91, every one of the Soviet Union's Warsaw Pact allies replaced its Communist government by an elected one, with remarkably little loss of life (see Table 13.1). A major reason for this was that Gorbachev (like the USA in the Philippines) pulled the rug from under them. Had the Soviet army intervened, as in East Germany in 1953, in Hungary and Poland in 1956 and in Czechoslovakia in 1968, there is little doubt that these popular demonstrations would have been crushed, but the beleaguered Communist governments knew that no such help was forthcoming.

POLAND

The Poles led the way, starting two years before Brezhnev died, and pursued their revolution for ten years without provoking Soviet intervention under the Brezhnev doctrine. In 1980 Solidarity, a free trade union, was formed under the leadership of Lech Walesa, a Catholic electrician working in the Gdansk shipyard. After nearly two years of reluctant tolerance, the Polish government introduced Martial Law in December 1981, and banned Solidarity in 1982, probably in order to pre-empt Soviet army intervention. General Jaruzelski became President. During the next five years, there was much unrest due to economic problems, but throughout this time Jaruzelski tolerated a thriving underground press, which was more widely read than the official censored press.[2] In 1987 Jaruzelski, realizing that the economy was collapsing, proposed an austerity package. Confident that the USSR (now under Gorbachev) would not intervene, he took the risk of calling a referendum, hoping to carry the public with him on these proposals, but they were rejected.

In April 1989, talks with Solidarity resulted in it being re-legalized and authorized to stand as a political party in parliamentary elections, which were held on 4 June. These elections were only partially free: of the 460 seats in the lower chamber, 55 per cent were reserved for candidates from the Communist Party and its allies, 10 per cent nominated by the Communist Party, and only 35 per cent open for contest by other parties as well. All the 100 senate seats, however, were free to be contested. Of the 161 seats contested, 160 were won by Solidarity.

On 19 July 1989, Jaruzelski was elected President under a new Constitution with a vote of 270 to 234 (with 34 abstentions) from the two houses. A respected academic who was a Solidarity man, Tadeusz Mazowiecki, was elected Prime Minister, Lech Walesa having shrewdly declined to stand. On 12 September a coalition Cabinet was elected by a unanimous vote in Parliament, with, in essence, Solidarity controlling the economy and the Communists controlling security.

It was agreed that there would be a new Constitution and fully free elections by 1991.

By the end of 1989, however, the economy was falling apart, with rising unemployment and a threat of galloping inflation. In January 1990, Mazowiecki introduced a crash programme to create a market economy (the 'Big Bang') in which prices were freed and the zloty made convertible at a fixed exchange rate with the US dollar. This brought a great deal of suffering in the short term, and by the end of 1990 the real GDP had fallen to 80 per cent of its 1987 level.[3] In December 1990 Jaruzelski stood down and Lech Walesa was elected President. The first free parliamentary elections were held in October 1991. By then unemployment had risen to 18 per cent of the workforce. Inevitably, Solidarity was blamed for the recession and lost much of its popularity. Parliament was fragmented into 20 parties, none with more than 13 per cent of the vote.[4] Nevertheless, by 1992 Poland's economy was beginning to recover, and its foreign trade was increasing.

HUNGARY

As in Poland, gradual moves towards liberalization had begun long before the 1989 crisis. When Gorbachev came to power in 1985 the Hungarian Communist Party leader (who, as in the USSR, held the real power) was Janos Kadar. First installed by

Khrushchev after the attempted Hungarian rising in 1956, Kadar had been in and out of power several times; he had allowed considerable economic liberalism, and small capitalist businesses played an increasing part in the economy. Like Deng Xiaoping in China, however, Kadar was more reluctant to allow relaxation of the political system. In particular, in 1986, he resisted the contagion of *glasnost* spreading from the USSR. He was, however, becoming out of tune with his party and in 1987 he was replaced by a reformist Communist, Karoly Grosz.

There was relatively free movement between East Germany and Hungary and on 10 September 1989, Grosz opened the borders with Austria. As a result, 22,000 East Germans crossed via Hungary and Austria into West Germany, thereby outflanking the Berlin Wall and The East/West German border. In the same month, Grosz announced that there would be parliamentary elections in Hungary early in 1990.

In March–April 1990, free elections were held for a 386-seat Parliament with a four-year term. A centre-right party, the Democratic Forum (DF) won 165 seats and formed a coalition with two other centre-right parties whose 64 seats gave them 229 out of the 386 seats. The second biggest was the liberal Free Democratic Party (FD) with 92 seats. The Socialists (Reformist Communists) got only 33 seats. This parliament elected a DF Prime Minister (Jozsef Antall) and a non-executive FD President (Arpad Goncz).

Politically, Hungary's change was the most orderly of all. As in Poland, however, the real GDP declined by 1992 to 80 per cent of its 1987 value and unemployment reached 17 per cent. East Europeans were paying a heavy economic price, reflected in real hardship, for shaking off Communist discipline, but they were mature enough to endure this without serious public disorder.

EAST GERMANY

Since its inception in 1949, East Germany's biggest problem was the constant drain of skilled workers – white and blue collar – to the West, mainly through Berlin. It was to restrain this that the Berlin Wall was built in 1961. But in 1989 the pressure to emigrate – encouraged by Gorbachev's liberal emigration policies – was becoming more insistent. Between January and August

1989, President Honneker attempted to defuse the situation by allowing 4500 to cross the border legally. The 22,000 who crossed via Hungary in September, however, increased the pressure, and Honneker's attempts to stem the flow merely aroused more fury. There were huge street demonstrations and a political opposition party openly announced its existence. From 1 to 4 October another 15,500 migrants squatted in the Czech Embassy and were eventually allowed to cross to West Germany via Prague.

On 18 October, Honneker handed over to a reformist Communist, Egon Krenz, a protégé of Gorbachev, who was said to have urged this move. Honneker took refuge in the USSR, where he was admitted to hospital. In 1992 he was deported for trial in the unified Germany, but was later released on grounds of health and age and emigrated to Chile.

Krenz fought a rearguard action for the next six weeks. On 23 and 24 October 1989, some 40,000 people demonstrated in East Berlin and Leipzig, demanding free elections. On 6 November the (still Communist) Parliament rejected a Bill for free travel. On 7 and 8 November the Cabinet and the Politburo resigned *en bloc*. Krenz remained President and ordered the dismantling of the Berlin Wall on 9 November; 3 million East Germans poured into West Berlin. Now knowing that they could cross at any time, most were content to make short visits, return home, and go again next day. For the next few days there were continuous and highly emotional celebrations on the streets by East and West Berliners, all confident that the reunification of Germany would soon follow. In the eyes of the world, 9 November 1989 was the day the Cold War ended.

On 13 November, Krenz appointed a reformist Prime Minister, but refused to bow to demands to disband the *Stasi* (secret police). On the 21st, 100,000 people demonstrated in Leipzig. On 6 December, Krenz resigned and it was announced that there would be free elections in the Spring of 1990. In March, an East German 400-seat Parliament was elected as a prelude to reunification. The two main parties paralleled those in West Germany. The Christian Democrats won 193 seats, the Social Democrats 87 and they formed a coalition with 280 seats. The Democratic Socialists (former Communists) won 65 seats.

Thereafter things moved quickly. In July 1990 the West Germans introduced monetary union on a basis of two Ostmarks to one Deutschmark, a heavy subsidy to the East because the free rate was many times higher than that. Gorbachev, after some initial misgivings, raised no objection to reunification, and agreed that the united Germany would remain a member of NATO. The Germans in turn agreed that Soviet troops could for the time being remain in East Germany, as it would be difficult to absorb such a large army in the USSR at short notice. Reunification was formally declared in October 1990 and all-German elections followed in December. The two main parties merged with their Western equivalents; Chancellor Kohl's Christian Democrats were elected with a large majority.

The economic problems, however, proved far greater than expected. Few people had realized how low was the quality of East German industries, and their products proved almost impossible to sell. Unemployment in East Germany soared. Accustomed to heavily subsidized food and other basic necessities, many East Germans suffered severely, and were bitterly resentful that they seemed to be second-class citizens. They also felt the loss of their pride and their identity, which had been built to a great extent on the international successes of their sporting stars, whose training had been heavily financed by the state.

Nevertheless, the East Germans are the best placed of all the East Europeans. West Germany is pouring investment into the East and doing its utmost to organize terms of trade which will make the economy viable. Though many West Germans resent the burden and regret the change, there is little doubt that the new enlarged Germany will become economically even more dominant in the EC than West Germany was in the past. A greater worry was the growth of neo-Nazi politics, both in East and West, resulting in some ugly explosions of racial violence in 1992, by East Germans resenting the admission of large number of refugees from the conflicts in the former Yugoslav states (see Chapter 15).

CZECHOSLOVAKIA

A whole generation of Czech and Slovak liberal activists had been repressed after the Soviet invasion of 1968 and had been kept repressed. Even the clandestine political opposition was very weak and no organized political parties existed. The hard line of repression was exceeded only by that in Romania. As a result, reforms came more slowly than in neighbouring countries.

In October 1989, the police broke up a demonstration of 10,000 in Prague, using some force but not killing anyone. The opening of the Berlin Wall on 9 November, however, encouraged a demonstration by between 100,000 and 200,000 in Prague on 20 November, and Vaclav Havel gathered together 12 small political parties to form the Civic Forum (CF). Havel, a world-famous dissident writer who had spent several years in prison, had enormous prestige. By that time, the Communist Party had appointed a reformist Prime Minister, Ladislav Adamec, who on 21 November had talks with Havel and other opposition politicians. The Politburo dismissed the party leader (Jakes) and seven other members, but on 27 November there was a two-hour general strike demanding the end of Communist government, which drew a massive response.

On 28 November, a New Constitution was declared under which the Communist Party's leading role would end; on 3 December, Adamec announced a Coalition Cabinet of 16 Communists and 5 others. This provoked a protest demonstration of 250,000 in Wenceslas Square, and Havel gave warning that, unless a Cabinet with a non-Communist majority was formed, there would be another general strike on 12 December. On 7 December Adamec resigned and Marion Calfa of Civic Forum became Prime Minister. On 9 December he formed a new Coalition Cabinet with 10 Communists and 11 others. On 20 December, this Cabinet unanimously elected Havel as President.

In June 1990 a 150-seat two-year Parliament was elected. Civic Forum (with its allied PAV Slovak Party) won an overall majority with 87 seats, the Communists 23, and the Christian Democrats 20, with 20 others.

Under his leadership and restraint, helped by Adamec's pragmatic cooperation in maintaining cohesion of the government during his stage by stage relinquishment of power, Havel achieved an orderly transition to democracy.

Havel, however, was a non-executive President and he lacked the power to hold the Czech lands (Bohemia and Moravia) and Slovakia together. In June 1992 Slovakia elected a nationalist Prime Minister, Vladimir Meciar, a former Communist whose national socialism had overtones of both Hitler and Stalin. Slovakia, in a one-third minority, had always been the poorer third, and Meciar resented Prague's domination. Though Slovakia had most to lose economically by a split, a divorce became inevitable and the Czechs were surprisingly generous in the terms of the separation in 1993 in which some links were retained. But Slovakia's large Hungarian minorities gave concern for trouble ahead under a vehemently nationalist Prime Minister.

ROMANIA

Romania was the only one of the former Warsaw Pact countries in which the 1989 revolution caused substantial bloodshed. Nicolae Ceauşescu had been President since 1965 and combined an independent trade and foreign policy with a rigid Stalinist domestic regime. In particular, his secret police, the Securitate, was exceptionally powerful and pervasive.

On 24 November 1989 two weeks after the opening of the Berlin Wall – when almost all his neighbours had reformist or even democratically elected Prime Ministers, Ceauşescu was unanimously re-elected President by his Communist Party. On 17 December, the army fired on a relatively minor demonstration (5,000–10,000) in the mixed Romanian-Hungarian city of Timisoara and killed an unrecorded number of demonstrators. Despite this, Ceauşescu left next day on a scheduled three-day visit to Iran, leaving his wife in charge. Presumably he felt that cancellation of the visit would be interpreted as a loss of confidence.

During the 19th and 20th there were more demonstrations so, on his return, Ceauşescu called a mass rally in Bucharest to demonstrate his people's loyalty. To his astonishment he was booed. The Securitate opened fire and a number of people were killed. In contrast to the other countries, Ceauşescu had refused to accept *glasnost*, the TV cameras and reporters, other than strictly controlled government media, covered none of these events.

On 22 December, the army quite suddenly changed sides, and joined the crowds, firing on Securitate marksmen who were shooting at demonstrators from the windows. Ceauşescu and his wife fled in an army helicopter, but the pilot notified his landing point and the Ceauşescus were caught, tried by the army and shot on 25 December. As soon as he was in custody on 22 December, a previously unknown group emerged and took control – the National Salavation Front (NSF) led by Ion Iliescu. For a few days fighting continued, with the Securitate exchanging shots with the army, presumably fearing that if they were caught they would share Ceauşescu's fate, but their resistance collapsed on 28 December. Some were sent to prison, but the new government abolished the death penalty.

In retrospect it became clear that Iliescu, who had been in trouble in the past for reformist tendencies, had been planning to oust Ceauşescu for some time before the opportunity arose. It is probable that the army's change of sides was planned by reformist officers, who will have had no difficulty in persuading their conscript soldiers to obey them, since they all feared and disliked the Securitate, and their own sympathies will have been with the crowd.

On 1 January 1990, the NSF announced elections in the spring of 1990. Other political activists now also emerged from clandestinity but were suspicious that the NSF consisted of former Communists who were attempting to 'steal the Revolution for the Communist Party', and there were demonstrations to this effect on 11 January. The election went ahead on 20 May 1990 for a 396-seat four-year Parliament, and the NSF won 66 per cent of the vote (233 seats). Iliescu was elected President with 85 per cent of the vote. In contrast to the others, Romania has an executive President, but in common with them it has serious economic difficulties with its reform programme and Iliescu will remain vulnerable to opposition accusations about his Communist past.

BULGARIA AND ALBANIA

The other Warsaw Pact country, Bulgaria, was slower than her neighbours in eliminating Communist government. Bulgaria ousted her hardline President Zhikov on 10 November 1989 and held an election on 1 February 1990 for a two-year Parliament with 400 seats. Nevertheless, the reformist Communists (renamed Socialists) won an overall majority with 211 seats against the anti-Communist Union of Democratic Forces (UDF) with 144, the other 45 seats going to other parties. In the second election in October 1991, for a 240-seat five-year Parliament, the UDF won 111 seats and the former Communists 106, with the balance of 23 seats held by the Turkish Party, reflecting Bulgaria's 10 per cent Turkish minority. Though reversion is unlikely, the balance is delicate.

Albania also shook off her Communism in two stages. She had left the Warsaw Pact in 1961 and allied herself with China. After the Stalinist leader, Enver Hoxha, died in 1985, popular demand for democracy gathered momentum, and was further stimulated by events in Eastern Europe in 1989–90. An opposition Democratic Party was formed in 1990 and the first multiparty elections were held in April 1991, resulting in a comfortable majority (68 per cent or 169 of the 250 seats) for the Socialist (former Communist) Party. On 22 March 1992, however, the Socialists were decisively rejected. The Democratic Party gained 67 per cent of the vote, and its leader, Sali Berisha, became Prime Minister. He faced enormous problems, with a near breakdown of order and basic supplies. Italy is doing her best to supply aid, not least to try to stem the flood of desperate refugees. And other troubles loomed over the Yugoslav treatment of the large Albanian ethnic majority in the province of Kosovo.

YUGOSLAVIA

Yugoslavia left the Soviet fold in 1948 but remained Communist under her wartime resistance leader, Tito, who died in May 1980. The six constituent republics (Serbia, Croatia, Slovenia, Bosnia, Montenegro and Macedonia) contain a bewildering mixture of ethnic and religious groups, many with long histories of rivalry. After Tito's death, they had a collective federal presidency with much power delegated to the six republics. Following the trend in Eastern Europe, the six republics held multiparty elections in 1990. While Nationalist Communists prevailed in Serbia, nationalist democratic parties won in Slovenia and Croatia. They declared their independence and so, later, did Bosnia and Macedonia. This led to an ongoing civil war and it is likely to remain an area of conflict for years to come, so the situation will be examined in Chapters 15 and 16.

THE DISINTEGRATION OF THE USSR

Under the Constitution of the USSR, all the 15 republics had the constitutional right to secede from the Union. In practice, however, the control of every republic by the monolithic Communist Party, with its bureaucracy, army and KGB, had made this an illusory right until Mikhail Gorbachev introduced *glasnost* and *perestroika*. The three Baltic states, annexed against their will in 1940 under the Hitler–Stalin pact of August 1939 were the first to declare their independence, in 1990. All had substantial Russian minorities, many Russian-operated industries, and some Soviet army presence, so the Soviet government challenged their declarations. This was Gorbachev's first major test, since his position as General Secretary depended on the support of the Communist Party and of its Politburo in particular. He ran a serious risk of being ousted if he were seen to be allowing the Union to disintegrate.

Lithuania led the way, holding her own multiparty election and declaring her independence in March 1990. The Soviet government responded by sending in troops to re-establish its authority. There was some fighting, and worldwide condemnation. Latvia and Estonia, with 33 per cent and 28 per cent ethnic Russian minorities respectively, were more cautious, but they too declared their independence in May 1990. All three had to wait until after the unsuccessful coup in August 1991 for their independence to be recognized by Gorbachev.

On 17 March 1991, Gorbachev had organized a referendum on the continuance of the need for the Union as a federation of 'equal sovereign republics in which human rights and liberties will be fully guaranteed for all nationalities'. The Baltic states and Armenia, Georgia and Moldova boycotted the referendum, though their Russian minorities were able to vote directly through their districts and workplaces. Others, such as Ukraine, altered the wording or asked additional questions, clarifying the interpretation of 'sovereignty' to mean full independence within a loose confederation (as was later developed in 1992 as the Commonwealth of Independent States). With these provisos, Gorbachev got a yes vote from 76 per cent of an 80 per cent turnout (about 60 per cent of those eligible) but in Moscow, Leningrad and Kiev this approval came only from 50 per cent or less.[5]

Meanwhile, there was growing alarm amongst some of the hardcore of the Soviet Communist Party, from the highest to the lowest. This was in general on three grounds: patriotic, social and personal. Party members could see the USSR disintegrating from a superpower to a loose collection of republics with neither power nor prestige; they feared that the failure of Gorbachev's economic policies, the shortages and the price rises, might lead to serious public discontent leading to revolution; and they resented the prospect of losing the personal privileges of office – the dachas, the priority for the best apartments, the access to special shops and so on – reserved for the *nomenklatura*.

On 19 August 1991, seven senior conspirators, including Gorbachev's Vice-President, Prime Minister, Defence Minister and the Head of the KGB attempted a *coup d'état* while Gorbachev was on vacation. On the evening of Sunday 18th, they sent a senior KGB delegation to his holiday home in the Crimea, and tried to persuade him to sign a letter of resignation. When he refused, he was placed under house arrest and all his communications were cut off. On Monday 19th, the plotters ordered the Chief of Soviet TV to broadcast (at 6 am) a communiqué stating that Gorbachev was sick and that his Vice-President had taken over in accordance with the Constitution. This communiqué later also appeared in the Press. It outlined the current problems in the USSR (loss of international prestige, economic hardships, crimes etc) and pledged to restore her to her former status in the world.

The surprising thing was that Gorbachev should have picked such men as his closest associates in the four most powerful appointments (other than his own) in the Union, but it must be assumed that this was part of the price he had to pay for the party's cooperation in continuing with his reforms. They were no doubt confident that they could oust him if the reforms went too far for them and furthermore that they could exploit not only the public discontent with food shortages, rising crime, and so on, but also the innate *Russian* patriotism. They hoped to get a majority of the public to rally round this reassertion of power and a restoration of law and order.

The plotters made the cardinal error of failing to arrest Boris Yeltsin – or at least to prevent him from getting to the Russian Parliament building in Moscow. At this time a very popular elected President of the Russians, he was surrounded by friends and any attempt to arrest him there would arouse public anger and massive publicity. And so it proved.

The plotters had meanwhile ordered two divisions of the Soviet army to move into Moscow. Just before noon on Monday 19 August they sent 12 tanks to take up positions in the road outside the Russian Parliament building, but with no orders to arrest Boris Yeltsin. He reacted characteristically, waving his bodyguard aside to jump up onto the turret of one of the tanks, shake hands with the tank commander and make a short speech condemning the coup to the cheering crowds – in front of the world's TV cameras. He was quite sure that the tank crews would not shoot him or arrest him, but it needed a great deal of courage, and thus captured the imagination of the Muscovites and the world. Up till then, the reaction of the Muscovites had been to stay at home until the situation had become clearer, but within a few hours of this incident they were thronging the Parliament Square and all the streets leading to it. By the second day, Tuesday, there were about 100,000 on the streets surrounding the Parliament building. There were similar mass demonstrations in Leningrad.

On Tuesday night and the early hours of Wednesday morning, the plotters made their second major error. They ordered a tank regiment to go and secure the Parliament building and (presumably) to capture Boris Yeltsin. The tank colonel asked that he be given these orders in writing, but neither the Defence Minister nor the army commander was prepared to sign them. When the tanks came to the barricades in streets blocked by dense crowds, they were not willing either to shoot or to run down their own people. (The only three fatal casualties of the coup occurred in a confused confrontation in the dark under a flyover bridge on the Moscow ring road.)

By Wednesday morning, the plotters knew that their coup had no hope of success: three of them went to the Crimea and brought Gorbachev back to Moscow. They were all arrested soon after their return except for one who committed suicide. On Thursday 22 August Gorbachev gave a press conference condemning the coup and announcing that he had resumed power.

Gorbachev knew that he owed his survival to Yeltsin and the two appeared together on the platform in the Russian Parliament on Friday 23rd. Yeltsin announced a package of decrees for the Russian Federation including the dissolution of the Russian Communist Party. Gorbachev publicly challenged this and urged Yeltsin 'not to make the mistake of dissolving the Party'. This was no doubt because he feared that the dissolution of the Russian Communist Party would increase pressure to dissolve the Soviet Communist Party, weakening his power base and (perhaps more important) dismantling almost the entire bureaucracy that administered the Soviet Union. Nevertheless, Gorbachev's statement of loyalty to the hated and despised Communist Party, again in front of the TV cameras, sealed his political doom. Within the next few months, all the republics declared their independence from the Union and the Communist Party structure disappeared. By the end of the year, the Soviet Parliament had also been dissolved, and there was no Soviet Union of which Gorbachev could be President, so his job disappeared too – only four months after the coup.

Early in 1992, Boris Yeltsin, as 'first among equals' of the independent republics, negotiated the formation of a loose Commonwealth of Independent States (CIS). The three Baltic states and Georgia opted out but the other 11 states did join, including Russia, Ukraine and Belorussia, the heartland for several centuries of Imperial Russia.

Many, however, had serious reservations, especially Ukraine, and there were arguments about the control of nuclear weapons and the command and allegiance of the armed services, especially the Black Sea Fleet: this was based in the Crimea which, though populated by a Russian majority, had been handed over from Russia to Ukraine by Khrushchev in 1954.

Thereafter, the same thing began to happen in the 16 autonomous republics within the Federation of Russia itself. The largest of these republics, Tartarstan, with a population of about 3 million, declared its independence in March 1992.

All of these unresolved tensions, plus the existence of ethnic minorities related to their neighbours (reminiscent of the Sudeten Germans in Czechoslovakia in 1938) in every one of the 25 new republics in East Europe and the former Soviet Union, mean that the situation will remain fluid and unstable for many years to come. This prospect is discussed in Chapter 15.

THE REVOLUTIONS IN RETROSPECT

'People power' proved more effective in 1989–92, than in most of past history, mainly because troops were not willing to fire on their own people nor to run over them with their tanks, nor were their officers and politicians willing to order them to do so. Scenes like those in Paris in 1848 and again in the Commune rising in

1871, when tens of thousands of demonstrators and rioters were mown down on the streets, did not occur. Though this was no doubt partly due to a less ruthless attitude towards human life, the more immediate reason was the presence of TV cameras amongst the crowd, especially from the foreign media. Instinctively the crowds themselves realized this and were ready to dare the tanks to run them down in front of the cameras.

The media, however, were not the only factor. Soldiers themselves are recruited from the people. Trotsky noted this in his analysis of the preliminary to the Russian Revolution in February 1917. He describes a demonstration of 2500, which the officers commanding the Cossacks tried to break up, but the individual soldiers, riding through the crowd, took no aggressive action, and got into conversation with the demonstrators. The officers quickly withdrew them into a line. The demonstrators sensed that the Cossacks were not going to shoot and not going to charge again, so they walked forward to pat the horses, duck between their legs and fraternize with the soldiers.[6] This kind of phenomenon had first been identified by the revolutionary Russian philosopher Tkachev in 1887 as a 'public sense of impunity', which he regarded as the moment when revolutions became assured of success. The phenomenon was apparent again in 1978–79 in Tehran, when the conscript soldiers in the Shah's army fired reluctantly and then only over the heads of the demonstrators.[7] In the Philippines in 1986, the soldiers of President Marcos did fire on occasions, but their hearts did not seem to be in it: this was again probably due to the anxiety of their officers about the reaction of the media (especially American TV) as well as to the soldiers' own attitudes.

Trotsky also pointed out the dilemma of the soldier required to shoot at the crowd in the awareness that his sergeant was pointing a pistol at the side of his head in case he failed to do so. But this approach to military discipline has gone out of fashion since the First World war.

Another trend-forming event was the Czechs' passive resistance to the Soviet tanks that invaded Prague in 1968. Up till this point, the USSR and her satellites had kept tight control of both their own and foreign media, so that their suppression of the risings in Berlin in 1953, and in Hungary and Poland in 1956, was more uninhibited.[8] As part of his 'socialism with a human face', however, Dubcek had given a free run to domestic and foreign media to photograph anything and interview anyone. For some weeks in the Spring of 1968, this had astonished the world public, able for the first time to look behind the 'iron curtain' and hear what the people thought. When the Soviet army invaded in August 1968, it took them several days to get the all-pervasive journalists out of the alleyways of Prague, and to close their outlets to the world's TV screens via Austria. Once again, however, it was evident that the tank crews had no desire whatever to hurt the people, who were arguing earnestly with them from the street below or climbing onto their tanks to argue face to face. There were virtually no casualties on either side.

In Poland, the manifestations of people power began in 1980, were temporarily checked in 1981–83, and resumed from 1984 onwards, with a growing 'sense of impunity'. The actual transition of power in 1989–91 was peaceful, as it also was in Hungary. People power in East Germany was of a different kind – the flood of emigrants voting with their feet. In Czechoslovakia, peaceful persuasion again won the day, and the demonstrating crowds of up to 250,000 had been exceeded only by those up to 1 million strong in Tehran in 1978. The crowds blocking all the approaches to Yeltsin's Russian Parliament building, and the army's reluctance to use force to disperse them, were decisive factors in the collapse of the Moscow coup in August 1991.

The reasons why things went differently in China were explained on pp. 161–4, and there may be another chapter to that story still to come. In Romania, the conscript soldiers, though obviously reluctant, did initially fire on the crowds in Timisoara and Bucharest because they feared retribution in the light of Ceauşescu's 24-year reign of terror; but they were happier to join the people when their officers opened the way. The Securitate, however, fired because they could see no other way of saving the structure that gave them their privileges, or even of saving their own lives from mob violence or judicial execution if that structure collapsed.

So *glasnost*, as foreshadowed by Dubcek in 1968, and launched by Gorbachev all over Eastern Europe and the Soviet Union, probably made the revolutions inevitable. Gorbachev may have been happy for this to happen, though he hoped to keep the existing administrative structure intact. *Perestroika*, which aimed to adapt but not destroy that structure, had the effect in USSR and East European countries, of a disruption of distribution of supplies, a growth of the black market and an increase in crime, which contributed to a serious decline in the GDP and in the standard of living and a sharp rise in unemployment. The possibility of future attempts at a coup to restore the status quo cannot be ruled out (see Chapter 15).

The reformist Communists themselves must be given credit for the generally peaceful transition of power. Gorbachev clearly set the pattern, but General Jaruzelski in Poland, Karoly Grosz in Hungary, Egon Krenz in East Germany and Ladislav Adamec in Czechoslovakia made positive contributions. It is still too early to pass judgement on Ion Iliescu in Romania. None save Gorbachev is likely to earn more than a footnote in history, if that, but their moderation in what was for them an agonizing crisis saved many lives.

The real heroes were the emerging democratic leaders, who were big enough men to cooperate with the reformist Communists in this orderly transition, rather than stoke up the flames of popular passion beyond control. Vaclav Havel, especially, handled the transition in Czechoslovakia with superb political skill and restraint. As a long persecuted writer and philosopher, he said that he did not want political power, but was drafted to become non-executive President by popular acclaim and elected by Parliament, leaving the Prime Minister, Marion Calfa, to hold the executive power. By 1992, however, Havel was becoming frustrated by his lack of power to tackle the country's problems and was seeking to get some executive powers transferred to the presidency. He was, however, too late to prevent the secession of Slovakia.

Czechoslovakia has also led the way in pragmatic clemency towards former Communist bureaucrats, most of whom have continued to do their jobs in the administration. The main exceptions were senior party officials, members of the Communist militias, secret police and their informants, who were barred from jobs in the government, the armed forces, the courts and the universities (but not Parliament) for five years. In Germany, where the secret police (*Stasi*) was even more pervasive than in Czechoslovakia, tensions have been increased by public accessibility to *Stasi* files, where many have been appalled to find that close relations and spouses were informing on them; in one case, an anti-Communist priest was being prescribed drugs that could lead to psychosis by his doctor, who was a *Stasi* agent. The

German government is, however, doing its best to restrain passions. Romania, not surprisingly, was the most vindictive. In 1980, 20 per cent of Romanians over 18 were Communist Party members. The figure in East Germany was 18 per cent, Czechoslovakia 14 per cent, Bulgaria 13 per cent, Poland 12 per cent and Hungary 10 per cent. The course of events reflected these differences.[9]

Gorbachev must undoubtedly have the major credit for the end of the Cold War, for the consequent massive disarmament and for the revolutions that followed in the 25 new democratic republics emerging from the Warsaw Pact. If these democracies fail, either economically or through a political backlash or reactionary military coup, or destroy themselves or each other in civil wars, he will also get his share of the blame.

His personal tragedy, of being squeezed out of power and seeing the Union dissolve, arose because he was an administrator rather than a leader, and feared that a collapse (as distinct from an evolution) of bureaucratic control, both within states and in maintaining a political union, would be disastrous. Whether or not these fears were justified will not be known for some years.

One of the first fruits of the end of the Cold War has been the new ability of the UN Security Council to take decisive action unhampered by the veto. This was proved in the Gulf Crisis of 1990–1, which will therefore be examined in the next chapter. After that, Chapter 15 will assess the prospects of future world stability in the wake of the dramatic changes of 1985–92.

14 The Gulf Crisis 1990–91

WARNINGS OF ATTACK

The run-up to the Gulf crisis in 1990 showed US foreign policy at its worst. Once Saddam Hussein had invaded Kuwait, however, US diplomacy and crisis management were brilliant; the handling of the war itself in January and February 1991 was a triumph of military science and generalship. On the aftermath leaving Saddam Hussein in power with enough military strength to crush an attempted Kurdish rebellion in the north and a Shia rebellion in the south – it is too early to make a final judgement.

Ten years previously, in 1980, Saddam Hussein had launched his invasion of Iran without provocation. After some initial advances, his armies were driven back. The cease-fire in 1988 seemed to leave Iraq with a slight advantage, and the Ayatollah Khomeini accepted it because he realized that his army and people were exhausted and worse would follow if he continued fighting. The cease-fire settlement left conflicting demands over the boundary and over control of the Shatt al-Arab, which were still not resolved when Saddam invaded Kuwait on 2 August 1990. When it became clear that the USA, with powerful Arab allies, and the support of the UN Security Council, were building up forces to challenge this occupation, Saddam Hussein abandoned the objectives for which he had started the 1980 war against Iran and conceded to the new pragmatic government in Tehran all they wanted – a return to the 1980 status quo. So Saddam had fought the entire war for nothing.

Although Iran had been the victim of flagrant aggression, the West generally, and the USA in particular, had provided arms for Iraq. They had feared that an Iranian triumph would lead to Iraq (with its Shia majority) becoming a Shia fundamentalist state aligned to Khomeini. The USA's Arab allies, notably Saudi Arabia, Kuwait and Bahrain, were even more alarmed at this prospect, and had lavishly underwritten the Iraqi war effort with their oil revenues. At the same time, the Soviet Union, embroiled in the early years of *perestroika*, alarmed at her own economic crisis, and courting the West, detached herself from her previous military sponsorship of Iraq. Amongst all these cross-currents was the bizarre 'Iran–Contra' saga, in which a White House team, without the knowledge of the US Congress, was conducting a clandestine arms deal with the 'moderate elements' they hoped would take over from Khomeini in Iran, and might influence the release of some 20 US hostages held by Shia terrorists sponsored by Iran in Lebanon. They used the money from the deal again without congressional authority – to finance Contra guerrillas attempting to overthrow the Marxist Sandinista regime in Nicaragua. All of this was a remarkable example of the pursuit by conflicting elements in a ponderous and bureaucratic government of their varying and often cynical interpretations of the national self-interest. President Reagan either turned a blind eye or went along with them.

Despite his apparent military advantage, Saddam Hussein ended the Iran war heavily in debt, and with much damage to be restored. The army and air force, however, were heavily armed with modern weapons and largely intact, so the Gulf states and the West were relieved that the ambitions of Khomeini (who was still alive – just) had for the time being been checked. When Saddam turned the full force of his chemical arsenal to annihilating Kurdish villagers whom he accused of having helped Iran, there was no more than a plaintive protest from the West.

Early in 1990, Saddam made a realistic reappraisal of his prospects. He desperately needed money for reconstruction, and, like all dictators, needed further spectacular foreign policy successes to revitalize the support of his people. For both these purposes, the annexation of Kuwait provided a perfect answer. Although, by then, Reagan had handed over office to his Vice-President, George Bush, it is not surprising that Saddam thought that, once again, he would get away with his aggression.

On 24 February 1990, Saddam began to test the water, and gave the first public indication of how his mind was working, in a speech in Amman to the Arab Cooperation Council (ACC) comprising Iraq, Egypt, Jordan and North Yemen. He drew attention to the disengagement and declining power of the Soviet Union and warned that the USA, through its influence on the Gulf states, was intending to dominate the region and manipulate the price of oil to suit themselves; the Arabs must counter this by using the oil weapon – the power to coerce Western and especially US policy by raising the price of oil (as in 1974) and by using the vast amounts of their oil money invested in the Western world.[1]

Saddam's speech was broadcast on Jordanian television, so it will not have escaped the notice of the US government, who also, no doubt, received a report from President Mubarak of Egypt, a staunch pro-American ally and recipient of US aid, who took such strong exception to the speech that he withdrew from the ACC conference. The US government, however, preferred to ignore Saddam's signal.

Saddam issued a second threat on 28 May in a belligerent attack on the Gulf states for pumping too much oil, thereby keeping the price low. With an output of around 1 billion barrels a year, Iraq lost $1 billion for every dollar fall in the price. Saddam desperately needed that money.

On 17 July, he switched his abuse to his real target, Kuwait. Since her liberation by the British from the Ottoman Empire at the end of the First World War, Iraq had always claimed a legal right to the territory of Kuwait; this claim was made more insistent by Kuwait's huge oil reserves and an output of 600 million barrels a year. In retrospect, he was clearly looking further ahead than this – to the oil reserves of Saudi Arabia and the other Gulf states. With by far the largest and most powerful army in the region (the fourth largest in the world), he saw himself in due course controlling all the Arab oil in the Gulf (5 billion barrels a year, more than a fifth of the entire production of the world) and, even more significant, a much higher proportion of the world's total known reserves, which are mainly concentrated under the soil of Saudi Arabia and Kuwait. A united Arab Gulf under Saddam's presidency could be a superpower, with the option to do almost anything he wanted to do.

His immediate demand was for control of two Kuwaiti islands (Bubiyan and Warbah) on the Kuwaiti–Iraq border, which would give him an alternative oil port to those on the Shatt al-Arab – the vulnerable waterway between Iraq and Iran. Kuwait had made conciliatory gestures about these islands, offering to discuss arrangements for guaranteed access for export of Iraqi oil, but without ceding sovereignty. Iraq, however, was now going further, accusing Kuwait of military incursions and of stealing oil from the Iraqi side of the border. *The Economist* commented (on 21 July) that it sounded 'alarmingly like a pretext for invasion'.

On 24 July, two Iraqi armoured divisions (30,000 troops) moved up to the Kuwaiti border.

Next day, 25 July, there was a remarkable interview between Saddam Hussein and the US Ambassador in Baghdad, Ms April Glaspie. She has been much criticized for this interview – which Saddam taped and released to the world – but she was clearly acting on instructions from Washington. Remarking that the US government sympathized with the Iraqi desire to get money for reconstruction, Ms Glaspie said that the Secretary of State, James Baker, had instructed her to say that 'the Iraq–Kuwait border issue is not associated with America' and that the US Government had no opinion on it; but that she should ask him 'in the spirit of friendship, not confrontation', about his intentions in massing troops on the Kuwaiti frontier.[2] Saddam replied that there was to be a meeting with the Kuwaitis in Saudi Arabia on 31 July, and gave his word that 'we are not going to do anything until we meet them. But if we are unable to find a solution, then it will be natural that Iraq will not accept death, even though wisdom is above everything else. There you have the good news.'[3]

'Protocol talks' between Kuwaiti and Iraqi officials took place in Saudi Arabia on 1 August, but soon collapsed. Saddam had promised Ms Glaspie that these would lead on to further talks in Baghdad, but he clearly had no serious intention of talking at all. The 'protocol talks' on 1 August were merely a cloak to cover the launching of the invasion, which began in the early hours of 2 August.

It is salutary to compare this crisis with the remarkably similar one in June–July 1961, when Kuwait emerged from being a British protectorate to full independence. President Kassem of Iraq had at once declared his claim to all Kuwaiti terrority (and oil) and massed his armoured divisions on the frontier. Britain, on departure, had signed a mutual defence treaty with the Emir of Kuwait, and maintained military bases in Bahrain and what is now the United Arab Emirates (UAE). A small British naval force, carrying a Royal Marine Commando and a squadron of tanks in landing craft, had moved into position three miles off the coast of Kuwait in anticipation of the Iraqi threat. At 11 am on 1 July, the Emir invoked the defence treaty and requested British assistance. This request was at once transmitted by radio to the ships. At 11.17 the first British commandos landed on the beach by helicopter, closely followed by the tank landing craft – surely the quickest military response to a treaty obligation in history. Air cover was provided from Bahrain. Soon afterwards, an infantry brigade (5000 men) was brought in, partly from Gulf bases and partly by air from the UKs, it dug in on the Iraqi frontier, where it was shortly joined by Saudi Arabian and Egyptian contingents.

Although the Iraqis could have quickly overwhelmed this force with their tanks, they held back. By deliberately putting a 'finger in the mangle', Britain had given unambiguous notice that any attack would draw in whatever response was eventually needed to expel it.

A similar deterrent deployment in response to Saddam's aggressive signals in the Spring and Summer of 1990 would probably have prevented the 1991 war. As an Israeli professor commented: 'In Saddam's world, when you issue a threat, you expect to get a counter-threat. If you don't, it means weakness, appeasement and eventual retreat.'[4]

INVASION AND CRISIS: AUGUST 1990 – JANUARY 1991

The Iraqi invasion, by about 100,000 troops, began at 2 am local time on 2 August 1990. The Kuwaiti armed forces, totalling 20,000 men, 275 tanks and 36 aircraft, were taken by surprise, presumably believing that talks were still in progress. Many officers and soldiers were at home in bed, and their units offered only brief resistance, in which one of the Emir's half-brothers was killed. Kuwait City was occupied before the day was out and the Emir and his Prime Minister had fled to Saudi Arabia. Saddam declared that Kuwait's government had been overthrown by a popular revolution whose leaders had invited him in (though no such leaders ever in fact emerged). A few days later, he announced that Kuwait had been annexed as a province of Iraq. Most of the Arab governments condemned the invasion, only Jordan (which had little option) and the PLO declaring positive support for Iraq.

As if to make up for the previously uncertain sound of their trumpet, the US government sprang into action, both militarily and politically, with furious energy. The UN Security Council's five permanent members (the USA, USSR, China, France and Britain) voted in unison, the only time they had done so without a veto on such a serious matter since the invasion of South Korea in 1950 (when the USSR was boycotting the Council) and the Argentine invasion of the Falkland Islands in 1982. During that day they passed Resolution 660, demanding that Iraq withdraw her forces and negotiate. The voting was 14 to 1 (Cuba) with Yemen abstaining.

On 6 August, Security Council Resolution 661 imposed mandatory sanctions and an embargo, on 9 August, Resolution 662 declared the annexation of Kuwait null and void. Within a few days, all oil pipelines out of Iraq had been closed, and no ships were entering or leaving her ports. Road traffic continued through Jordan, but the blockade was soon extended to the Jordanian port of Akaba.

Meanwhile, President Bush ordered 4000 US combat troops, with ships and aircraft, under operation DESERT SHIELD, to Saudi Arabia on 7 August. They were joined on 11 August by British and Egyptian aircraft and troops, and British warships. France, Italy, Belgium, the Netherlands, Turkey and Syria also announced that they would send contingents of various kinds. The declared mission of DESERT SHIELD at this stage was to defend Saudi Arabia, not to liberate Kuwait. The build-up continued. At this point (15 August) Saddam Hussein wrote off all his gains from the 1980–88 war, offering Iran 'everything you want'.

Throughout the crisis, Saddam insisted that any negotiation for a settlement must be linked to discussions on Palestine, and there would be no withdrawal without a withdrawal of Israel from the occupied territories – a condition consistently rejected by the USA and her Arab allies. Saddam clearly hoped to harness anti-Israel and anti-US feeling amongst the Arab peoples in the hope that they would rise and overthrow their leaders, especially in Saudi Arabia and Egypt, but these hopes never looked like being realized.

On 16 August, Saddam Hussein ordered the rounding up of all British (4000) and US (2500) residents and their families in Kuwait, and declared his intention of holding them as hostages, some as human shields in military installions to deter Allied bombing. On 18 August, the UN Security Council passed Resolution 664 demanding that all foreigners be allowed to leave Iraq and Kuwait. (The worldwide disgust at this use of hostages eventually led Saddam to release them in November and December.)

The Security Council did not specifically authorize the use of military force to enforce the embargo, due to the reluctance of China, but on 25 August (in Resolution 665) it did authorize a naval blockade 'using measures commensurate to the specific situation'. This, in practice, gave the growing naval forces in the Gulf, and off the port of Akaba, all the powers they needed. (Later, Resolution 666 authorized humanitarian food shipments to be distributed through international aid agencies.)

On 25 September, Security Council Resolution 670 imposed a similar air blockade; on 29 October, Resolution 674 made Iraq accountable for war crimes and damage in Kuwait. This became an important factor in enforcing reparations as a condition of the eventual cease-fire.

The most important resolution of all, however, was Resolution 678 of 29 November authorizing the use of 'all necessary means' to drive Iraq out of Kuwait if she failed to withdraw by 15 January, and to restore international peace and security. This was the climax of four months of successful diplomacy, which had proved that the Security Council could, at last, act to counter aggression against any UN member by united action, as envisaged by its founders in 1945.[5]

THE WAR

By this time, Allied forces had reached a strength that would enable them to launch an attack with virtual certainty of success. Iraq had 1 million men under arms (60 divisions with 5000 tanks and 600 combat aircraft) of whom 650,000 with 4000 tanks were in Kuwait. The Allies had (by the start of hostilities in January 1991) 680,000 men, of whom 415,000 were Americans, 45,000 British, 14,000 French, with contingents from 25 other countries – some of them token ones. Contingents from 11 countries took part in the ground offensive in February, including Saudi Arabia, Kuwait, UAE, Bahrain, Qatar, Oman, Syria and Egypt.[6] Though the Allies were inferior in numbers, their technological superiority, especially in the air, gave them a decisive edge. Their main dilemma was that it would be urgently necessary to complete the final victory before the onset of sandstorms and almost unbearable heat (made worse by the prospect of troops having to wear protective clothing against Saddam's chemical weapons). The war must be over by May at the latest, preferably April. The UN's deadline for starting it 15 January seemed to be cutting this dangerously fine.

On 30 November, the day after the UN deadline was set, President Bush offered direct talks with Saddam. After weeks of wrangling over dates, the US Secretary of State and the Iraqi Foreign Minister did meet for six hours in Geneva on 9 January, but it was clear that Iraq had no intention of withdrawing and was merely playing for time, hoping, no doubt, to defer Allied action beyond the point of no return for completing it by April.

In both the USA and West Europe, there were determined lobbies urging the Allies not to take offensive action, but to give sanctions more time to work. These lobbyists were, however, in a minority; the majority of the public appreciated the significance of the oncoming hot season and public opinion polls in both Britain and the USA showed clear support for military action if Saddam did not withdraw by the deadline.

The US Congress, dominated by Democrats who were reluctant to leave the initiation of offensive operations to a Republican President, stalled for a long time. The President's patient attempts to negotiate, culminating in Saddam's intransigence on 9 January, led them to vote on 12 January by a narrow majority to authorize him to go ahead if the deadline passed (midnight 15/16 January New York time or 8 am on the 16th Iraq time).

In the event, the Allies launched their massive air strike at 2.30 am Iraq time on 17 January 1991, less than 24 hours after the deadline expired. For the first 38 days (17 January – 23 February) the offensive was entirely in the air, except for clandestine operations by Special Forces, particularly the British SAS, behind enemy lines. The primary purpose, of both the air offensive and the Special Forces, was to gain air supremacy prior to launching the ground offensive.

In this they were totally successful. Some 70,000 sorties were flown for the loss of 36 aircraft (26 US, 6 British, 2 Saudi, 1 Kuwaiti and 1 Italian) and 284 Cruise guided missiles were fired. Low level attacks on airfields by British Tornados and precision bombing of bunkers, command and control centres and bridges quickly paralysed the Iraqi Air Force. Very few Iraqi combat aircraft took off: when they did they were shot down. About 150 Iraqi aircraft, including many of their most modern fighters, took refuge in Iran, and the Iranians announced that they would not return these, retaining them against unpaid reparations for the Iran–Iraq War. This, coupled with the lack of resistance, may have indicated that Saddam Hussein had already abandoned hope of holding Kuwait, and was thinking ahead to conserving the military strength to maintain control of his own country after the war.

The Iraqis did, however, fire more than 60 Soviet Scud missiles, most of them on residential areas in Israel, where they caused many injuries but very few deaths. The aim of these was clearly to provoke Israel to join the war, which Saddam hoped would cause a massive switch of Arab support to his side. Under strong pressure from the USA, however, Israel did not hit back, and the chief effect of the Scud missiles was to prove the effectiveness of the US Patriot anti-missile missiles in shooting them down.

Altogether, in this period, the Iraqis lost more than half their aircraft – mainly destroyed on the ground – and had to abandon any attempt at a coordinated air defence, since their radar and their command and control systems had been made completely inoperative. The only resistance was from locally directed anti-aircraft artillery.

At the same time, the Allies destroyed more than one-third of their tanks by air attack and by Special Forces raids into Iraq before the land war began (1685 out of the 4000 tanks in Kuwait and southern Iraq). Iraqi front-line conscript soldiers were demoralized by continuous bombing against which they had no defence, and large numbers crossed the lines to surrender. The elite Republican Guard, who were being held back in a counter-attack role, were also demoralized so that when the ground offensive began, there was neither any serious resistance nor any counter-attack.

The ground war was launched in the early hours of 24 February 1991. In 100 hours exactly, all of Kuwait had been liberated and a large part of the Republican Guard was cut off by an outflanking force comprising the US 82nd Airborne Division and the French Foreign Legion, which had advanced unopposed through the desert 100 miles west of Kuwait and reached the Euphrates River and the main Basra–Baghdad road.

At 8 am on Thursday 28 February, the Allies declared a conditional cease-fire. To obtain this, Saddam Hussein was forced to agree publicly to accept all the 12 UN Resolutions, which included abandoning his annexation of Kuwait (all of his troops having already been driven out, killed or captured) and accepting the obligation to pay reparations. These were going to be very heavy indeed, because he had deliberately set fire to most of Kuwait's oil wells in a final outburst of malice before he left: Kuwait's oil production will not be fully restored for many years to come.

There was very little serious fighting. The conscripts in southern Kuwait and Iraq, in many cases abandoned by their officers, surrendered as fast as they could indicate their desire to do so. The much feared Republican Guard did little better. Over 2000 more tanks were destroyed or captured, and the survivors of the Republican Guard withdrew to the area between Basra and the coast with their remaining tanks; however, though there were still about 1000 tanks with the troops in the rest of Iraq, around Baghdad and the Kurdish areas, which had not been involved in the war.

In the entire seven weeks of the war, on land, sea and air, the Allies had destroyed most of Saddam's tanks and captured an estimated 170,000 prisoners at a cost of 150 men killed in battle – surely the most convincing endorsement of the power of modern war technology. The strategic and tactical handling of the Allied forces by the US General Norman Schwarzkopf was masterly: in terms of a massive victory for a minimal cost in lives, it must go down as one of the most brilliant campaigns in military history.

THE AFTERMATH OF WAR

As with the lack of serious resistance by Saddam's air force, the almost total failure of his army to resist the Allied offensive suggests that he had written off Kuwait and was concerned only to keep as many as possible of his Republican Guard intact for use in maintaining his personal power in Iraq.

The Allies had appreciated for some time that there were likely to be two major revolts as and after the war ended: first, by the Kurds in the north; second, by Shia Muslims led by fundamentalists in the south. So there was every likelihood of Iraq splitting into three.

This presented the Allies with a dilemma. Such a split would probably result in the fall of Saddam Hussein; but most of the productive oil fields are in the north (around Kirkuk and Mosul) and the south (near the Kuwaiti border) so whoever took over the surviving centre of the country would inherit a crippled economy deprived of the source of revenue to rebuild it and with no means of paying reparations.

Moreover, such a split would generate acute anxiety amongst Iraq's neighbours. If Iraqi Kurdistan became independent, Turkey would face an intensification of the demand for autonomy or independence by her own even larger Kurdish population. Similarly, if southern Iraq became an independent Shia Muslim state, it would have close ties with Iran, which would alarm Saudi Arabia, Kuwait and the other Gulf states. The spectre of an even stronger Iran, without the restraint of a powerful neighbour in Iraq, might have made the Gulf even more unstable than it had been before. It had been to prevent this very situation that they had so lavishly supported Iraq in her 1980–88 war against Iran.

Possible solutions to both problems offered themselves, but there is no evidence that either was seriously considered by the Allies. Turkey could have expressed her support for the idea of an autonomous Kurdistan, federated with Turkey, incorporating both Turkish and Iraqi Kurds. The Kurds would almost certainly have welcomed this, and Turkey would have benefited from the incorporation of the rich oil fields around Kirkuk and Mosul. Regarding the south, the Allied armies had every justification for remaining in occupation of the whole of southern Iraq in order to enforce the payment of reparations to Kuwait. This could have been achieved by operating the oil fields in southern Iraq at full capacity (their staffs would have cooperated because they would have enjoyed both security and full salaries). The revenue would have been paid to Kuwait until such time as reparations were paid in full. These would have included the ongoing loss of production of Kuwait's own oil fields which Saddam had set on fire and would remain out of action for a very long time, so this repayment – and hence the occupation – would have lasted for many years. Though some US and British participation – especially in naval, air and other high technology areas – would have been necessary, the main army element in the occupation could have been provided by Saudi, Egyptian and other Gulf troops, whose extra costs would have been a further charge on the reparations bill.

If such ideas were ever contemplated, they were never officially proposed, though a former British Ambassador to the UN did suggest that Allied troops should remain in southern Iraq until Saddam had fulfilled certain conditions.[7]

Three days after the shooting ended (3 March) the general commanding the Iraqi troops who were cut off north of Kuwait signed cease-fire terms. Public expectation had been that these troops would have to hand over all their tanks and other weapons and then be transported unarmed through Allied lines to Baghdad. Instead, though this was not publicly announced, they were allowed to keep their weapons and remain intact as units – presumably to suppress any attempted rising by the Shia population – which they did during the subsequent three weeks.

In northern Iraq, Kurdish partisans occupied most of Iraqi Kurdistan, including the oil town of Kirkuk, but within four weeks the Iraqis, using helicopter gunships and tanks, had recaptured Kirkuk and most of the villages. Kurdish refugees, remembering the Iraqi mass slaughter by gas attacks on the villages in 1988, streamed north towards Turkey and Iran. Faced with the prospect of 1 million refugees, the Turks closed their borders, and the mountain sides were packed with Kurdish families under makeshift shelters. Cold and hunger took a heavy toll, especially of Kurdish children. Eventually Allied troops moved into northern Iraq to set up 'havens' in the valleys to which the refugees were encouraged to move, under military protection against the Iraqis, until it became safe for them to return to their own villages. These troops were relieved by UN monitors by early July.

All this was a heavy price for the people of Iraq to pay for the Allies' preference for leaving Saddam Hussein in power with the military strength to suppress his dissident minorities. The Kurds felt particularly bitter; during the war they had been encouraged to rebel to draw off Iraqi troops, and it had not occurred to them that the Allies would calculatedly leave Saddam in control. Meanwhile, the UN sanctions remained in force: as well as the Kurds and Shia Muslims, many ordinary Iraqis in Baghdad and elsewhere were equally bitter that the Allies had not carried through their victory to remove Saddam Hussein and thereby enable the UN blockade to be lifted.

CONCLUSIONS

The Western world was extremely slow in reacting to the very clear signals that Iraq was giving from February to July 1990 of her belligerence towards Kuwait and the other Gulf states, and towards the USA. These signals were undoubtedly given by Saddam Hussein to help him to decide how far he dared to go. The United States had been trying to encourage Saddam to believe that he had most to gain by re-entering the trading world of the West now that the Soviet Empire and its sponsorship of radical Arab states had declined. Saddam, however, was impatient for power: he was quite convinced not only that he could solve his internal economic problems by seizing Kuwait, but also that this would lead inexorably to his control of all the world's richest oil-producing area and, with it, superpower status. His actions offered the closest parallel yet seen to Hitler's step-by-step challenge from 1936 to 1939.

Just as France and Britain, wary of another war, and seeing Hitler as a potential barrier to the USSR, failed to react to the reoccupation of the Rhineland in 1936, then of Austria and Czechoslovakia, so the Western Allies failed to take the risk of deterring Saddam Hussein. Had they followed the example set by Britain, Saudi Arabia and Egypt in 1961, and put a force a fraction of the size of the eventual task force into Kuwait, or even into Saudi Arabia, Saddam would have backed off from his invasion. The ultimate fear was probably that the USA might be drawn into 'another Vietnam'.

The low point came on 25 July, when Saddam had massed his troops on the border of Kuwait and the US State Department had instructed its Ambassador to reassure Saddam that the USA did not consider herself involved in the dispute between Iraq and Kuwait. Saddam judged this to be the green light to invade a week later.

The contrast between this and the subsequent firm response to the invasion led by the United States, in the UN, and later in the military operations, arose because (like the Allies in 1939) they at last realized that Saddam was not going to stop unless checked by force. Another factor was probably that, during the 1988 US election campaign and afterwards, President Bush had been sneered at by his opponents as a 'wimp'. The dismal lack of resistance to Saddam in July, and its results, had seemed to substantiate this sneer, making Bush feel that he had to retrieve his reputation amongst the US public and in the world.

The weak handling of the aftermath was again probably prompted by President Bush's fear of being dragged into an open-ended commitment to keep the peace in a complex and disturbed country whose fate was no longer of vital concern to the USA. There is little doubt, however, that the very rich Arab oil states, financing also a large contingent from Egypt, would have been ready to bear the bulk of the burden of the occupation of southern Iraq, though the USA and Britain would have had to provide most of the high technology support, especially naval and air and in the field of intelligence and surveillance. They were, however, unwilling to accept even this relatively small risk and commitment: they may later have reason to regret this decision.

Overall, however, the Gulf crisis of 1990–91 has made a major contribution to world stability. It has proved that, after 45 years of impotence, the UN can act effectively to turn back a powerful and aggressive dictator; also that, in contrast to the failure of the military technology of the 1960s and 1970s to prevail in Vietnam, the military technology of the 1990s can be supreme if properly directed by able commanders.

If the permanent members of the UN Security Council can remain united, if the USA can keep her nerve, and if Western Europe is prepared to play its full part, the Holy Grail of Collective Security, which has, over the ages, eluded the world, could be within reach. But the pattern of conflict is constantly changing and the newly united major powers must adapt the application of their decisive military and economic strength to the future spectrum of conflict, from nuclear threat and conventional war to religious conflicts, drug trafficking, terrorism, peacemaking and peacekeeping.

Part V

Today and Tomorrow

15 Patterns of Future Conflict

THE BALKANIZATION OF EASTERN EUROPE

The Cold War is irrevocably dead. Even if a *coup d'état* were to restore the totalitarian government in Russia, with the old Communist bureaucracy back in control, the other former Soviet and East European states would never reconstitute the Warsaw Pact, and the military threat which underlay it will not reappear. Nor could the Russian economy, now reliant on the West, afford to renew the challenge.

Despite this, the world has never been so unstable since the 1950s. The fear of nuclear escalation had, from 1945–90, caused both sides to try to resolve confrontations and restrain their client states, but nuclear weapons may now proliferate and be harder to control. And small wars abound; at the end of 1992 there were at least 33 armed conflicts in progress all over the world (see Table 15.1).

The breakup of the USSR and Eastern Europe has created 25 new independent democratic republics, all trying to switch to market economies. Every one of these has ethnic minorities within its borders who are related to major communities on the other side of those borders; some, such as Yugoslavia before she split, and now Bosnia, have mixtures in which there is no overall majority, and many have dangerous religious mixtures (see Table 15.2). Politicians seeking electoral votes are likely to exploit the patriotic passions aroused by these situations.

The Russian Federation itself is also threatened with disintegration. Of its 147 million population, some 25 million live in 20 autonomous republics (see Table 15.3), some of which are demanding complete independence. Some have explosive population mixtures: Tartarstan, for example, has 49 per cent Tartars and 43 per cent ethnic Russians.

Instability or economic chaos in Russia and in some of the other republics such as Ukraine could well result in a swing to Fascism (national socialism), which has a very close affinity to

Table 15.1 Contemporary armed conflicts, September 1992*

	Civil wars or wars of secession	*Insurgencies*
LATIN AMERICA	*Colombia*	
		Guatemala
		Peru
AFRICA	Angola	*Chad*
	Liberia	Djibouti
	Somalia	Mali
	Sudan	
	Western Sahara	
EUROPE	Azerbaijan	Georgia
	Bosnia	*Spain*
	Croatia	Turkey
	Moldova	*United Kingdom*
ASIA	*Afghanistan*	*Bangladesh*
	Cambodia	*India*
	Lebanon	*Indonesia*
	Papua New Guinea	Iraq
	Sri Lanka	Israel
		Myanmar
		Philippines
		Tadjikistan

*Those in *italics* have been in progress for ten years or more

Communism. Their agonizing transition to democracy and a market economy may be under new leaders, but the middle levels of the bureaucracy, including middle-ranking army officers, are the same; they cannot be replaced overnight. Most of them were chosen as good party members: they deplore lack of control and yearn for national discipline. They face an abyss of chaos and resent the loss of their power and privileges; some fear the loss of their jobs and some, haunted by their past, may fear for their lives, as their opposite numbers did in Romania. Many of them might gladly rally behind the kind of 'strong man' –

Table 15.2 Ethnic and religious minorities in former Soviet republics and Eastern Europe

Russian minorities in former Soviet republics

Kazakhstan	41%	Belorussia	12%
Latvia	33%	Uzbekistan	11%
Estonia	28%	Tadjikistan	10%
Kirghizia	26%	Lithuania	9%
Ukraine	21%	Azerbaijan	8%
Moldova	13%	Georgia	7%
Turkmenistan	13%	Armenia	2%

Other potential explosive mixtures in former Soviet republics

Armenia	Azeris (5%)
Azerbaijan	Armenians (8%) concentrated in Nagorno Karabakh
Georgia	Armenians, Azeris, Abkhazians and South Ossetians
Kazakhstan	Ukranians (6%)
Kirghizia	Uzbeks (12%)
Lithuania	Poles (7%)
Moldova	Romanians (64%), Ukrainian (14%), Gazauz (4%)
Russia	Ruthenians, North Ossetians, Chicheno-Ingushetians, Cossacks, Bashkirians and Tartars (mainly in autonomous republics, regions and areas)
Tadjikistan	Uzbeks (23%)
Turkmenistan	Uzbeks (9%)

Potentially explosive mixtures in other East European states

Yugoslavia (former)	*Racial*:Serb (40%), Croat(20%), Slovene (8%) Albanian (6%), Macedonian (6%) *Religious traditions*: Orthodox (50%), Catholic (40%), Muslim (10%)
Albania	*Religious traditions*: Muslim (70%), Orthodox (20%), Catholic (10%)
Bulgaria	Turks (10%); Orthodox/Muslim mix
Romania	Hungarians (8%)
Turkey in Asia	(Kurds not recognized as such. Estimates vary from 7% to 25%; many with mixed blood)

political or military – who often emerges in such circumstances with a promise of restoring order. The public at large might well follow suit, in sheer exasperation, whether the strong man called himself nationalist or socialist or (like Hitler) both. Russia might

Table 15.3 Minorities in the Russian Federation

Russian republics	*Population (000)*	*% Titular nationality*	*% Russians*
Bashkiria	3943	22	39
Buryatia	1038	24	70
Checheno-Ingushetia	1270	(C) 58 (I) 13	23
Chuvashia	1338	68	27
Dagestan	1802	(Avars) 28	9
Kabaroino-Balkaria	754	(K) 48 (B) 9	32
Kalmykia	323	45	38
Karelia	790	10	74
Komi	1251	23	58
Mari	749	43	47
Mordovia	963	32	61
North Ossetia	632	53	30
Tartarstan	3462	49	43
Tuva	308	64	32
Udmurtia	1606	31	59
Yakutia	1094	33	50
Adygei	432	22	68
Gorno Altai	191	31	60
Karachai-Circassia	415	(K) 31 (C) 10	42
Khakassia	567	11	79
All Russia	147,400		82

Source: *The Economist*, 14 March 1992.

again become a Fascist state, as it was, in effect, under Stalin and Brezhnev, with much of the old *nomenklatura* back in control.

Meanwhile, miniature 'strong men' will continue to emerge amongst the plethora of ethnic or religious minorities in any of the new states, as they already have in what was Yugoslavia. An extreme example of the intractability of this problem is illustrated in Map 15A, showing Bosnia as she was at the time she became independent from Yugoslavia in March 1992. No community had as many as 50 per cent of the population, the Muslims having 40 per cent, Serbs (Orthodox Christian) 32 per cent, and Croats

(Catholic) 18 per cent. But these figures are imprecise because there has been much intermarriage. Even in areas where one community had more than 50 per cent, it was seldom a large majority. In many places, including the capital, Sarajevo, no community had as many as 50 per cent. In some apartment blocks, there were members of all three communities living one above the other. Though many carried guns, they had lived reasonably happily together for generations, but when the Bosnian government called a referendum in 1992, the Muslims and Croats voted solidly for independence and the Serbs boycotted the referendum.

At this stage all sides, and especially the Serbs, were copying Hitler's sinister policy of 'ethnic cleansing'. It is in fact an inaccurate phrase in this instance, since most of the inhabitants are of fairly similar Serbo-Croat blood, sometimes with some Montenegrin, Albanian, etc, and the difference is rather one of communal traditions and religion. In 1991 the Croats were using it to try to drive Serbs out of their border areas and they, having lived in a Fascist puppet state under Hitler's occupation, also called it ethnic cleansing, so the term is now in general use.

It was the Serbs, however, who excelled in it in Bosnia with, for them, very successful results. They used a combination of local Bosnian Serb militias in the mixed areas, supported by units of the regular Federal Yugoslav army, whose officer corps was traditionally Serbian. Some of these regular units were stationed in Bosnia, recruited mainly from Bosnian Serbs, and had remained in barracks in Bosnia when it seceded in March 1992. These regular units sometimes joined in the fighting or loaned heavy weapons to the Serb militias. The militias mainly used small arms, grenades and mortars, while the regular units supported them with artillery, tanks and aircraft (from bases in Serbia). Both Serb and Croat militias had regular armies on whom to call for heavy weapons. The Bosnian Muslims had not, so they were at a serious disadvantage, only slightly redressed when Turkey and other Muslim countries got some heavy weapons through to them. This, of course, encouraged the Muslims to do more ethnic cleansing themselves.

The Serbs avowedly aimed to get two-thirds of Bosnia under their control and, within four months of Bosnia's declaration of independence, they had largely achieved this (see Map 15.B). By July 1992, the Serbs (with 32 per cent of Bosnia's population)

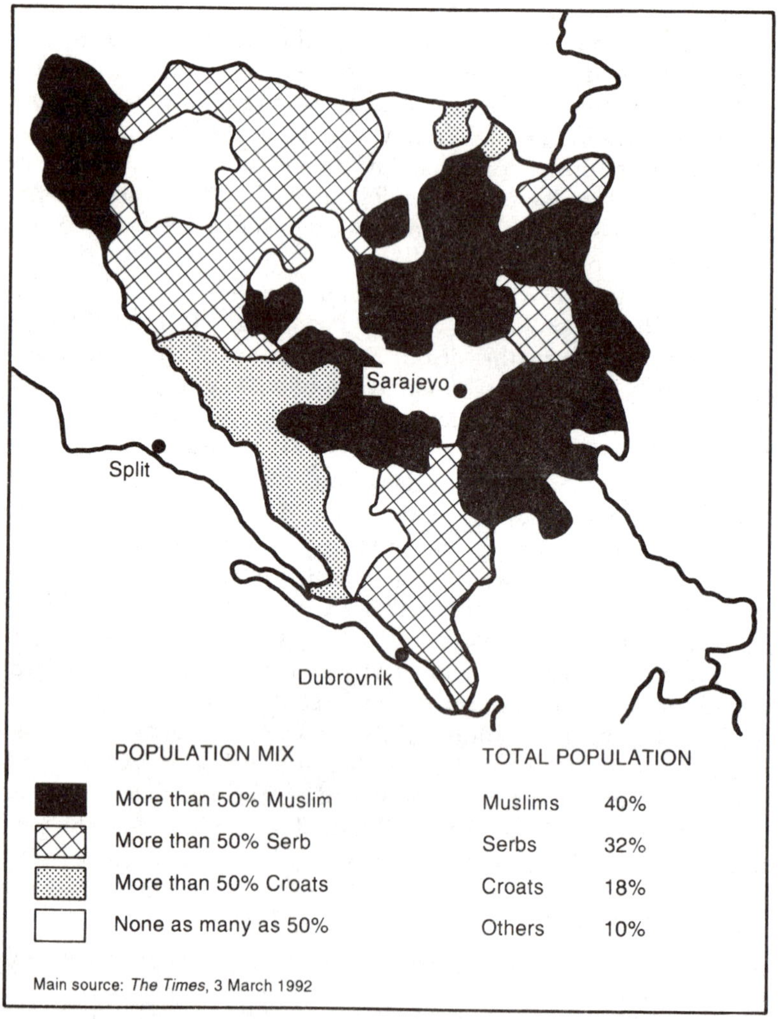

Map 15A Bosnia: population mix March 1992

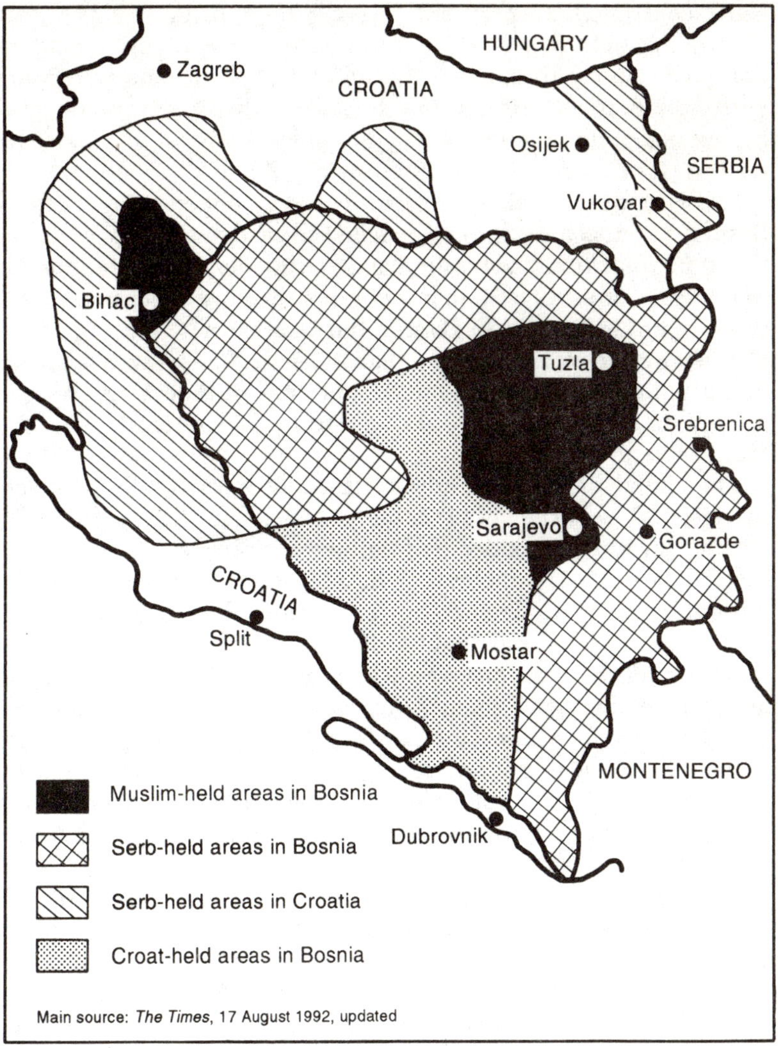

Map 15B Bosnia: military control September 1992

controlled 65 per cent of the country, and the Croats (with 18 per cent) controlled 30 per cent, leaving the Muslim 40 per cent controlling only 5 per cent – an area in the east just including Sarajevo (closely threatened by the Serbs), with tenuous contact with small areas around the besieged cities of Gorazde and Srebrenica, and another area 150 miles away in the extreme northwest of Bosnia around the town of Bihac.

By September 1992 there were nearly 2 million refugees from Bosnia, Croatia and Serbia, expelled from their homes, but still living in what had been Yugoslavia, with friends or relations, or in refugee camps. Over half a million of these were Bosnians of all three communities still in Bosnia, but in areas now under control of their own community (see Table 15.4). There were another half a million in other European countries outside Yugoslavia – mainly in Germany, but also a lot in Switzerland, Austria, Hungary and Sweden.

The actual processes of ethnic cleansing were vividly depicted by intrepid reporters and camera teams on the world's TV screens: several were killed or wounded in doing so. Their reports showed how the staunchest of Bosnian fathers, however determined he was to defend his home and his locality under continuous sniping and bombardment, would eventually decide that his children and their mother mattered to him even more, so he would either send them away from the combat zone to try their luck as refugees or – for fear that they would not get through without him – he might decide to go with them. But in a war with no front lines, this would mean getting safe conduct on a bus through the Serb roadblocks. To get this, he would be required to sign over his house, 'voluntarily', to the Serb militia or to a Serb family nominated by them. The sum of human misery of 2.5 million refugees (80 per cent of them still dispersed in Yugoslavia and 0.5 million in West Europe) has shocked the world.

As each family flees from its home, the remaining minority in their village or urban district get smaller and feel more vulnerable. A minority of Bosnian Muslims of 30 per cent becomes 20 per cent, and then more quickly 10 per cent and finally only a handful. The Serbs intend then to present the UN with a *fait accompli* and demand that the frontier be changed.

Ethnic cleansing is clearly here to stay, under whatever name. Stalin used it regularly to drive his ethnic communities (e.g. the Tartars) out of areas where he did not want them. He used it

Table 15.4 Yugoslav refugees

Yugoslav refugees still within former Yugoslavia (September 1992)

Present location	*From Croatia*	*From Bosnia*	*Total*
Croatia	271,798	335,985	638,109 *
UN-patrolled areas	87,000	-	87,000
Serbia	162,337	252,130	414,467
Bosnia	93,000	588,000	681,000
Montenegro	6,743	50,857	57,600
Slovenia	1,000	69,000	70,000
Macedonia	2,500	28,800	31,300
Total	**624,378**	**1,324,772**	**1,979,476 ***

*Includes 30,326 refugees from Serbia

Yugoslav refugees outside Yugoslavia (August 1992)

Germany	220,000	Netherlands	6,000	Poland	1,500
Switzerland	70,450	Czechoslovakia	4,000	Luxembourg	1,200
Austria	57,500	Norway	2,617	France	1,108
Hungary	50,000	Britain	2,000	Spain	120
Sweden	47,600	Finland	1,892	Ireland	10
Italy	17,000	Belgium	1,800	Greece	7
Turkey	15,000	Denmark	1,795	Elsewhere	30,013
		Total	**531,412**		

Killing

Up till September 1992, 10,000 had been killed in Bosnia, with 50,000 missing

Source: *The Economist*, 19 September 1992, p. 54, citing UNHCR, Zagreb Public Information Unit

again in 1945–46 to drive more than 1 million Germans out of western Poland and other areas of Eastern Europe to fit the new frontiers, and Poles and others out of areas ceded to the USSR. After Hitler had used it against the Jews in the 1930s, Jewish extremists followed his example in 1948 in a series of killings of Arabs. The massacre of 254 Arabs in the village of Deir Yassin on 9 April 1948, for example, was an important factor in causing some 600,000 Arabs to flee the country in the weeks before and after Israel was founded on 15 May 1948.[2]

Attempts by the EC and the UN to prevent ethnic cleansing in Bosnia and Croatia and the problems of peacekeeping are further discussed in Chapter 16. The repercussions of Serb terror in Bosnia, however, may be only a foretaste of the problems that will face Western Europe in the next few years.

WESTERN EUROPE

The biggest threats of destabilization in Western Europe in the 1990s will come not only from the pressure of refugees wishing to enter from Eastern Europe and across the Mediterranean, but also from the neo-Fascist backlash that this may provoke.

In the mid-1980s, before Germany was reunified and before the Shengen Agreement opened the frontiers between France, Germany and the Benelux countries, it was estimated that about 100,000 people were arrested on Germany's frontiers each year, about half being on wanted lists and the other half questioned on the hunches of police officers, customs and immigration officials. Though Germany's eastern frontiers, being EC external frontiers, should be as tight as the old borders between East and West Germany, the opening of internal frontiers will mean that many of those 100,000 will either have to be caught by police and customs spot checks, or will remain at large. Frontier checks, including those at ports, airfields and main road crossings, were never really watertight, but they did provide bottlenecks through which everyone had to pass, greatly assisting police officers and other officials in spotting wanted or suspicious persons. Assuming that such people were also arrested at other EC frontiers, we must expect a massive increase – running into six or seven figures – in the number of illegal immigrants (in addition to genuine refugees and asylum seekers) drug-runners and other criminals at large in the EC at any one time; it will be very much easier for them to evade the police as soon as they sense that they have become vulnerable, simply by crossing into the territory of another police and judicial system.

West European police and intelligence services are well aware of this problem, and are diligently improving their cooperation. There is strong pressure to develop harmonized identity card (ID) and visa systems; and to include machine-readable biometric data unique to the card holder, such as digitally recorded fingerprint, retina, hand geometry or vein-pattern data on ID cards and visas. This will make it possible to check in a few seconds whether the person presenting them is the person to whom they were issued.

Over half a million refugees entered Western Europe in 1991 (see Table 15.5). Of these, over half entered Germany, mainly from Eastern Europe. Figures for 1992, when finalized, will be much larger. The total number of refugees processed at one reception station on Germany's eastern frontier had already reached 350,000 in the period January to September 1992, and another 50,000 entered in October, so that the total for Germany alone was about half a million in 1992.

Processing refugees is a long and arduous business. In Germany, refugees can stay up to five years while their cases are being investigated. Of 45,000 who applied for asylum in Britain in 1991, only 10 per cent were initially judged to have genuine grounds to fear persecution if they returned home but, because of the prolonged appeal procedures, there was in November a backlog of 60,000 applications for asylum awaiting appeal; but, over the years, 60 per cent of those who apply have in the end been allowed to remain in Britain.[3]

Conflict, persecution, hardship, hunger and – even without these – the wholly understandable desire of people to seek a better life for their families, are likely to lead to several million refugees trying to enter Western Europe during the next few years. Only a minority will qualify for asylum, and others will be given temporary residence permits while their appeals are considered. All EC countries, including Germany and Britain, are tightening their immigration laws to avoid arousing anti-immigration reactions and overstraining their social services. Many immigrants, therefore, fearing rejection if they apply, will enter illegally and try to find a clandestine means of survival. Unable to get regular work without risk of revealing themselves, and unable to draw social security payments, they will provide a pool of labour, reluctant but eventually desperate, for criminal and drug-running gangs. Some will be drawn into terrorist groups, particularly international groups operating in Europe, such as Palestinians and East European ethnic groups fighting their battles on West European streets, as other groups have in the past.

Most of the conflict and instability engendered by these problems will be internal, but international conflicts do spill

Table 15.5 Refugees to Western Europe, 1988 and 1991

Refugees	*1988 from*			*1991 from*			
to	*Eastern Europe*	*Africa*	*Asia/Middle East*	*Eastern Europe*	*Africa*	*Asia/Middle East*	*Total*
Germany	71416	6548	24711	166662	36004	52826	255,492
France	8915	14725	5747	14662	16172	13738	44,572
UK	891	1822	2384	3735	27485	12945	44,165
Switzerland	11187	823	4304	22758	5728	13485	41,971
Scandinavia	6319	3015	13009	21330	5696	9056	36,082
Benelux	2601	5209	4230	12523	10916	11191	34,630
Austria	14574	74	1017	19184	1901	6124	27,209
Italy	97	635	543	20676	2307	323	23,306
Turkey	412	16	56504	400	38	9036	9,474
Spain/Portugal	1772	678	907	2947	2388	675	6,010
Greece	4608	1266	2549	1110	172	1391	2,673
					Total	1991	525,584

Britain in 1991 had 45,000 claims for asylum, 90% unfounded, but 60% remain due to slow appeal procedures (60,000 backlog)

Visa now required for ex-Yugoslavs *except* Croatians and Slovenes

Germany has total of 210,000 refugees from former Yugoslav states, 50,000 refugees entered Germany in October 1992

Source: *The Times*, 6 November 1992

over into the international arena, especially if there are ethnic, nationalist, ideological or religious undertones, for example, when neo-Fascists persecute domestic ethnic or religious minorities on the grounds that they are sheltering illegal immigrants. Such persecution can quickly arouse passions amongst people in neighbouring countries who are religiously or ethnically related to the minorities or immigrants being persecuted.

In the long term, there remains a disturbing possibility, albeit a distant one, of more of the German people becoming frustrated and posing a real threat of electing a nationalist and perhaps authoritarian government. If the mainstream political parties find themselves facing an alarming haemorrhage of voters to a neo-Nazi party, they too might be forced into adopting more nationalist policies. Unfortunately, the growing racist violence by a small fringe of neo-Nazis suggests that the German people (and possibly also the French) may be more readily roused in this direction than most.

It must be said that no one is more aware of this than the Germans themselves, and especially their political leaders. That is why they, with the French, are so anxious to tie Germany irrevocably to a politically and militarily united Europe, tight enough to contain such a nationalist surge, and to curb the military capabilities available to any nationalist Chancellor brought to power by their democratic process.

The risk of Germany attempting for a third time to exercise military hegemony over Europe is a remote one, as their two disastrous military defeats have cut deeply into their international attitudes. Yet it must be remembered that Hitler was brought to power by the democratic process, and succeeded in striding over the military restraints of Versailles to create the military strength to over run most of Europe within seven years of becoming Chancellor.

The likelier shape of the threat lies in Germany's economic dominance. The strains of reunification and the recession of the early 1990s will be behind them by 1994–95, and the Germans will thereafter continue to outstrip their fellow Europeans. Frustration with being expected in perpetuity to bear an unfair share of the EC's burdens, and to hand out more and more of the fruits of their success to others who have done little to earn them, could further fuel the fire of German nationalism. That in turn could produce more violent disturbances on the streets of Europe, as foreshadowed by such outbursts as those by angry French farmers as well as by East German neo-Nazis in 1992 and 1993.

RELIGION, CONFLICT AND WAR

Many of the most vicious wars in history have been fought in the name of a religion on one or both sides. Religious fanatics believe that they are acting in the name of their God and cannot therefore be wrong. Some leaders have claimed to hold that belief to justify actions prompted by more cynical political aims. An orthodox Jew sincerely believes that his people have a God-given right to all the pre-Roman lands of the Children of Israel (including Judea and Samaria – the occupied West Bank) as strongly as a Shia fundamentalist believes that he has the right and holy duty to kill those who have held and then abandoned his faith, or who stand stubbornly in the way of its spread. Some Sikhs and Hindus are equally fanatical, though few Christians have been so for some hundreds of years, and Buddhists virtually never.

Marxists recognize no god, though many (especially the Khmers Rouges in Cambodia) have had a Marxist secular philosophy as cruel as that of the most extreme religious fanatics. Stalin, with the highest extermination record in history, quite cynically cited the Marxist philosophy without otherwise practising it at all, to justify the murder of some 19 million of his own people to enforce his political will. And many of the terrorists who have claimed similar justification in more recent years have been equally cynical.

Perhaps because it was secular, Marxism's roots were shallow and it did not endure. From the time it first blossomed into a significant political force (1917) until its collapse (1991), it survived little more than the average lifetime of one human being. The professed adherence of China's leaders to Marxism also owes more to political expediency than to philosophical conviction, and Chinese society has borne little resemblance to the Marxist model for a great many years – if it ever did. The Chinese did, however, perfect the Leninist technique for totalitarian control, and that model is likely to be followed again and again by tyrants and revolutionaries across the spectrum of political aims, as in the past.

Marxism is unlikely ever again to be the ideological motivation of major international or domestic conflict. Nor are any of the sects of Christianity or Buddhism. Hinduism and Sikhism are mainly confined to India or Indian communities overseas. Fanatical Jews, or those Jews who pretend Jewish orthodox principles to justify political aims, are few in number but still poison the prospects of peace and cooperation in the Middle East, though they are now less likely to ignite a conflict outside their own region.

Islamic fundamentalism continues to spread and causes much violence, though it may have passed its 1980s peak of terrorism. Time will tell.

ISLAMIC FUNDAMENTALISM

In the 1980s, Islamic fundamentalism surpassed Marxism as the primary generator of international terrorism. This terrorism went into abeyance after 1991, for pragmatic reasons. But the pressures and philosophies behind it still exist and it remains a strong potential source of violence.

The Islamic revival has had a particularly powerful appeal to poor and frustrated people in the Third World. Islam has 600 million adherents, second only to Christianity with 1000 million and, like Christianity, it is split. The mainstream, 90 per cent, adhere to the Sunni sect (*sunna* means 'the well-trodden path'), which has its heartland in Muhammad country, Saudi Arabia. The Shia sect attracts 7 per cent, and for 400 years Iran has been its heartland. There is also a Shia majority in Iraq and substantial minorities in Lebanon, Syria, Bahrain, Yemen, East Africa, India and Pakistan. There are also both Sunni and Shia fundamentalists amongst the mujahideen competing for power in Afghanistan.

The split dates from the unexpected death of Muhammad in AD 632. Rival Caliphates (*Khalifah* means 'successor') were set up by the Prophet's father-in-law, Abu Bakr, and his son-in-law, Ali, who was also the father of the Prophet's only two grandsons, Hassan and Hussein. (*Shi'at Ali* means 'the party of Ali).' Ali was assassinated in 661 and Hussein and most of the remaining Shia males were killed in battle in 680. The bitterness and the rival hierarchies remain to this day.

Both sects have their fundamentalists, the Muslim Brotherhood, for example, being Sunni and Hezbollah being Shia. Fundamentalism implies strict adherence to the *Sharia* ('the way'), as expounded by Allah to Muhammad and recorded (from his jottings) by his disciples to become the Koran. Just as there has never been a Christian government which complied rigidly with the Gospels, there has never been a totally fundamentalist Islamic government. Saudi Arabia (Sunni) and Iran (Shia) have come closest to it. Pakistan and Sudan claim to rule by Islamic law, and the Islamic Salvation Front (FIS) would do so if it came to power in Algeria. A cardinal principle is that the ecclesiastical structure of government, carrying the authority of the word of God to Muhammad through his successors and down to the Mullahs in the Mosques, overrides any secular ministers or officials, who are merely civil servants employed to implement the clerics' interpretation of the *Sharia*. For this reason, democratic elections are regarded by the purists as totally inconsistent with Islamic law. Though the FIS in Algeria tried to use the democratic process to come to power, they made it clear that democracy would at once be abolished if they did.

Fundamentalists, especially Shia, also cite the Koran as authority for the right and duty of every Muslim to kill in specified circumstances to preserve or spread the faith. (Many Sikhs and Hindus, and, in the past, Christians, have claimed the same right.) In the first century of Islam, between AD 622 and 714, Muslim armies imposed Islamic government by force along the North African coast into Spain, and through Central Asia to India. Anyone who becomes a martyr in carrying out assassination or military conquest to spread the faith is assured of eternal bliss in Paradise.[4]

This is the basis of Shia terrorism, and accords with the offer of a reward of $1 million by the followers of the Iranian Ayatollah Khomeini to anyone who assassinated the British-Indian writer Salman Rushdie (an apostate). Despite the pragmatic attempts by the Iranian government to secure Western economic cooperation, this offer was increased by Khomeini's successors to $2 million in 1992.

Following Khomeini's bloody repression of internal dissent after his revolution in 1979, and the seizure of the US Embassy with 50 hostages in 1979–81, the spread of Shia terrorism emanated from his dispatch of about 1500 fanatical young Revolutionary Guards to join the Syrian army base in the Beka'a Valley in Lebanon in 1982. Espousing the cult of martyrdom, they in turn trained and inspired the Lebanese 'Army of God' – Hezbollah – which carried out a series of 15 mainly suicide bombings in Lebanon and Kuwait in 1983, killing more than 350 people; then a number of spectacular bombings and hijacks between 1984 and 1988, and the seizure of 35 Western hostages in Lebanon between 1984 and 1989. Some of these were held incommunicado for more than six years, surpassing all previous records of hostage-taking in its prolonged cruelty.

Though there is evidence that some of these hostages were used by the Iranian government as bargaining counters in 1986–88 for obtaining arms for their war against Iraq, they provided no other dividends. They were eventually released (except for two who had been murdered) in 1990–91, as part of President Rafsanjani's policy of developing relations with the West to help him in recovering from the war.

The subsequent lull in Islamic terrorism was encouraging but, if the pragmatic reasons for this dissolve, or if any of the fundamentalist governments or movements (including the FIS in Algeria) find their aims or activities frustrated, they will have no moral restraints in invoking the Koran to justify a resumption of violence. The complexions and attitudes of Islamic governments will need to be vigilantly watched to give warning of this.

OTHER ONGOING CONFLICTS

The Arab–Israeli conflict will not go away. Even if the peace talks were to lead to a settlement accepted by both the Israeli government and the PLO there would be extremists on both sides who would reject it and do their best to rekindle violent conflict to overturn it.

Despite the defeat and military and economic weakness of Iraq, and the social, economic and religious problems in Iran, there will always be tensions and grounds for local conflict in the Gulf. The rivalry between Saudi Arabia and Iran will continue and if either side sees an opportunity – for example to gain control of islands or navigation rights or offshore drilling rights – they will take it. Iraq will never abandon her claim to better maritime access at the expense of Kuwait – or indeed to Kuwait herself. Many countries, notably Saudi Arabia and Kuwait, are vulnerable to internal revolution and to its international repercussions. Affluence never reduces the prospects of conflict – on the contrary.

Muslim–Hindu–Sikh conflict, in southern Asia and sometimes spilling over elsewhere, will not go away either, and is responsible for thousands of deaths each year. As Punjab is on the Indo-Pakistan frontier, it is also a potential source of international conflict.

Greeks and Turks have a similarly deep and historical hostility, which will always add an explosive element to tensions on their common frontier, on disputed islands and in Cyprus.

Opium and heroin production and trafficking involves such huge profits that it finances private armies in some cases more powerful than national armies, for example that of Khun Sa in the Karen country of Myanmar. This is the heartland of the opium-growing 'Golden Triangle' which incorporates also Laos and Thailand, with trafficking through Hong Kong, China, Malaysia, Indonesia and Vietnam. The other main heroin-producing area, the 'Golden Crescent', involves the North-west Frontier of Pakistan, Afghanistan and Iran, with trafficking through Lebanon and the Central Asian Republics that were formerly part of the Soviet Union. With so much big money involved, people will fight.

Similarly, cocaine production and distribution generates billions of dollars each year in Colombia, Peru and Bolivia, and in transiting through Venezuela, Mexico, the Caribbean and the USA, for criminals and terrorists.

It is an abiding disgrace that the richest countries in the world, notably in North America and West Europe, still allow the drug addicts on their streets to provide the money which almost wholly finances the violence and political and economic disruption in Asia and Latin America; but they still show little sign of taking effective measures to cut the demand, so the consequent conflicts will continue.

CIVIL WAR AND INSURGENCY

The Balkanization of Europe has taken the predominant pattern of human conflict back to one of its earliest forms – tribal warfare. The great majority of the armed conflicts listed in Table 15.1 (p. 198) are not between states but between communities within states, whether classed as civil wars, wars of secession or insurgencies. These wars are historically the most vicious, as they involve more intense and personal hatred between individual participants than do wars between national armies.

Such wars are generally fought between informal groups of armed citizens or local militias, mainly with hand-held weapons and bombs, including rocket-propelled weapons. Intervention by national armed forces and paramilitary formations is common, and they bring in tanks, artillery, ground-attack aircraft and sometimes high-technology weapons, but the fighting is generally confused, without front lines, amongst inhabited streets and buildings. The aim is sometimes to capture key hilltops, crossroads, radio stations, and so on, whereby to consolidate control over an area; but in current situations the aim is more often to terrorize some or all of the local population so that they submit to the gunmen (e.g. in Somalia) or, if they are of the 'wrong' ethnic group, abandon their homes and flee (e.g. in Bosnia).

Professional armed forces will need to accept that this *is* now the predominant form of conflict, and to reshape their organization, training and tactics to deal with it. This must include the armies and police forces of the countries concerned and also those of powers which might intervene, on their own or as part of an international force.

Sometimes that intervention may take the form of aggression, as when Serbian regular units intervened on behalf of armed Serbian irregulars fighting to gain control of areas of newly independent Croatia or Bosnia. Some regarded Syrian army intervention in Lebanon as aggression, others as a restoration of order welcomed by the majority of the population. The same was said about the dispatch of US troops to Somalia in December 1992, albeit with UN approval.

Similarly conflicting judgements can be applied to the Basque region of Spain and to Northern Ireland. In each case, approximately 10 per cent of the population think it justifiable to use violence to break away, another 10 per cent will support terrorist violence to preserve the status quo, while the other 80 per cent just yearn for peace for their families. There may be a moral case for frontier adjustments in small and clearly defined areas in which the overwhelming majority wish to change (e.g. in the frontier village of Crossmaglen and its immediate hinterland in Northern Ireland), but the situation is rarely as tidy as this, as was illustrated in the map of Bosnia (Map 15A), or in the patchwork of Protestant and Catholic housing areas in the predominantly Protestant city of Belfast.

The most dangerous insurgency in the world in 1992 was in Peru, where a puritanical Maoist movement, *Sendero Luminoso* (SL), had begun a vicious insurgency in 1980 in which, by 1992, over 25,000 people had been killed, with an estimated economic cost to Peru of $22 billion.[5] Founded and led by a charismatic philosophy professor of mixed blood, Dr Abimael Guzman, SL first took root amongst the Quechua Indians in the Inca country around Ayacucho, but later spread to the shanty towns around Lima. As with other Maoist movements (e.g. in Vietnam; see

Chapter 11) its primary technique was to murder or terrorize community leaders, local officials, judges, and so on, to make the government and law enforcement system collapse, which in many places it did.

Peru produces more than 50 per cent of the world's coca, so the Colombian drug cartels found that it was in their interest to finance SL, in order to keep the army and police away from the coca fields. This suited the peasants well, because they earned more from growing coca than any other crop. It also suited SL, as it gave the peasants an incentive to support them and to provide them with a secure rural base. SL also took full advantage of the government's inability to provide facilities for the 5 million inhabitants of the shanty towns around Lima. They were further helped by the high degree of corruption amongst politicians and public officials, including the army and police. By the summer of 1992 it seemed quite probable that government would collapse completely in some areas, including parts of Lima, leaving *de facto* control in the hands of SL; there were fears of a military coup to pre-empt this.

On 12 September 1992, Guzman and a number of his Central Committee were captured in Lima, and several hundred other *Senderistas* around the country, but SL's regional organizations had considerable autonomy, and some able leaders survived. Some will continue to operate.[6] SL also has organizations in neighbouring countries and, with its appeal to the Indian and *Mestizo* populations, its ideas might spread if it were to recover in Peru.

Civil wars and insurgencies have a record of spreading internationally. This may take the form of intervention, overt or clandestine, by neighbours who favour one side; or it may involve the use of international terrorism designed to induce other neighbouring countries to change their policies towards the conflict.

TERRORISM

Terrorism has come to stay as a tool of foreign policy as well as of domestic dissent. The spirit of terrorism was best captured in a proverb ascribed to Sun Tzu 2500 years ago: 'Kill one – frighten 10,000'. The art lies, not so much in killing soldiers or police officers as in killing vulnerable officials (including mayors and judges) or indiscriminate victims, so that everyone fears he might be the next target, as in Peru. It is remarkably effective in gaining publicity out of all proportion to the actual damage or deaths that may be caused. Because of the emotion aroused by sensationalized 'human interest' coverage by the media, governments are more ready to concede to a threat to the lives of 100 passengers in an aircraft, or even to the life of a single hostage, than to a threat of bombardment or invasion which might take 10,000 lives.

Terrorism – to kill a few to frighten many – is a technique used by all sides: by dissidents within a country, with political, ideological, religious, communal or ethnic motivations; by paramilitary or guerrilla organizations in a civil war or insurgency situation; by international terrorist movements such as Hezbollah or the Palestinians; by governments against their own dissidents, either openly or indirectly (e.g. by sponsoring 'death squads'); or by governments encouraging or supporting terrorist movements, domestic or international, operating in other countries where they judge that these activities will further their foreign policy aims.

Terrorist movements rise and decline. Frustrated or fanatical people are attracted to terrorism by its spectacular short-term dividends: political blackmail (especially getting prisoners released); money (from ransoms, extortion, protection money or 'revolutionary taxes'); and, above all, massive publicity. Most terrorists, however, become disillusioned within a generation or less due to their failure to advance their long-term aims. Palestinian terrorism has not recovered one square metre of Palestine for the Arabs; IRA terrorism has not brought the unification of Ireland any closer; indeed, in both cases their terrorism has been counter-productive, in hardening opposition and forfeiting world sympathy. Both have been campaigning on their current lines for about 25 years. Hezbollah has been operating for a little over 10 years.

Nevertheless, because of the emotions aroused, small terrorist incidents can have a disproportionate effect on international affairs. Especially, they can set back the prospects of a settlement of the underlying conflicts. Since settlements usually involve compromise, sabotage of a settlement is often a primary aim of the fanatics who have turned to terrorism.

Most terrorist movements confine their operations to their own countries, though they may be supported and encouraged by foreign governments or by sympathetic foreign communities (eg the IRA receives about 2 per cent of its funds from sympathetic Irish Americans).

The movements that seem (1993) most likely to operate outside their own frontiers include many well-known ones. From Spain, ETA[7] may continue to operate in France. From Ireland, north and south, the IRA will attack British targets in continental Europe as well as in Britain. From Italy and the USA, the International Mafia will operate worldwide (though aiming primarily for criminal gain, the Mafia also use their terror to exercise political influence). From Turkey, PKK[8] work in countries with large Kurdish immigrant communities, such as Belgium, Germany and the Netherlands. From the Middle East, Palestinian groups such as Abu Nidal, PFLP-GC and PLF[9] will try to poison peace talks that could lead to acceptance of the legality of Israel, to influence foreign governments and to seek publicity. Hezbollah, though pursuing political power by orthodox means in Lebanon, will also operate internationally to punish or deter those whom they consider enemies of the spread of the Shia faith. From Sri Lanka, the Tamil Tigers will also operate in India, as in the past. From Hong Kong, the Triads (Chinese secret societies) will combine criminal gain with political influence like the Mafia, especially through international drug-trafficking. SL may try to develop their activities further in foreign countries if they are frustrated in Peru. And the international drug cartels based in Colombia have sufficiently massive assets all over the world to continue to operate like the Mafia, whatever may happen in Colombia.

Many of these movements will decline, as most of the Marxist terrorist movements in Western Europe have declined. Other movements, however, will undoubtedly arise, especially from minority groups in the former Soviet and Yugoslav states (see Tables 15.2 and 15.3) who, if frustrated at home, may fight their battles on foreign streets and seek publicity on the world stage, as Croats and Armenians did in the 1980s, and as Muslims and Hindus did in the wake of the destruction of the Mosque at Ayodhya in India in December 1992. Islamic fundamentalists from Algeria, Iran and Sudan may do the same, as Palestinians, Sikhs and Hezbollah already do. There is a strong need, therefore, for the world to coordinate its response to terrorism; this will be discussed in the next chapter.

REGIONAL WARS

There has been no year since 1945 in which there has not been a regional war going on somewhere in the world in which tanks, artillery, missiles and aircraft have been used and in which casualties have run into thousands or tens of thousands. There are sadly few reasons for thinking that this will improve. Despite violent fighting in Croatia, Bosnia, Georgia, Moldova, Azerbaijan, Armenia, Sudan, Peru, Colombia, Somalia, India, Sri Lanka and Cambodia, 1992 probably saw fewer fatal casualties than most of those before it, yet they still ran into thousands.

The response to Saddam Hussein's invasion of Kuwait in 1990-91, politically by the UN and militarily by the USA and her allies, showed what the world can now do if it turns its mind to it, and it could be that this will point the way to effective response to military aggression in the future. But until the lessons of the Gulf War have sunk in, and have perhaps had to be repeated once or twice more, it must be assumed that other dictators will try to get their way by aggression. This response is further discussed in the next chapter.

NUCLEAR WEAPONS

Nuclear proliferation is now more likely than ever in the past, chiefly because of the breakup of the USSR. Faced with insoluble economic problems, some of the new states which have access to complete nuclear weapons, or to the raw materials, components and manufacturing plants, will be sorely tempted to pass some of these on at high prices to the likes of Gadafi and Saddam Hussein, or to new ambitious leaders as yet unknown. Or they may prefer to be more discreet by selling the knowhow rather than the hardware. Or individual scientists, engineers and technicians, formerly involved in development and manufacture, but now underemployed and short of money, may be willing to make their knowledge privately available to other countries ready to pay for it.

No nuclear weapon has been fired to kill since 1945, and it remains unlikely that anyone – even with the mentality of Saddam Hussein – will embark on a confrontation with the *intention* of firing one. The danger lies in 'brinkmanship', that is, in a fanatical leader being confident that his adversaries will concede rather than allow a nuclear exchange to take place, and calculatedly carrying his confrontation to a point at which they will realize that he cannot withdraw without unacceptable loss of face or credibility in the eyes of his own people. If such a leader does get control of nuclear weapons, he must be left in no doubt that there will be no concessions to a threat to use them and that, if he does, his destruction will be certain and immediate. The nuclear powers can take this line so long as they act in unison, and the use of nuclear weapons need be no more likely in the new world order than it was in the Cold War. But the nuclear capability of China is the one that may cause most concern.

CHINA

In the long term – in the twenty-first century – the greatest threat to world tranquillity may come from China, especially if she makes best use of the economic and technological potential of Japan and the newly industrialized nations of east Asia. There can be little doubt that the economic and therefore the political centre of gravity of the world will shift increasingly to the Far East. The question is whether this shift can be accommodated peacefully.

China, in five centuries as a 'sleeping giant', never had an effective nationwide government until Mao Zedong came to power in 1949. In retrospect, Deng Xiaoping's revolution of 1978 may prove to be even more of a landmark. Since then, China's real GNP has grown by an average of 9 per cent a year, and will be four times bigger in 1994 than in 1978, matching the fastest rate of growth achieved in Japan's 'economic miracle'. On current form, it is likely to be eight times bigger by 2002, and the world's largest economy by 2010.[10]

This economic success was in stark contrast to the severe economic problems following the revolutions in Eastern Europe and the USSR in 1989–92. The Chinese, however, made no serious attempt to liberalize politically, and such relaxations as they had allowed were summarily reversed in 1989 by the ruthless suppression of pro-democracy demonstrations in Tiananmen Square. The sustained social and economic difficulties of the former Soviet and East European states will reinforce the

Chinese government's determination to clamp down on any further stirrings of democracy.

The Chinese are an able, industrious and disciplined people. They have no traditions of liberalism, and may be content with their mixture of totalitarian government, state capitalism and market economics so long as prosperity continues to grow. They are also, however, a proud people, and will expect to exert more influence in the world. Growing economic strength may make them more aggressive and, if they are frustrated, they are probably one of the few nations posing a risk of using or threatening to use their nuclear capability. Short of this, they also have long experience in fostering and directing the international weapon of subversion and revolutionary warfare within countries on whom they wish to exert pressure.

China is, on present form, the best long-term field for investment and trade in the world. As her economy and consumption grow, her huge potential both as a producer and as a market could revitalize the world's economy. If handled wisely, China will value the cooperation of the rest of the world as her market and her source of technology and investment. The Chinese are no fools. If handled unwisely, frustrated, provoked or insulted, however, they could become a formidable enemy.

Within a generation, therefore, China could become the world's greatest contributor to prosperity or the world's greatest nightmare. Which this is to be depends as much on the behaviour of the rest of the world as on the behaviour of China.

16 Keeping the Peace

PAX AMERICANA?

With the United States as the only surviving superpower, is there a prospect of a 'Pax Americana' comparable to the 'Pax Britannica' of the nineteenth century?[1] The USA, while militarily and technologically supreme, no longer dominates the world economically. The European Community in 1991 already had a bigger population (320 million) and an industrial base 25 per cent larger than the USA. The EC is operating as an economic union even though not yet as a political one. If later joined by Austria, the Scandinavian countries and by some of the Central and East European countries, its population will exceed 400 million.[2]

Nevertheless, the USA can still use her power as a decisive balancing factor. This was all Britain really contributed to the 'Pax Britannica', with her economic strength and naval predominance (see Chapter 3). In this respect, with the Gulf War as a model, the USA will be able, if she so chooses, to play a decisive role in deterring or suppressing aggression in regional conflicts. And the dispatch of 28,000 US troops to Somalia in December 1992 showed that the USA was prepared to use force to rescue the people of a country suffering death and starvation as a result of the disintegration of its government into armed anarchy. And in Somalia, unlike the Gulf, the USA had no particular national interests involved.

Even in the Gulf War, however, the USA could not have achieved success without allies, notably Saudi Arabia and Bahrain, nor would her action have enjoyed the support of the Arab world. Though the Saudis' military contribution was limited, their role as a base was indispensable: the USA was in fact acting on behalf of Saudi Arabia and Kuwait with the approval of the UN Security Council. And in Somalia, too, US troops were under US command, again with the approval of the UN Security Council. US armed forces, especially air forces, may also prove decisive in the former Yugoslav states but, here again, they are likely to act only with allies and with UN approval, probably under NATO command.

PEACEMAKING AND PEACEKEEPING

'Keeping the peace' is a broad term incorporating both the prevention of armed conflict and the countering of aggression. In modern parlance, 'peace*making*' is used to describe the restoration of peace (as in the Korean War of 1950–53, and in the Gulf War of 1990–91), while 'peace*keeping*' defines the process of maintaining peace once it has been restored.

The UN has been extremely reluctant to conduct peace*making* operations. The Korean War was an exception when, in the absence of the Soviet delegation to veto the Security Council resolution, a UN force was set up to counter the North Korean invasion (see Chapter 6). Nevertheless, although it contained contingents from many countries, its decisions were in practice governed by those of the President of the USA, acting on behalf of the UN. It was President Truman who decided to dismiss General MacArthur, not the UN.

Up till 1991, the only other approximation to peace*making* by the UN was in the former Belgian Congo (now Zaire) in 1960–64. The country became independent in 1960 but was at once disrupted by an army mutiny and by rival leaders forming their own armies (with an element of Belgians and other mercenaries) and attempting to seize power or to form secessionist states. At the request of the elected Prime Minister, Patrice Lumumba, the UN deployed 4000 troops in July 1960. Its actions were hamstrung by conflicting requests from Lumumba and other rival leaders, and the country was without any unified or stable government. In January 1961 Lumumba was murdered, and the Security Council on 21 February authorized the UN troops to use force in the last resort to prevent civil war. They did carry out a number of offensive operations against secessionist forces but they were never given a free hand, due to UN deference to any Congolese leader who had any claim to legitimacy in any part of the country, and to disagreements amongst Security Council members.[3] The inevitable conclusion was that the UN was not designed to exert executive power in the day-to-day handling of a crisis unless, as in Korea, one government was, in effect, made responsible for the operation. More recent experience, for example, in the Gulf and Somalia (see later in this chapter) has underlined this point.

Probably for this reason, the UN has tried to avoid sending peace*keeping* forces to any country until the warring factions (whether in an inter-state or a civil war) have agreed to a truce, and if that truce is holding. It has not been easy to stick to this principle. If the truce has been seriously broken, the UN peacekeeping force has threatened to withdraw. Such a force has generally operated only in territories in which the government requested it to do so – as happened in Sinai in 1967 (see Chapter 9). UN peacekeeping forces have been deployed in many countries under these conditions. Those still in operation at the end of 1992 are shown in Table 16.1. The estimated annual cost in 1992 was £1.7 billion, but operations in Cambodia, Somalia and the former Yugoslav states will certainly make it larger than this in 1993. Neither the USA nor the USSR had provided UN peacekeeping troops prior to 1992. Canada has always been a generous contributor. Britain has consistently provided troops for UN peacekeeping in Cyprus since 1964, and was providing the largest contingent in the escort force for humanitarian aid in Bosnia at the end of 1992. Neutral countries, such as Finland, the Irish Republic and Sweden, have regularly provided troops; this is often their only form of active service.

This pattern began to show a change in 1992, when the UN continued to operate in Croatia and Bosnia in face of Serbian armed harassment. The US troops in Somalia, though acting with UN support, were not strictly a peacekeeping force, and they too made it clear that they would use armed force to restore order.

The UN has calculated the cost of one peacekeeping soldier to be $998 per month,[4] but this is not a reliable figure, since costs vary a lot, for example the pay of a Finnish soldier is ten times more than that of an Indian soldier. In all, the UN forecast for its peacekeeping operations in 1992 was over $3 billion. UN members have agreed on a scale: for example the USA pays 30.7 per cent, Japan 12.5 per cent, Germany 8.9 per cent, and some of the smaller countries only 0.002 per cent. But many were in arrears – the USA by $141 million.[5] The previous UN Secretary-General, Perez de Cuellar, suggested that the UN should maintain a 'peace fund' of $1 billion, to be topped each year.

Table 16.1 UN peacekeeping operations 1992

	Year first deployed	*Strength 1992*	
Angola	1991	440	
Bosnia[a]	1992	7,000	from 9 countries for humanitarian relief
Cambodia	1992	16,000	plus 3,600 police and 2,400 civilians
Croatia[b]	1992	15,000	from 25 countries. Peacekeeping in areas of Croatia occupied by Serbian forces
Cyprus	1964	2,200	
El Salvador	1991	1,000	
India, Pakistan	1949	40	
Iraq, Kuwait	1991	540	
Israel, Jordan	1948	300	
Israel, Syria	1974	1,300	
Lebanon	1978	5,900	
Somalia[c]	1992	34,000	
Western Sahara	1991	2,700	

Notes: [a] Including Britain (2,400), Canada (1,200), France (1,100), Netherlands (940), Spain (700), USA (300 – field hospital in Zagreb), Denmark (151), Belgium (100), Norway (35) and Portugal (10–15)

[b] Including France (2,619), Canada (1,260), Netherlands (1,130), also Argentina, Denmark, Jordan, Kenya, Nepal, Nigeria, Poland and Russia (900–925 each)
and Bangladesh, Belgium, Brazil, Britain, Colombia, Czechoslovakia, Egypt, Finland, Ghana, Luxembourg, Norway, Sweden, Switzerland and Ukraine.

[c] 28,000 US troops under US command with contingents from France (2,000), Italy (1,500), Canada (900), Egypt (600), Belgium (550), Pakistan (500) and others

Source: The Times 12 May 1992 and 27 October 1992; *Independent on Sunday* 6 December 1992

CAMBODIA

The most ambitious conventional UN peacekeeping operation up to 1992 was in Cambodia, under the agreement reached in Paris in October 1991. It illustrates the complexity that such operations can involve, and the endless patience and determination required to carry them out.

By 1991, Cambodia had endured 17 years of strife since the end of the Vietnam War. In 1975, Pol Pot and his Khmers Rouges (KR) had overturned the US-supported government of Lon Nol, and launched a reign of terror in the name of primitive rural Maoism, and China, to her disgrace, supported it. The result was the almost total destruction of both the urban and rural economies; 1 million people died, including the majority of Cambodia's professional and technically qualified personnel.

In 1978, the Vietnamese army occupied the country, driving out Pol Pot and installing their own version of Communism under a puppet Prime Minister, Hun Sen. This led to 13 years of civil war, in which a triple alliance between KR, the Khmer People's National Liberation Front (KPNLF) and Cambodia's former ruler, Prince Sihanouk, operated from Thailand and northern Cambodia in an attempt to oust the Vietnamese and the Hun Sen government. The triple alliance was supported by China; the Vietnamese and Hun Sen by the USSR.

The first hopes of a solution were raised on 20 January 1990, when the five permanent members of the UN Security Council agreed on a plan to end the war. This came about because both the USSR and China wanted to be rid of the burden of supporting their clients. It was agreed that the UN would run the country for a year, after which there would be UN-supervised elections.

It was, however, another 21 months before the Security Council and the governments concerned could agree on how such a plan might be implemented. While the USSR (and Russia when she inherited her UN seat) seemed sincere in her intentions, China and Vietnam were determined to rig the plan so that their own client (KR or Hun Sen respectively) would in fact inherit power.

Finally, however, an agreement to implement the plan was signed in Paris on 23 October 1991 by all the governments and organizations involved and 18 other governments. Under this agreement, a UN Transitional Authority for Cambodia (UNTAC) would move in to supervise government by a Supreme National Council (SNC) made up of Hun Sen, Prince Sihanouk, KPNLF (represented by Son Sann) and KR (represented by

Khieu Samphan – Pol Pot remaining in the background). UNTAC would be supported by a UN peacekeeping force (PKF),[6] for which the UN would raise a budget of about $2 billion. The armies of all four sides would hand over their arms to the PKF and elections would be held in May 1993 under UN supervision.

UNTAC, headed by the UN special representative, Yasushi Akashi (a Japanese diplomat) brought an advance party of 268 to the Cambodian capital, Phnom Penh, with the first 37 soldiers (Australians) on 10 November 1991. The plan was for UNTAC to become fully operational by the summer of 1992, with the PKF by then comprising 22,000 (16,000 soldiers, 3600 police and 2400 civilians). The tasks of UNTAC were as follows

1 To monitor a cease-fire.
2 To supervise the concentration of troops of all sides (200,000) into cantonments, where they would hand over their arms. For this purpose, all four (Hun Sen, Sihanouk, KPNLF and KR) agreed to give UNTAC/PKF unhindered access to all areas occupied by their troops in Cambodia and Thailand. They agreed to cooperate in clearing mines (about four million).
3 To resettle some 700,000 refugees from camps close to or beyond the Thai border, to which, again, unhindered access was promised.
4 To run government ministries in cooperation with the SNC.
5 To prepare for elections to a Constituent Assembly in May 1993, to include agreement on eligibility and registration of voters.

An early hint of trouble to come occurred on 27 November 1991, when the KR representative on the SNC, Khieu Samphan, had to be rescued from a mob intent on lynching him. Some people suspected that the Hun Sen government may have allowed this to happen to indicate the intensity of the feeling amongst the relatives of the 1 million killed by KR in 1975–78 but, after the incident, Hun Sen gave a guarantee that KR representatives would be protected.

By June 1992, most of the UN PKF (22,000, provided from 30 countries and commanded by an Australian, Lieutenant-General John Sanderson) had arrived. The four sides had previously agreed to a deadline of 13 June to move their troops into cantonments ready to disarm. At the SNC meeting on 10 June, however, KR refused to move or disarm their troops, demanding that there must first be a check that there were no longer any Vietnamese troops in Cambodia, or still serving in Hun Sen's army.

It became clear to UNTAC that KR had no intention of keeping its promises unless it was convenient to do so. As well as wishing to retain its territory and power, KR also enjoyed considerable financial benefit from trade across the Thai border. Although a civilian government had replaced the military government in Bangkok, Thai generals were still in *de facto* control in border areas, and it was claimed that this trade (mainly in timber and gems) was worth $400 million a year to Thailand, and its cessation would cost 100,000 Thai jobs.[7]

In a further attempt to put pressure on KR, 33 countries meeting in Tokyo on 27 June 1992 pledged $800 million in aid to Cambodia, mainly to reconstruct the infrastructure (roads, water, electricity, etc.), announcing that none of this would go into KR areas unless their troops disarmed.[8] On 2 July, KR replied that they would disarm only if the Hun Sen government were dismantled; 10 per cent would be disarmed when the Departments of Defence and Interior were closed down; a further 20 per cent with the dismantling of the Foreign and Finance Departments; and the remainder when all other departments and Hun Sen himself stood down.[9] But there was no reason to believe that KR would honour this promise any more than their previous ones.

On 5 August, the other SNC members agreed that anyone with one Cambodian parent would have the right to vote, but KR tried to block this too. It became clear that the election would either have to go ahead outside the KR areas (to which UNTAC were still denied access to register the voters) or be postponed.[10] KR, with 35,000 well-disciplined troops, were extending their area of control, impeding access by further mining of the roads. On the other hand, they controlled less than 15 per cent of the country (3 of the 21 provinces) and the other 85 per cent was now accessible to UNTAC. Of the 5 million voters, 65,000 had been registered and the process was continuing. KR no doubt realized that they had no hope of success in free elections, and Hun Sen was probably also resigned to defeat. The likeliest winner was

Sihanouk's son Prince Ranariddh, who headed a new party using the acronym FUNCINPEC. Sihanouk therefore favoured going ahead with the elections.

Sihanouk said he wished to stand outside party politics and proposed that the new Constitution should include an elected presidency, for which he would stand, and no one doubted that, if he did, he would be elected by a large majority.[11] He might well make a deal with both KR and Hun Sen (who still had 55,000 troops), enabling the UN to withdraw without total loss of face, but again, if KR were left intact, there would be no reason to expect that they would keep their word, so there would be a risk of Cambodia disintegrating into a situation like that in Lebanon in 1975–90.

As the election approached in the spring of 1993, KR withdrew their representatives from the SNC in Phnom Penh, claiming that they were no longer safe. They assassinated a number of UN officials, to disrupt preparations for the election, and began a concerted campaign of ethnic cleansing, which resulted in a mass exodus of ethnic Vietnamese to Vietnam. This was popular with many Cambodians, who have a historic hatred of the Vietnamese (Khmers/Tongkingese). Despite KR intimidation, 97 percent of the eligible population registered as voters, but there can be little hope of an end to disruption and civil war in Cambodia.[12]

SOMALIA

The crisis in Somalia began on 26 January 1991, when the Communist President, Siad Barre, after 21 years of dictatorial rule, fled from his capital, Mogadishu, in the face of a *coup d'état* led by General Mohamed Aideed on behalf of the United Somali Congress (USC), a loose alliance led by Ali Mahdi. To the chagrin of Aideed, the USC appointed Mahdi President. Each had his own private army, with Aideed controlling the southern part of Mogadishu and Mahdi the northern half. Fighting began, although both came from the same Hawiye tribe. The north of the country, the old colony of British Somaliland and populated by the Isaak tribe, broke away in August 1991 to form an independant Republic of Somaliland. In the rest of Somalia, 25,000 had been killed by February 1992, and another 250,000 made homeless. A further 800,000 had fled to Ethiopia.[13]

On 14 February 1992, representatives of the warring factions met in the UN Building in New York and agreed a cease-fire – which was promptly broken. Another cease-fire was agreed in March, and a UN special envoy, Mohamed Sahnoun (from Algeria), was sent in with 50 military observers to monitor it. The warlords, however, maintained their fiefdoms and growing numbers of freelance gunmen, mainly teenagers, got hold of weapons. Some mounted machine-guns and light anti-aircraft cannon on stolen jeeps (known locally as 'technicals'), and looting and banditry spread over the countryside, leading to widespread starvation.

Battling with this were a number of heroic international non-government organizations (NGOs), such as the International Red Cross (IRC), the British Save the Children Fund (SCF) and the French-based *Médecins sans Frontières* (MSF). The IRC was running 35 kitchens feeding 600,000 people each day. SCF ran 16 health centres and MSF ran six in Mogadishu and others in the countryside.[14] UNICEF also ran feeding centres, but otherwise the UN left the task largely to the NGOs.

To do this at all, the NGOs had to negotiate their own terms with the private armies and individual gang leaders on the ground, and for this they paid the only currency valid in Somalia at the time – food. The IRC therefore allocated 15 per cent of the food they imported to 'security', a polite term for protection money; they lost at least another 10 per cent to looters, but this still left about 75 per cent for distribution.

The Somali warlords and private armies seemed indifferent to the fate of the rest of the population, provided that they got enough themselves – better still more, so that they could use the balance as currency. The only gleam of light was in some of the 'elders' of the clans, who still had some influence on the people, and did care what happened to them. Mohamed Nor Shodok, the octogenarian Governor of Hodor, had a militia of 2500 men, for whom he requested and received a substantial cut (varying from 10 per cent to 35 per cent) of the food delivered by the World Food Programme; but he saw that the rest did reach the people in his province, and that looting was kept in check.[15] Regular flights of two Hercules aircraft carried 2000 tons of food per month to Belel Huen, and were fairly distributed. Such arrangements, however, depended on negotiation with courageous local leaders, of whom there were very few. In any case, this added up to only a fraction of the 50,000 tons per month needed to feed the population, and 5000 Somalis, mainly the old and very young, were dying every day.

Amongst the suggestions that came from one of the NGOs was simply to flood the beaches with food from the huge unwanted EC food mountains. Even if 50 per cent were looted, the food would be so plentiful that it might cease to attract looters. But with food as the only currency, this was probably a pious hope, and the plan never materialized.

On 27 July 1992, the UN Security Council voted to mount a massive airlift, and to dispatch 500 troops, later to be increased to 3500, to guard the depots and convoys.[16] General Aideed, however, refused to agree to this, claiming that he had 30,000 armed troops of his own, and controlled 11 of Somalia's 18 districts.[17] The UN still stuck to the principle of not deploying peacekeeping troops unless the 'national government' agreed. Eventually, with Aideed's reluctant agreement, 500 Pakistani troops were deployed: they could do little but defend the airfield, and even here they were periodically attacked by Aideed's gunmen. The food convoys were unguarded except for the 'guards' hired by the NGOs, many of whom looted a great deal for themselves. The people continued to starve.

By October 1992, a further private army had emerged in the south, led by the former President Barre's son-in-law, Mohamed Siad Hersi Morgan. He captured Baidera, previously held by General Aideed, about 300 kilometres west of Mogadishu. This put many other routes to the interior under threat.

In November 1992, Mohamed Sahnoun resigned as UN special envoy, complaining that he was not getting the support he needed from the UN bureaucracy. He was replaced by Ismael Kittani, an Iraqi diplomat with long involvement in the UN.[18]

Up to this point, 300,000 Somalis had died of starvation; this would soon reach half a million unless something drastic were done. President Bush, with the support of President-elect Clinton, offered to send 28,000 US troops under US command to organize and protect the distribution of food. The UN Security Council approved, and a number of other countries offered contingents, bringing the total to 35,000 (see Table 16.1). The troops began deployment in early December. Bowing to *force majeure*, General Aideed and Ali Mahdi pledged cooperation and met under US auspices to declare a truce. Some of the heavily armed 'guards' were less welcoming, realizing that they were about to lose their livelihood; the roving gunmen and looters were also put out, but the US Marines quickly showed that they meant business when their helicopter gunships annihilated two 'technicals' that had fired on them. As the US troops extended their deployment to Baidoa (where masses of refugees were dying of starvation every day), most of the gunmen buried their guns or retired to remoter areas from which to continue their looting when opportunities arose.[19]

By March 1993, the US-led force had confiscated 5000 small arms and 90 heavy machineguns, but there were still many more at large. The UN called a conference in Addis Ababa of 300 Somalis, including representatives of the warring factions, of which there were 15 (4 loyal to Aideed and 11 to Ali Mahdi). They agreed to lay down their arms in 90 days and to form a Transitional Council of 74, one from each of the 15 factions, 3 from each of the 18 regions and 5 from Mogadishu. This Council would govern for two years pending elections; during this time it would appoint heads of administrative departments for the central government and oversee the formation of regional and district councils. The US-led force would be replaced during the summer of 1993 by a UN force of 28,000.[20]

LIBERIA

Perhaps because of the complexity and frequent frustration of peacekeeping efforts, there has recently been a growing tendency for neighbouring countries to send in troops to help resolve internal conflicts in their regions. Usually, however, this kind of peacekeeping force has a bias to one side or the other.

Liberia is an example. Late in 1989, a small force of rebels from the Gio and Mina tribes formed up amongst fellow tribesmen in the adjacent French-speaking countries of Burkina Faso and Côte d'Ivoire. They entered Liberia on 24 December under Charles Taylor, who declared his intention of ousting the Liberian dictator, Samuel Doe. By May 1990, thanks to overreaction by Doe's army (7000 strong), the rebel force had grown to 5000 and largely controlled the north-eastern part of the country. In July, a rival force broke away from the rebels under 'Prince' Johnson, and surrounded the President in his palace in the capital,

Monrovia. The neighbouring English-speaking countries of the Economic Community of West African States (ECOWAS), led by Nigeria, Ghana and Sierra Leone, sent in a peacekeeping force initially 2500 strong, increasing a few weeks later to 4000. Welcomed by President Doe and Johnson, they largely stopped the fighting. Then, in September 1990, Doe, while visiting ECOWAS headquarters in Monrovia, was ambushed, taken away, tortured and finally killed by Johnson. Johnson thereafter maintained a loose alliance with ECOWAS, which secured Monrovia (in which one-third of the population lived) and its airport. Taylor, whose army had grown to 15,000, controlled 12 of the 13 rural counties, including the International Airport some 38 miles outside Monrovia. ECOWAS meanwhile installed an interim President, Dr Amur Sawyer. The conflict badly disrupted food supplies to Monrovia, which was getting only half the food it needed: an average of 20 children were dying of starvation every day in its hospitals.[21]

The ECOWAS force, reinforced by extra troops from Nigeria, had reached a strength of 7000 by April 1991, and brought about an uneasy cease-fire, though the interim government control was limited to the area around the capital, By September 1992, a third force from Samuel Doe's tribe, the Krahn, had secured control of the two northern provinces, while most of the rest of the rural areas were still controlled by Charles Taylor. Fighting flared up again and ECOWAS appealed to the UN Security Council to impose an embargo on arms supplies to all the rebel groups. The Security Council agreed to this in November 1992, and sent a UN special representative to monitor it.

By the spring of 1993, Charles Taylor's forces had been driven back into a smaller area east of Monrovia, though he still had tribal contacts with friends in Francophone Africa. The cease fire had broken down, and the ECOWAS force had grown to 15,000. Liberia's economy had gone from bad to worse. Neverthless, ECOWAS had proved that a regional force was probably more likely to succeed in this kind of situation than an equivalent UN force.[22]

Francophone Togo, however, facing its own horrific disorder and sandwiched between Nigeria and Ghana, asked no such help for fear of the spread of Anglophone influence, especially where (as in this case) there are tribes straddling the frontier – a constant problem in West Africa.

COMMONWEALTH OF INDEPENDENT STATES

The Commonwealth of Independent States (CIS), formed in 1991 by Russia with ten of the republics of the former USSR, made provision for regional cooperation in maintaining the internal and external security of the area of the previous Soviet Union, including dispatch of peacekeeping troops to republics whose governments requested it. In practice, only Russia, and to a lesser extent, Uzbekistan and Kazakhstan, have sent significant peacekeeping forces. Russia has generally agreed to requests only when the safety of ethnic Russian minorities is involved (e.g. in Moldova and Tadjikistan). A request from Armenia for Russian troops to help resolve the conflict in the Nagorno Karabakh region in Azerbaijan was refused. Although Georgia had declined to join the CIS, its President Edward Shevardnadze, the former Soviet Foreign Minister, requested Russian troops to intervene in rebellions in Abkhazia and South Ossetia, both of which were trying to secede (see Tables 15.1, 15.2 and 15.3, pp. 198–200).

BOSNIA

The fighting in the former Yugoslav states began when Slovenia and Croatia became independent in 1991, and it spread when Bosnia-Herzegovina declared its independence in March 1992. This was discussed in Chapter 15 in the context of the Balkanization of Eastern Europe following the disintegration of the Soviet Empire.

By September 1991, the Serbs had occupied large areas of eastern Croatia which had a high Serb population, and ethnic cleansing was in full flood. By the time the Serbs had occupied the areas they wanted, both armies were exhausted, and they bowed to pressure from the EC to accept the deployment of foreign observers to monitor a cease-fire. The Serbs, however, extracted a condition that they would enforce law and order in the areas of Croatia occupied by their army, which amounted to *de facto* annexation. Initially 123 observers were deployed, and these were built up early in 1992 to a UN protection force, UNPROFOR 1, of 15,000 from 25 countries (see Table 16.1). Based in Zagreb, this force helped to stop the fighting as the Serbs were content to have the situation stabilized where it stood.

Fighting and ethnic cleansing began in Bosnia as soon as she declared her independence in March 1992, and monitors were sent from UNPROFOR 1 in Zagreb to the Bosnian capital, Sarajevo, with the theoretical agreement of all concerned, that is, the state governments of Serbia, Croatia and Bosnia and the leaders of the Bosnian Serbs, Bosnian Croats and Bosnian Muslims. The Serbs, however, had no intention of keeping their word. They signed 15 cease-fires between March and September 1992: all were broken. As in Croatia, they set about occupying the areas in Bosnia which they wished to annexe for their Greater Serbia, amounting to two-thirds of the country (see Map 15B). By September, the official death toll had reached 10,000, with another 50,000 missing and nearly 2 million driven from their homes (see Chapter 15). The Serbs then intensified their ethnic cleansing and attempted to starve the population out of the Muslim towns and villages. Some of these, such as Gorazde and Srebrenica, close to the border of Serbia, were surrounded by Serb militia from April onwards.

In September, the UN decided that it must take action to escort food convoys to these and other towns, and a second peacekeeping force (UNPROFOR 2) was dispatched – again with the theoretical agreement of all concerned. This force, 7000 strong, initially occupied Sarajevo Airport – though both the troops and the transport aircraft bringing in food and medical supplies were fired upon. The governments and militias usually denied responsibility; it is hard to say how many of these incidents were planned and how many were due to ill-disciplined militias firing on their own initiative. The Bosnian Muslims themselves were not wholly innocent; on one occasion they deliberately ambushed a UN food distribution convoy and killed two French UN soldiers.

As the UN force built up to its full strength (by November 1992) it deployed to protect the airfields and ports (including Split in Croatia – see Map 15B) and established military bases at intervals on the roads to escort the convoys as they came through. Though the Serb military commanders paid lip-service to supporting distribution of humanitarian supplies, their men did not hesitate to block roads when they wished to squeeze one of the towns held by their rivals. Sometimes this was done by demonstrators – often women and children – occupying bridges or defiles to block the convoys. The commanders of the UN escorts had to negotiate the passage of each individual convoy, and their orders were not to shoot except in self-defence. This made the soldiers very vulnerable targets as they drove along, prey to the whims of Serb snipers, mortars or artillery observers in the hills astride the road. The first convoy did not reach Srebrenica until the end of November 1992, by which time the inhabitants had been without deliveries of food and medical supplies for seven months.

In such mountainous country, the safest way for the UN convoys to move would have been to leapfrog pickets from hill to hill either side of the road ahead of the convoy, as the British had done on the North-west Frontier of India in imperial days, and as the Soviet army did in Afghanistan, but this is a time-consuming process involving a large number of troops and the individual pickets can be very vulnerable to guerrilla fighters.

Meanwhile, the UN had imposed a ban on oil to Serbia and on weapons to all the warring factions. To support this, the navies of the Western European Union and NATO deployed ships in the Adriatic, but initially these had power only to 'monitor', that is, to question approaching ships by radio. They had no power to search a ship if her Captain gave even a patently false statement of her cargo. Initially the sanctions caused an oil shortage in Belgrade, but by November 1992 the Serbs had found many ways round the embargo, into ports in Montenegro, up the Danube and overland. Belgrade was no longer short of oil, and large quantities of weapons were getting in. The UN therefore authorized the navies to stop and search ships to enforce the blockade and tightened up the border checks over land and up the Danube.

As winter approached, there was growing pressure in the UN to escort convoys of refugees in buses out of Croatia and Bosnia. Most of these were Croats and Muslims and, of course, this suited the Serbs well as it assisted their process of ethnic cleansing. But all European countries, including Germany, began to tighten their regulations for granting asylum.

The tragedy of Bosnia-Herzegovina is that the three communities are not ethnically very different and, even if they were, they are interbred after generations of sharing the same country. Their differences are in their traditions and religion. Racially, all are predominantly South Slav. The Serbs, though long part of the Ottoman Empire, fought stubbornly to retain their identity, of which their Orthodox Christianity was a distinguishing mark. The Croats were until 1918 part of the Catholic Austro-Hungarian Empire, while a substantial proportion of the Slav population in Bosnia-Herzegovina embraced the Muslim religion of the Ottoman Empire, with a good deal of intermarriage with Turks and other Muslims. For the last three generations, the Serbs have dominated (even though Tito was a Croat), and clearly intend to continue to do so. So long as one or more of the three prefers to kill the others or terrorize them into leaving their homes rather than live together, no purely peacekeeping operation is likely to succeed.

Nor are full-scale military operations on land: the Germans tried this from 1941 to 1944. The mountainous terrain absorbs troops like a sponge, and is ideal for guerrilla warfare, at which the Serbs are adept. The Germans never controlled more than the towns, with armed convoys running between them, despite deploying more than 100,000 troops.

There remains the threat that the Islamic world, exasperated by the failure of the UN to protect the Bosnian Muslims in contrast to their actions in Somalia, might mount a massive arms delivery or even a military intervention. This could lead to a serious risk of escalation and clashes with UN troops.

The UN did declare a 'no-fly zone', as they had done successfully over Iraq. Although the Serbs held back from using combat aircraft over Bosnia, they continued to fly helicopters, transporting weapons and supplies to the Bosnian Serb militia. The UN was reluctant to shoot these down in case the Serbs retaliated against UN troops escorting humanitarian aid convoys so that the Bosnian Muslims would suffer more in the end.[23]

In January 1993 the leaders of all three communities meeting under joint UN/EC chairmanship in Geneva agreed in principle to a federal Bosnia with ten autonomous provinces, each community governing three with the tenth (around Sarajevo) governed jointly. They could not, however, agree on the borders, the Serbs reluctant to give up any of the 70 per cent of Bosnia they had overrun, and the Muslims refusing to recognize Serb control of areas gained by ethnic cleansing.

In April 1993, all three leaders signed their agreement to the provisional borders, the Vance-Owen plan. Then the Bosnian Serb leader's signature was over-ruled by a so-called 'Bosnian Serb Parliament', despite intense pressure from the Serbian President

Milosevic in Belgrade, who was alarmed by the tighter sanctions imposed by the UN and the imminent treat of NATO airstrikes. Milosevic thereupon declared his intention of cutting off all funds and supplies to the Bosnian Serbs other than food and medicine. NATO cancelled the despatch of 75,000 peacekeeping troops it had organized on behalf of the UN to police the Vance–Owen plan. Despite its intense disappointment, however, the UN had developed during the Bosnian crisis: the Security Council had not been blocked by vetos, albeit after long discussions behind the scenes; and it had accepted the principle of NATO acting on its behalf. Boris Yeltsin, despite Russia's historic sympathy for the Serbs, had supported the tough sanctions and promised a Russian contingent for the NATO peacekeeping force.

THE FUTURE OF PEACEMAKING AND PEACEKEEPING

Experience in Cambodia, Somalia and Bosnia has thrown doubt on the principle that UN peacekeeping forces would not be deployed, or would withdraw, unless all parties to the dispute agreed to their presence; the division between peacemaking and peacekeeping has become blurred. People like the Khmers Rouges in Cambodia, the warlords in Somalia, Milosevic and the Serb militia leaders in Bosnia would honour agreements only when it suited them to do so or when faced by *force majeure*. If UN humanitarian aid convoys are not permitted to use force to remove gunmen blocking their way, they will fail to relieve the suffering and will earn only contempt. If they are required to run the gauntlet, waiting to be shot at, they are sitting targets, and it puts the UN troops at an unacceptable disadvantage.

The UN Charter already allows the Security Council to authorize collective use of force against actions anywhere in the world which it considers threaten peace and security. Offensive operations by UN forces were carried out in Korea (1950–53) and to a limited extent in the Congo (1960–64). The reversal of Saddam Hussein's invasion of Kuwait was achieved by an Allied force under Security Council authority, but not under the UN flag. The same applied to the US and Allied forces in Somalia.

There is, however, a great deal more that military forces can do under UN authority short of military occupation, first by uncomprising enforcement of blockades and, if necessary, by naval and air attack to destroy the military capability of those using force to defy UN Resolutions.

The blockade must if necessary be extended to other countries which assist the offenders. If the Thais do not cease harbouring and (by trade) financing the Khmers Rouges, Thailand must herself be subjected to a blockade. If arms and other war materials continue to enter Serbia and Bosnia by air or by sea (via Montenegro), across land frontiers or up the Danube, this should be prevented by the necessary degree of force. If neighbouring countries, such as Hungary, Romania, Bulgaria and Greece, fail to prevent the passage of embargoed traffic, they too should be subjected to sanctions and blockade. If Serbian armed forces attempt to get round the blockade, they and their bases should, after warning, be attacked from the air as effectively as were those of Iraq in 1991. The UN members have the power and, rather than tolerate the suffering inflicted on the peoples of Bosnia, Somalia and Cambodia in defiance of the UN, they should use it.

The use of force, whether to enforce a blockade or to damage the military power of an aggressor, or to occupy territory, requires a decisive and coherent direction. Every experience illustrates that, for anything beyond peacekeeping voluntarily accepted by the parties to the conflict, the UN Secretary-General, his special representatives on the ground and the commanders of mixed forces in blue berets, cannot exercise command in what amounts to a war. Effective direction in these circumstances requires a single chain of command in which, at each level, the political and military decisions can be delegated to one person, instantly, with responsibility only to the person (colonel, general or politician) above him in the chain.

This has worked best when the UN has delegated responsibility to a single member government, such as to the US government in Korea, the Gulf and Somalia. This, however, is appropriate only when the armed forces used are predominantly provided by that member.

Where more collective forces are required, there is a well-established and well-practised organization in being, able to exercise both political and military control over mixed forces under battle conditions: NATO.

A NEW ROLE FOR NATO

NATO is admirably suited to act as an executive agency for the UN Security Council or the CSCE. Its 16 members have for many years worked together in planning military operations in accordance with the political policies of its governments. For this purpose, the NATO Council brings together government ministers and officials to agree on policy, and each member has an Ambassador accredited to NATO who is involved full time in decision-making and liaison with his parent government. The Supreme Allied Commander in Europe (SACEUR) has a staff made up from the 16 members; they have the power and authority to act in accordance with these decisions. They can operate in emergency, for example if one of their members is attacked, and are *restrained by no veto*, except that an individual government could withhold the use of its own troops for a particular task. While consultation upwards and downwards would be continuous as far as time allowed, the NATO Headquarters (Supreme Headquarters Allied Powers in Europe – SHAPE) is geared to act immediately in emergency. It was formed from the Allied Headquarters in Europe on the Western Front in 1944–45, whose commander, General Eisenhower, became NATO's first SACEUR, with an Allied staff. Formed in the post-war crisis atmosphere, when there seemed to be a real threat that the Soviet army might advance into Western Europe, SHAPE was geared for active operations, with the momentum built up from practical experience still in being.

NATO could well have provided the commander and staff for the Gulf War, but did not, because many non-NATO countries (especially Arab) were involved, and the operations were outside NATO territory. NATO, however, played a major part in mounting the US, British and other contingents, making up their equipment from other NATO members, and organizing a great deal of their movement and logistics. NATO has since accepted that it may now often have to operate 'out of area'.

When they became free to do so in 1989–90, several former Warsaw Pact countries applied to join NATO. This was refused because the sixteen NATO members are committed by the treaty to respond to an attack on one as an attack on all, and they were understandably unwilling to extend this guarantee to any more countries. In 1991, however, eight East European countries which had applied to join NATO were invited instead to meet with NATO members in a North Atlantic Cooperation Council (NACC). In March 1992, eleven more states from the former USSR (now CIS) also joined NACC. At that meeting, the new total of 35 sovereign states collectively offered to provide troops for peacekeeping and to act, if so requested, on behalf of the UN or CSCE.

This opens up exciting possibilities. NACC already has access to a functioning executive headquarters in SHAPE. Liaison officers from the 19 non-NATO countries would initially suffice if SHAPE undertook operations to which their countries were contributing, and later the staff could be strengthened by permanent representation, though it would be important not to make the headquarters too cumbersome. The best solution would probably be to set up a tactical headquarters manned from NATO (with liaison officers as needed) to command operations, as the Allies did under the US General Schwarzkopf in the Gulf War. Indeed, if intelligence information indicated that operations were likely to be needed in a certain area, NATO could send a small staff to make contingency plans, and this would later form the nucleus of the tactical command headquarters when the time came to deploy troops.[24]

NATO and NACC roles should henceforth be much wider than planning and commanding Allied forces in conventional operations like the Gulf War; they should also extend to terrorism, the drug war and disaster relief. For each of these tasks they should set up planning cells, possibly with detachments permanently in crucial areas, for example to coordinate interception of drug trafficking in the Caribbean.

Disaster relief is especially important for three reasons: first, because there are disasters, somewhere, every year; second, because the armed forces are better organized and equipped than anyone else to provide immediate response, for example air and ground reconnaissance, field hospitals and medical evacuation, land, sea and air transport, heavy engineering and rescue, reopening roads and bridges, and telecommunications; third because the month-by-month deployment on disaster relief would give the governments, staffs and troops practice and training in reacting quickly in a real life-and-death situation, and in working together in readiness for more warlike operations when they are needed.

Financing of international operations should be done on a pool basis. For frequent regular operations like disaster relief, the drug war and anti-terrorism, all UN countries should pay an agreed *pro rata* sum into the pool each year. A country providing troops, ships, and so on would provide the basic costs – for example, the pay of the troops and maintenance of ships and aircraft – which it would be paying whether or not they were deployed on this task. It would draw the 'extra costs' – for example of fuel, ammunition, transport and logistics – from the pool.

NACC should later be widened (presumably with a change of name) to include appropriate North and Central European countries and Japan, Australia and New Zealand – what could be described as 'donor countries'. There are strong arguments against accepting more than 30 or 40 countries into the NACC operational headquarters, as it might lose its executive capability – as the UN has done, with its 164 members. NACC would most commonly act on behalf of (or with the approval of) the UN.

If used wisely, this organization could revolutionize the world's response to aggression, terrorism, organized crime and disaster relief. And it will clearly have to develop its tactics and techniques for peacemaking (as well as peacekeeping) in the numerous and messy conflicts that will continue to arise all over the world, and especially astride the borders of the East European and former Soviet states.

17 Crisis Management

ASSESSMENT OF THE CRISIS MANAGERS

It takes one to make a war, but two to avoid it. Crises have – or will be – resolved only if both parties choose to resolve them rather than fight. If either leader prefers to launch his people into war rather than compromise, and is confident that he will win, war it will be; Bismarck, Hitler and Saddam Hussein all demonstrated that. Handling a crisis effectively therefore depends more on understanding the adversary, how his mind works and how he will react, than on principles.

To sum up on some of the crisis managers assessed in the case studies: Bismarck was a past master at provoking his adversary to strike the first blow (e.g. in 1866 and 1870) at a time that suited him. He had clear aims, sized up his opponents and created a better war organization than theirs, so he was confident. He always looked ahead to the next step, including the offer of peace terms which his defeated enemy could live with. Napoleon III was vain, weak and indecisive, headed a poor organization and therefore lacked confidence; he dared not face the political consequences of compromise, and allowed himself to be manipulated by Bismarck.

The First World War began because the two people who made or ultimately approved the decisions were neither of them fit for high office, still less for autocratic power. The Kaiser was vain and petulant, and had a deep inferiority complex which led him to be assertive. The Tsar was a gentle family man and was totally out of his depth in affairs of state.

The Second World War was made inevitable by the Treaty of Versailles, which resulted from the vindictiveness of Clemenceau and from the ideals of Woodrow Wilson, which were so unworldly that he could not get the US Congress to approve them. The terms of Versailles created the conditions to throw up a militant nationalist to lead a German resurgence, but failed to provide a machinery for restraining him. Adolf Hitler had charisma, immense organizing ability and the stomach and determination to fight if he did not get what he wanted – a Greater Germany – and there is no doubt that he inspired the majority of Germans to support him. The British and French leaders, with the memory of 1914–18 still vivid, were not prepared to fight. Appeasement gave Hitler time to build up his strength, so when the Allies eventually realized that they had no option but to resist, they began the war at a disadvantage.

Over the Berlin blockade in 1948, President Truman showed confidence and judgement worthy of Bismarck. He prevailed by determination and good organization. He knew that Stalin was on the verge of testing an atom bomb, and took account of this in leaving him a way out.

Kennedy was a classic winner in the Cuban Missile Crisis of 1962. The principles he followed were codified by one his diplomats: 'Keep your objectives limited; decide how far you would go; creep up carefully on the use of force; widen the community of the concerned' (see p. 112). Kennedy kept his own options open, and ensured that he left Khrushchev a tolerable option other than war. Kennedy was also willing to fight if necessary and was fairly sure that Khrushchev was not. Kennedy's intelligence was excellent and the human intelligence (from Penkovsky) decisive.

In 1967, Nasser may or may not have wanted war, but his rherotic was entirely counter-productive. So were his 'crisis signals' to Israel – expelling the UNEF and seizing Sharm el Sheikh. With the experience of 1948 and 1956, he should certainly have been more realistic about the chances of the Egyptian army defeating the Israelis in the open desert. The Israelis' divided leadership may paradoxically have helped to confuse their adversaries: they were lucky that their military efficiency and national morale carried them through.

In 1973, the Israelis were stupidly overconfident. Their intelligence was surprisingly bad, probably due to their failure to separate fact-finding from analysis. If one person handles both, there is a danger that he will convince himself that facts conflicting with his ongoing analysis must be wrong. Again, the Israelis were saved by the flair and dedication of their army. Sadat was shrewd; he had to rise above the shadow of Nasser. He foresaw that he must get a bilateral peace with Israel for both security and economic reasons; he also clearly aimed to switch his custom as a client from the USSR to the USA. He hoped for both without fighting, but realized that he would not get either unless he convinced Israel that the Egyptian army was willing to fight and might win. Whether he also foresaw that the superpowers, in their alarm, would join forces to ensure that he kept what he had initially won, must still be open to conjecture.

The champion in Vietnam was the North Vietnamese General Vo Nguyen Giap, who masterminded a classic Maoist campaign, first against France and then against the USA, for 29 years. His achievements were remarkable. The tragedy for the Vietnamese people is that the Communist ideal for which he and they fought so devotedly was a flawed one, which has brought them only suffering and poverty. President Johnson was the conspicuous failure. He failed to understand that the war was about the people in the villages, not about soldiers and bomber aircraft. And he judged wrongly how his own American people would react to their sons and brothers being sent to fight it.

In Bangladesh in 1971, Yahya Khan had honourable intentions, but failed to reach a reasonable settlement when it was there for the taking. Later, when it became clear that India intended to resolve the problem by force, he should have realized that the situation of his army made defeat inevitable and should have settled for the best he could get without fighting, even if this meant that he would be ousted from power (which he was anyway). Mrs Gandhi, who held all the cards, showed courage and confidence in going on her world tour to 'widen the community of the concerned' on the eve of the war.

In Cyprus in 1974, the Greek Colonels and Nicos Sampson should have foreseen what the Turks would do; the deployment of the 600 Turkish troops in Cyprus gave a clear indication of this. The Greeks were stupid to start something that they could not possibly win.

In 1982, British intelligence concerning the threat to the Falkland Islands, or perhaps their analysis of it, was as poor as that of the Israelis in 1973. Both General Galtieri and Mrs Thatcher knew that they would lose power if they gave way, so both were willing to fight. But neither believed that the other would do what he or she did. As with the Israelis, the brilliance of the military performance carried Mrs Thatcher through, but her coolheadedness and determination deserved their reward.

Over the Gulf crisis of 1990–91, President Bush's crisis management was inept in the run-up to the Iraqi invasion, when he misread the signs and sent the wrong signals. The diplomatic phase *after* the invasion was well handled (as with the British after the Falklands invasion). The military performance was superb, but Bush was wrong to give way to Turkish and Saudi Arabian fears and his own anxieties about Iran in letting so many of the fruits of victory slip away.

Saddam Hussein was a crisis manager only in that he so handled his diplomacy up till August 1990 that no one was ready to take action to resist his invasion of Kuwait, or even to threaten him with the consequences if he did it. His handling of the crisis thereafter lost him all he had gained and impoverished his country but he did, through Allied timidity, retain his power and the military resources to exercise it internally.

Of the leaders in Cambodia, Somalia, Liberia, the CIS and the former Yugoslav states, only Hun Sen and Prince Sihanouk in Cambodia and Presidents Yeltsin and Shevardnadze in the CIS have made any serious attempt to resolve their crises without fighting. In Bosnia, Milosevic and the Serb militia commanders closely followed Hitler's example in their ambitions as leaders of a 'master race' to build a Greater Serbia, and were able to arouse Serbian popular support on that basis. The warlords in Somalia and Liberia, however, seemed to have no wider aims, and did not care how many of their people died from violence or starvation in their contest for personal power.

CRISIS MANAGEMENT IN YEARS TO COME

The lessons from these varied crises in the nineteenth and twentieth centuries have themselves varied, but one thread is common to all of them – the importance of looking through the eyes of the adversary and judging correctly what he will do and how he will react. Good intelligence is therefore the biggest single factor: if *both* sides have good intelligence there will probably not be a war, because, if one side *knows* it would lose, it will probably find a way to settle, saving what face it can. Technical intelligence is valuable, but only as an adjunct to human intelligence from sources within or with links to the adversary's inner circle.

In predicting the behaviour of a political or politico-military leader, it can best be assumed that his primary motivation is to stay in power, since he cannot achieve any of his other objectives unless he does that. His other objectives will include those that best advance his national interests. These can be realized by international power described in terms of options to have his own way as described in Chapter 1 of this book.

Chapter 15 examined the likeliest circumstances and patterns of war: arising from the Balkanization of Eastern Europe and the former USSR; from the opening of Western Europe's frontiers; from religious fanaticism; from abiding animosities such as Arab–Israeli, Greek–Turk and Muslim–Hindu–Sikh; and from the international drug Mafias. The patterns of civil war, insurgency, terrorism and regional conflicts were examined, and the hazards arising from nuclear proliferation.

Whether these predictions of circumstance and pattern prove correct or not, the historical examples in the earlier part of the book, placed against the experience of the twentieth century, suggest that the underlying causes of war are deep-rooted and endemic to the human species; they will not go away.

Affluence increases rather than reduces the prospects of war: the 1914–18 war dwarfed all previous massacres in history and the 1939–45 war dwarfed even that.[1] Yet these wars were between the richest countries, not the poorest. All wars have had some element of competition for resources, from the earliest tribal wars onwards, but affluence increases greed and greed stimulates conflict and crime. Greed, pride and the thirst for power have now transcended competition for the resources needed for survival as causes of conflict. The twentieth century has been by far the most violent in history, and the challenge is to prevent the twenty-first century being even more so.

Amongst the circumstances surrounding the conflicts of the twentieth century, a contributing factor has often been the decay of an empire and the aftermath arising from its disintegration (eg in the Balkans in 1908–14, the ethnic minorities in Czechoslovakia and Poland in 1939 and the chronic instability left behind by the European empires in Africa). The disintegration of the Soviet and Yugoslav empires has disturbing parallels. And the callousness towards their own people of contemporary competing warlords rivals that of Stalin.

Apart from the personal and family suffering that these internal conflicts cause, they often spill over internationally, so we will need to keep our seatbelts fastened, improve our crisis management procedures and revise our attitudes and organizations (including the UN, CSCE, EC, CIS and NATO) for intervention in keeping the peace.

Notes and References

Preface

1 M. D. Donelan and M. J. Grieve, *International Disputes: Case Histories 1945–70*, London, Europa, 1973, analyse 50 cases in the first half of the Cold War, and there were at least another 50 – 2 or 3 each year – in the second half.

1 International Power and Crisis Management

1 To avoid repeated use of 'he or she', 'man or woman', etc, the reader is asked to assume that 'he' means 'he or she' and that 'man' means 'humankind' where appropriate.
2 Thomas Hobbes, *Leviathan* (1961) Harmondsworth, Penguin, 1968, pp. 183–8
3 James E. Dougherty and Robert L. Pfaltzgraff Jr, *Contending Theories of International Relations*, Philadelphia, Lippincott, 1971, Chapter 3, gives an excellent analysis of the views of the political realist philosophers
4 For examples of this dedication see Lee Kuan Yew, *The Battle for Merger*, Singapore Government Publications, 1961, pp. 19, 21 and 85, cited in Richard Clutterbuck, *Conflict and Violence in Singapore and Malaysia*, Singapore, Graham Brash and Boulder, Colorado, Westview, 1985, p. 64. See also Richard Clutterbuck, *Riot and Revolution in Singapore and Malaya*, London, Faber & Faber, 1973, p. 271
5 Coral Bell, *The Conventions of Crisis*, London, Oxford University Press, 1971, p. 116
6 This accords with Hans Morgenthau's philosophy, see p. 5
7 Attributed to Hilaire Belloc
8 Coral Bell, op cit, p. 9
9 Ibid, p. 14
10 Phil Williams, 'Crisis Management', *International Affairs*, May 1973
11 Harlan Cleveland, 'Crisis Diplomacy', *Foreign Affairs*, New York, July 1963
12 Heidi Avery, 'Industrial Society and International Order: Sir Norman Angell's Analysis', unpublished Master of Studies Thesis, Faculty of Modern History, Oxford University, June 1990, gives a concise and lucid account of this theory. She cites Sir Norman Angell's books, *The Great Illusion*, London, Heinemann, 1912, and *After All*, London, Hamish Hamilton, 1951; also J.D.B. Miller, *Norman Angell and the Futility of War*, Hong Kong, Macmillan, 1986

2 Historical Roots of International Conflict

1 Desmond Morris, *The Naked Ape*, London, Jonathan Cape, 1967. See also MacFarlane Burnet, *Dominant Mammal*, Harmondsworth, Penguin, 1971. Morris traces man's behaviour from his animal roots, Burnet through biology and demography. Both throw a great deal of light on man's tendency, rare in the animal world, to slaughter large numbers of his own species.
2 For an excellent analysis of European power at its peak, see John Terraine, *The Mighty Continent*, London, BBC, 1974
3 Michael Shanks, *What's Wrong with the Modern World*, London, The Bodley Head, 1978, gives a fuller explanation of this 50–year cycle. See also Richard Clutterbuck, *Industrial Conflict and Democracy*, London, Macmillan, 1984, pp. 8–10
4 Alexis de Tocqueville, *The Ancien Régime and the French Revolution* (Paris 1852), London, Fontana, 1971
5 Crane Brinton, *The Anatomy of Revolution*, New York, Vintage, 1957
6 Crane Brinton's book was originally published in 1938. In the 1957 edition he made some significant changes, underlining the differences between the Russian Revolution and the pattern he originally based on the French Revolution, op cit, pp. vi–vii
7 John Terraine, *The Mighty Continent*, London, BBC, 1974

3 The Balance of Power

1 Alan Palmer, *Metternich*, London, Weidenfeld & Nicolson, 1972, pp. 190–5
2 Winston S Churchill, *A History of the English Speaking Peoples*, London, Cassell, 1958, vol IV, pp. 36–8
3 Ibid, p. 11
4 Ben Whittaker, *The Police in Society*, London, Eyre Methuen, 1979, p. 38
5 David Ascoli, *The Queen's Peace*, London, Hamish Hamilton, 1979, pp. 121–2
6 R.C. Birch, *Britain in Europe 1789–1871*, London, Pergamon, 1969, p. 156
7 Palmer, op cit, pp. 302–4
8 Birch, *1789–1871*, pp. 161–2
9 Palmer, op cit, p. 323
10 Birch, *1789–1871*, pp. 159–60. This is a recurring pattern in French history. After the Paris Commune in 1871 and again after the strike and student riots in Paris in 1968, the French electorate swung strongly to the conservatives
11 Ibid, p. 163
12 Ibid, p. 171
13 Martin Gilbert, *Russian History Atlas*, London, Weidenfeld and Nicolson, 1966, p. 18; Churchill, op cit, p. 291
14 Birch, *1789–1871*, p. 187–90

15 *Encyclopaedia Britannica*, 1981, vol 8, pp. 104–5
16 David W Ziegler, *War and Peace in International Politics*, Boston, Little, Brown, 1977, pp. 12–14
17 Birch, *1789–1871*, p. 196
18 Prussia's dynamic approach to the organization of mobilization was to play a major part again in the outbreak of war in 1870 and again in 1914, as will be described
19 A.J.P. Taylor, *How Wars Begin*, London, Hamish Hamilton, 1979, p. 83
20 Birch, *1789–1871*, pp. 198–9
21 Ibid, pp. 202–3; Taylor, *How Wars Begin*, pp. 89–95
22 Birch, *1789–1871*, pp. 201–2
23 Taylor, *How Wars Begin*, p. 95
24 Birch, *1789–1871*, p. 204
25 The decisive vote came, as usual, from the petty bourgeoisie and small farmers, yearning for security
26 *Encyclopaedia Britannica*, 1981, vol 7, p. 668. Other sources put the number as high as 40,000 – see note 28
27 A proud nation, defeated and humiliated, is often thereby galvanized to heroic efforts to recover its pride, as the Germans and Japanese were in 1945
28 R.C. Birch, *Britain and Europe 1871–1939*, London, Pergamon, 1966, p. 46. Birch also puts the numbers killed in the Commune rising at 40,000
29 F.S. Northedge and M J Grieve, *A Hundred Years of International Relations*, London, Duckworth, 1971, p. 27. See also *Encyclopaedia Britannica*, 1981, vol 8, p. 113
30 Taylor, *How Wars Begin*, p. 61
31 *Encyclopaedia Britannica*, 1981, vol V, p. 883
32 Ibid, vol IX, p. 21
33 Leonard De Vries, *History as Hot News*, London, Murray, 1973, p. 26
34 American Heritage, *The Civil War*, New York, Doubleday, 1960, p. 348
35 The *Encyclopaedia Britannica* records those killed in the two world wars as follows:

First World War (*Encyclopaedia Britannica*, 1981, vol 9, p. 966) Allies 5 million, Central Powers 3.4 million, total 8.4 million
Second World War (ibid, p. 1013)

	Combatants	*Civilians*	*Total*
USSR	11,000,000	7,000,000	18,000,000
Poland	?	?	5,800,000
		(excluding 3,200,000 Jews)	
Jews	–	5,700,000	5,700,00
		(including those in Poland)	
Germany	3,500,000	780,000	4,280,000
China	1,300,000	22,000,000	23,300,000
			(estimates 'dubious')

	Combatants	*Civilians*	*Total*
Japan	1,310,224	672,000	1,982,224
Yugoslavia	305,000	1,200,000	1,505,000
UK	264,443	92,673	367,116
USA	292,131	6,000	298,131
Approx Totals	20 million	40 million	60 million

Allowing for omissions a very rough approximation for the Second World War dead would be 20 million military and 40 million civilians, though in some cases these figures may have been exaggerated, especially the civilians. Nevertheless, the *minimum* total estimated by the *Encyclopaedia Britannica* (35 million) would still dwarf the figure for any other war in history

36 K.J. Holsti, 'International Theory and War in the Third World', in Brian L Job (ed) *The Insecurity Dilemma: National Security of Third World States*, Boulder, Colorado, and London, Lynne Reinner, 1992, estimates that between 1945 and 1989 there were 21,809,000 casualties in 'interstate and internationalized civil wars' of which 99.2% were in the Third World

4 The Outbreak of the First World War

1 John G Stoessinger, *Why Nations Go to War*, London, Macmillan, 1990, pp. 21–4
2 F.S. Northedge and MJ Grieve, *A Hundred Years of International Relations*, London, Duckworth, 1971, pp. 71–90, gives an excellent analysis of the approach to the First World War
3 Ibid, pp. 26–8. Bismarck had also negotiated a non-aggression pact with Austria and Russia in 1881, usually known as the *Dreikaiserbund.* The three monarchs were related to each other by blood or by marriage, mainly through Queen Victoria and her sons and daughters
4 Ibid, pp. 31–2
5 Ibid, pp. 80–3
6 John Lawrence, *A History of Russia*, New York, Mentor, 1962. Chapter XVIII (pp. 197–205) 'The Foundations Crack' puts the Russian Revolution in historical perspective
7 *Encyclopaedia Britannica*, 1981, vol IV, p. 61. See also Birch, *1871–1939* p. 107
8 A.J.P. Taylor, *War by Timetable*, London, Macdonald, 1969, pp. 54–6
9 A.J.P. Taylor, *How Wars Begin*, London, Hamish Hamilton, 1979, p. 106
10 Stoessinger, op cit, p. 3
11 Taylor, *War by Timetable*, p. 65
12 Stoessinger, op cit, pp. 5–7

13 Taylor, *How Wars Begin*, p. 107
14 Stoessinger, op cit, p. 8
15 Taylor, *How Wars Begin*, p. 108
16 Stoessinger, op cit, p. 9
17 Ibid, pp. 12–13
18 Germany could put 5 million fully trained men into the field, France 4 million and Austria 2.5 million. Russian reservists were unlimited in that they vastly exceeded the capacity of the railways to move them or of the armies to receive them. Britain had planned to send 100,000 men to France with another 100,000 to go elsewhere overseas. R. C. Birch, *Britain and Europe 1871–1939*, London, Pergamon, 1966, p. 131
19 Taylor, *War by Timetable*, gives the best analysis of this problem
20 Stoessinger, op cit, p. 16
21 Taylor, *How Wars Begin*, p. 10
22 Stoessinger, op cit, p. 14
23 Ibid, p. 17
24 Robert Asprey, *The German High Command at War*, New York, William Morrow, 1991, p. 42. This is the most recent and probably the best analysis of the German conduct of the First World War by the government and General Staff.
25 In the event the Russian army, mobilizing on 30 July, crossed the frontier on 19 August, but it was totally unready for war, many units being short of officers and NCOs, horses and equipment. They were disastrously defeated at Tannenburg on 30 August, before any German divisions had been moved over from the west, by a much smaller army under two generals who thereby made their reputations and rose to great heights – Hindenburg and Ludendorf
26 Taylor, *How Wars Begin*, p. 100
27 Stoessinger, op cit, p. 19.
28 *The Guns of August* (New York, 1962)
29 Stoessinger, op cit, p. 5
30 Asprey, op cit, pp. 21–2

5 The Rise of Hitler

1 Robert Asprey, *The German High Command in War*, gives a vivid new assessment of the roles of Hindenburg and Ludendorf, both militarily and politically, in Germany's survival of this crisis
2 R. C. Birch *Britain and Europe 1871–1939*, London, Pergamon, 1966, p. 148
3 Ibid, pp. 152–80
4 James Joll, *Europe since 1870*, Harmondsworth, Penguin, 1976, p. 279
5 Ibid, pp. 358–61
6 Joll (pp. 331–8) gives a detailed account and analysis of Hitler's rise to power

7 Martin Gilbert, *Recent History Atlas 1860 to 1960*, London, Weidenfeld & Nicolson, 1967, pp. 53 and 61. Like Serbs and Croats in the new states created by the disintegration of Yugloslavia in 1991–92, these Germans were, of course, intermingled with Czechs and Poles, so no 'fair' border could be drawn. In the areas transferred to Germany by the Munich Agreement in September 1938, there would have been a two to one majority vote in favour of joining Germany, but Hitler revealed that his true intention was merely to use these areas as a stepping stone when, within five months, he marched his soldiers into Prague.

8 *Encyclopaedia Britannica*, 1981, vol 8, p. 118

9 Joll, op cit, p. 336

10 Richard Bessel, '1933: A Failed Counter-Revolution', in E. E. Rice (ed) *Revolution and Counter Revolution*, Oxford, Blackwell, 1991, pp. 109–25. He contends that Hindenburg and the conservative politicians led by Von Papen were attempting a counter-revolution against what they saw as a dangerously liberal programme proposed by Schleicher's administration. Bessel suggests that they aimed to use Hitler as a tool, but that he hijacked their counter-revolution.

11 Joll, op cit, p. 339

12 J P Stern, *Hitler: The Fuhrer and the People*, London, Fontana, 1975, p. 135

13 Birch, *1871–1939*, pp. 192–4

14 Joll, op cit, p. 268

15 F.S. Northedge and M.J. Grieve, *A Hundred Years of International Relations*, London, Duckworth, 1971, p. 126

16 Ibid, p. 134

17 Gilbert, op cit, pp. 47 and 51

18 *Encyclopaedia Britannica*, 1981, vol IX, p. 26

19 Northedge and Grieve, op cit, p. 214

20 Leon Blum's Popular Front government in France wanted to supply the Spanish Popular Front government with arms, but Britain persuaded him not to do so, and the League of Nations passed a non-intervention resolution. Joll, op cit, pp. 352–4

21 Gilbert, op cit, p. 55

22 Gilbert, op cit, p. 54. Gilbert also records that, as well as 2,820,000 Germans, 1,150,000 Czechs (the minority in the Sudeten areas) were transferred to Germany. After the war the East Europeans got their own back with a vengeance, in the most ruthless of 'ethnic cleansing' operations in modern times, expelling 9.5 million Germans to be absorbed into the defeated Germany. Of these, 3.5 million were expelled from Czechoslovakia, 2 million from East Prussia, which Poland had annexed, 3 million from the rest of Poland, and the remainder from Hungary, Romania and Yugoslavia

23 Ibid, p. 56

24 Birch, *1871–1939*, pp. 295–7

25 Ibid, pp. 274–5

6 The Cold War

1 Winston S Churchill, in *The Second World War*, London, Cassell, 1954, vol VI, published much of his correspondence with Stalin. No one reading this can doubt Stalin's ill will, duplicity and determination to force Communist government on Eastern Europe, especially Poland. Perhaps most chilling is Stalin's message of 5 May 1945 (pp. 435–7) in which he admitted the arrest of the entire delegation of 16 Polish politicians from the Polish government-in-Exile in London. They had been invited to go to Poland to take part with Polish Communist politicians in arranging free elections for a government of national unity. Stalin also declared his intention of having them tried for war crimes. The tone and content of letters like this make it astounding that Roosevelt should have trusted Stalin's good faith for so long

2 Truman's advisers estimated that the defeat of Japan by conventional means would have cost 500,000 more American lives and well over 1 million more Japanese lives (*Encyclopaedia Britannica*, 1981, vol 18, p. 725). Others have estimated that the deaths would have been at least double these figures

3 James Joll, *Europe since 1870*, Harmondsworth, Penguin, 1976, p. 423. Their new realism was indicated in May 1945 with the abrupt cancellation of the lease-lend programme, under which the USSR had received $9.1 billion in US Aid and the UK $13.5 billion

4 Ibid, p. 452

5 Peter Calvocoressi, *World Politics since 1945*, London, Longman, 1982, pp. 141–2

6 Corelli Barnett, 'Total Strategy and the Collapse of British Power', *Royal United Services Institute Journal*, Winter 1991, p. 6

7 F.S. Northedge and M.J. Grieve, *A Hundred Years of International Relations*, London, Duckworth, 1971, p. 236

8 *Encyclopaedia Britannica*, 1981, vol IV, p. 355

9 Joll, op cit, p. 435

10 The author was in the planning department of the War Office (Ministry of Defence) at this time

11 *Encyclopaedia Britannica*, 1981, vol 9, p. 1171

12 Ironically, it was this overstrain of the economy which led to the collapse of the Soviet system in 1989–92

13 M.D. Donelan and M.J. Grieve, *International Disputes: Case Histories 1945–70*, London, Europa, 1973, p. 58

14 Ibid, p. 59. Following this, the UN General Assembly on 3 November 1950 passed its 'Uniting for Peace' Resolution, whereby it could *recommend* action if the Security Council was prevented by a veto from doing so.

15 *Encyclopaedia Britannica*, 1981, vol 10, p. 514

16 Ibid, p. 513

17 It seems something of a paradox that Democrat Presidents committed US troops to Korea and Vietnam, and Republican Presidents took them out

18 A hydrogen bomb, more accurately described as a thermonuclear bomb, relies on nuclear fusion, as distinct from nuclear fission in the original and much less powerful 'atom bomb'

19 The 7 million estimated to have been killed on the Great Purge, added to the 12 million killed in the enforced collectivization of farms in the late 1920s and early 1930s brings Stalin's total to 19 million of his own people put to death to enforce his policies and keep him in power – a record of tyranny which puts even that of Hitler in the shade

20 Donelan and Grieve, p. 178

21 Ibid, p. 171

22 Robert Asprey, *War in the Shadows*, New York, Doubleday, 1975, vol II, pp. 1404–5

23 Ibid, pp. 1211–12

24 Majid Khadduri, *The Gulf War*, New York, Oxford University Press, 1988, pp. 195–8

25 Ibid, pp. 199–207

7 Czechoslovakia and Berlin 1948

1 The US army had already reached the German–Czech frontier and could easily have responded to a request for aid when the Czech nationalists tried to seize power from the Germans four days before Soviet troops arrived, but President Truman ordered strict loyalty to the Yalta agreement. Stalin held the Soviet army back until the Czech nationalists had exhausted themselves against the Germans, who were fighting desperately like cornered rats, no doubt hoping to keep control until the Americans came in. When they judged the time to be right, the Soviet troops moved in and arrested the Czech nationalist leaders. See *Encyclopaedia Britannica*, 1981, vol 2, p. 1197. They had used precisely the same technique in the Warsaw Rising in August 1944, when they held back and encouraged the Polish nationalists to rise and destroy themselves against the Germans before the Soviet army moved in (ibid, vol 14, p. 653)

2 Peter Calvocoressi, *World Politics since 1945*, London, Longman, 1982, p. 130

3 Ibid, p. 13

4 James Joll, *Europe since 1870*, Harmondsworth, Penguin, 1976, p. 431

5 Calvocoressi, op cit, p. 13

6 Philip Windsor, *City on Leave: A History of Berlin, 1945–62*, London, Chatto & Windus, 1963, p. 52

7 Joll, op cit, p. 454

8 M.D. Donelan and M.J. Grieve, *International Disputes: Case Histories 1945–70*, London, Europa, 1973, p. 29

9 Calvocoressi, op cit, p. 13
10 Ibid, pp. 13 and 14
11 Donelan and Grieve, op cit, p. 31
12 Calvocoressi, op cit, p. 14

8 Cuba 1962

1 Robert Beggs, *The Cuban Missile Crisis*, London, Longman, 1971, p. 20. A large part of this book comprises a detailed diary of events published by the *New York Times* on 3 November 1962
2 The ICBM works on a totally different system: the missile goes into orbit and circles the earth until ordered to descend and strike any point in the world. The range is therefore unlimited and, with the development of submarine launched ballistic missiles (SLBMs), the importance of land launching bases around enemy frontiers rapidly declined. In 1962, however, MRBMs and IRBMs played a vital part in nuclear capability. Despite the tremor caused by the Soviet Sputnik in 1957, the USA, both in nuclear missile technology and access to land bases, was vastly better placed than the USSR and Khrushchev was well aware of this.
3 Nigel Forward, *The Field of Nations*, London, Macmillan, 1971, p. 121
4 Ibid, p. 122
5 Beggs, op cit, p. 19
6 Roger Hilsman, *To Move a Nation*, New York, Doubleday, 1969, pp. 195–6, cited in Forward, p. 123. Hilsman was at the time Director of Intelligence and Research at the US State Department
7 Forward, op cit, p. 124
8 Ibid, p. 124
9 The author was, from 1961 to 1963, teaching at the US Army Staff College in Fort Leavenworth, Kansas. He saw this television broadcast, and was also aware of the huge extent of the military build-up in readiness for an invasion, should it prove necessary. He formed the strong impression, throughout the crisis, that President Kennedy was fully prepared to go to war, without limits, but that he was quite confident that there would be no war so long as Khrushchev realized that this was so. The author was at this time, of course, unaware of the existence of the spy Penkovsky, as a prime basis for Kennedy's confidence
10 Beggs, op cit, pp. 23–5
11 Forward, op cit, p. 126
12 Beggs, op cit, p. 26
13 Forward, op cit, p. 126; Beggs, op cit, pp. 26–7
14 Forward, op cit, pp. 126–7
15 Ibid, p. 127
16 Beggs, op cit, p. 27
17 Forward, op cit, pp. 127–8

18 Khrushchev's letter No 1 was so emotional and personal to Kennedy that Kennedy never published it in full: only selected proposals and phrases were ever made public
19 Robert Kennedy, *13 Days*, London, Pan, 1969, p. 106
20 Forward, op cit, p. 128
21 Beggs, op cit, p. 29
22 Amongst the best books and articles on crisis management are: Harlan Cleveland 'Crisis Diplomacy', *Foreign Affairs*, New York, July 1963; Nigel Forward, *The Field of Nations*, London, Macmillan, 1971; Coral Bell, *The Conventions of Crisis*, London, Oxford University Press, 1971; Phil Williams, 'Crisis Management', *International Affairs*, London, 1971; Robert Beggs, *The Cuban Missile Crisis*, London, Longman, 1971

9 The First Arab–Israeli Wars 1948–67

1 The worst example of ethnic cleansing was the massacre of 254 Arabs in Deir Yassin on 9 April 1948, leading to a mass flight of other Arabs from the area. This massacre was carried out by two fanatical Jewish terrorist movements. At the time, the Deir Yassin massacre was 'condemned as . . . utterly repugnant' by Ben Gurion, who became Israel's first Prime Minister, by the Jewish Agency from which the 1948 government was formed, and by the Haganah, which became the Israeli army (Sydney D Bailey, *Four Arab–Israeli Wars and the Peace Process*, London, Macmillan, 1990, p. 11). As well as denouncing the raid, Ben Gurion sent a message of apology and sympathy to King Abdullah of Jordan. Nevertheless, these incidents have ever since made the Israelis vulnerable to counter-accusations when they have complained of Arab terrorism or the 'ethnic cleansing' to which the Jews in Germany were subjected by Hitler; and they injected a virulent poison into Arab–Israeli relations which has affected subsequent efforts at reconciliation
2 Martin Gilbert, *The Arab–Israeli Conflict: Its History in Maps*, London, Weidenfeld & Nicolson, 1976, pp. 67–9
3 Bailey, op cit, p. 189
4 Indar Jit Rikhye, *The Sinai Blunder*, London, Frank Cass, 1980, p. 41. General Rikhye was Commander of the UNEF in 1967
5 Gilbert, op cit, p. 68
6 Bailey, op cit, p. 214
7 Ibid, p. 276
8 Ibid, p. 285

10 The Arab–Israeli War of 1973

1 Sydney D Bailey, *Four Arab-Israeli Wars and the Peace Process*, London, Macmillan, 1990, p. 288
2 Insight Team, *The Yom Kippur War*, London, *Sunday Times* and André Deutsch, 1975, pp. 36–8

3 Bailey, op cit, p. 289
4 Ibid, pp. 291–2
5 Insight Team, op cit, pp. 55–6
6 Bailey, op cit, p. 294
7 Insight Team, op cit, p. 110
8 Ibid, pp. 73–4
9 Ibid, pp. 105–6
10 Ibid, pp. 101–2
11 Ibid, p. 107; Bailey, op cit, p. 303
12 Insight Team, op cit, p. 125
13 Ibid, p. 136
14 Gilbert, op cit, p. 92
15 Bailey, op cit, pp. 313–18
16 Gilbert, op cit, p. 98
17 Insight Team, op cit, pp. 347–63
18 Bailey, op cit, p. 331
19 Gilbert, op cit, p. 102
20 Ibid, p. 100
21 Bailey, op cit, p. 335
22 Insight Team, op cit, p. 450
23 Ibid

11 The Vietnam War

1 Bernard Fall, *Street without Joy*, Harrisburg, Stackpole, 1961, gives an excellent assessment of the French campaign
2 Malcolm Browne, *The New Face of War*, London, Cassell, 1965, vividly describes the way these agit-prop teams operated
3 John Girling, *People's War*, London, Allen & Unwin, 1969, pp. 141–4
4 Sir Robert Thompson *Defeating Communist Insurgency*, London, Chatto & Windus, 1966, p. 27. On p. 25, Sir Robert (who headed a British Advisory Mission to Vietnam 1961–64) describes the tactics against village officials:

> On one occasion in Quang Ngai Province, when the Viet Cong regained control over a village which had been in government hands for some time, they seized the headman and his family, disembowelled his wife in front of him, hacked off his children's arms and legs and then emasculated him. This method of dealing with 'traitors' is certainly an effective way of winning that 'popular support' which so endears insurgent movements to less well-informed critics of the local government.

It might also be added that these atrocities certainly discouraged others from volunteering to replace the local government officials and probably ensured that anyone who did take the job would make a secret deal not to interfere with terrorist activities in that village. See also Sir Robert Thompson's 'Foreword', in Richard Clutterbuck, *The Long Long War*, London, Cassell, 1967, p. ix

5 Robert Asprey, *War in the Shadows*, New York, Doubleday, 1975, vol II

6 These views are based on the author's attachment to the US army and a visit to Vietnam during the period. He was assigned as British instructor at the US Army Command and General Staff College, Fort Leavenworth, Kansas, 1961–63. During this time, having previously served in Malaya (1956–58), he was also asked to lecture regularly at the US Army Special Warfare School, Fort Bragg, and the US Marine Corps School, Quantico. Thereafter he corresponded with US advisers serving in Vietnam whom he had taught in the USA, culminating in a week's visit to Vietnam in 1967, when he was taken around by other officers he had taught, who by then were lieutenant-colonels. He first published these views in *The Long Long War* (New York, Praeger, 1966; London, Cassell, 1967) and included, with their permission, many quotations from US captains and majors serving in Vietnam in 1962–64

7 Asprey, op cit, pp. 1211–12

8 Interview by the author with 'Tom' in Washington in May 1968

9 *World Almanac*, 1981, New York, p. 317

10 The author spent that week in Vietnam. He later learned that it was a record week for casualties, but he found the intensity of the fighting far less than the media had led him to expect. This, however, is a common feature of war reporting by a free press

11 Asprey, op cit, p. 1510

12 Ibid, pp. 1508–10

12 Bangladesh, Cyprus and the Falklands Islands

1 The six points are set out more fully in Robert Jackson, *South Asian Crisis*, London, Chatto & Windus, 1975, pp. 166–7

2 Kalim Siddiqui, *Conflict, Crisis and War in Pakistan*, London, Macmillan, 1972, p. 196

3 Ibid, p. 197

4 Ibid, p. 199

5 Jackson, op cit, p. 33

6 Ibid, p. 102

7 Siddiqui, op cit, p. 207

8 M.D. Donelan and M.J. Grieve, *International Disputes: Case Histories, 1945–70*, London, Europa, pp. 118–19

9 There is a vivid description of the work of one of these UN battalions in Frank Kitson, *Bunch of Five*, London, Faber & Faber, 1979

10 Peter Calvert, *The Falklands Crisis*, London, Frances Pinter, 1982, gives a clear and readable account of the background to the war

11 Christopher Dobson, John Miller and Ronald Payne, *The Falklands Conflict*, London, Coronet, 1982, p. 21

12 Calvert, op cit, pp. 47–8
13 Ibid, pp. 90–108
14 Dobson et al, op cit, pp. 173 and 190
15 Calvert, op cit, p. 113
16 BBC TV *News*, 12 May 1992

13 The European Revolutions of 1989–92

1 The main sources for this chapter were *The Economist* and the London *Times*. Individual items of news have not been documented unless they include valuable or controversial comment, or they contain facts that were not generally reported elsewhere. Other opinions expressed by the author were in many cases formed during three conferences between representatives of West European countries and of the USSR, held in Moscow, St Andrews and Paris in 1990 and 1991 to discuss cooperation against terrorism, drug-trafficking and other forms of crime. It was agreed that views expressed at these meetings would not be attributed
2 A Polish journalist friend of the author, who was an active member of Solidarity, made regular visits to the UK from 1981 onwards. After the introduction of martial law in December 1981, he worked for an 'underground' journal, to which the authorities deliberately turned a blind eye, and it was sold quite freely, circulating more widely than the government-controlled media, so its journalists became increasingly prosperous. This particular journalist concerned continued to oppose the government, but he regarded Jaruzelski as 'first a Pole, second a soldier and only third a Communist'. The author formed the opinion that Jaruzelski knew the way things were developing in Poland – four years before Gorbachev came to power – and kept them in check only sufficiently to avoid provoking Soviet interference. He must take credit as the first of the Communist reformists, and for Poland's gradual and bloodless transition to pluralism
3 *Europe: The Revolution of 1990–92*, London, *The Economist*, 1992, p. 19
4 Ibid, p. 17
5 *The Economist*, 23 March 1991
6 Leon Trotsky, *The Russian Revolution*, New York, Doubleday, 1959, pp. 100–1
7 The Shah's generals also had a very poor sense of public relations. The author was in Tehran at this time, and was in frequent contact with a British TV news crew. They told him that, on their arrival, they were met by a team of 12 from the Mujahideen, who promised to guide them to where the action was and to take care of them. By contrast, when they were seen to set up their cameras in the street, the soldiers were ordered to aim their guns at them and fire over their heads. Later in discussion with the author, the Shah's Chief of Staff, General Oveisi, complained of the anti-government bias of the foreign media. He seemed quite unable to understand that the contrast in their treatment might at least partially account for this bias. It is also an axiom

amongst TV reporters that viewers will normally identify with the side from which the cameras are filming – in this case from amongst the crowd. A wise police or army officer will offer facilities and protection to the news crews, as the Mujahideen had done in this case.

8 Another factor was that the Germans, Hungarians and Poles are historically more combative as people than the Czechs, who have always relied on passive resistance. This can be more effective, as Gandhi proved in India in the 1930s. It does not come easily to individual soldiers and police officers to use rifles or batons against people who are themselves threatening no violence

9 *The Economist*, 21 March 1992, pp. 25–7

14 The Gulf Crisis 1990–91

1 *The Economist*, 29 September 1990, p. 19

2 *The Gulf Crisis: The First Sixty Days*, Manchester, *Guardian*, 1990, p. 10

3 *The Economist*, 29 September 1990, p. 20

4 Ibid, p. 22

5 Three other Resolutions (667, 669 and 677) were passed during this time, making twelve in all. These three concerned Iraqi raids on diplomatic premises, assistance to other nations affected by the embargo and measures to prevent Iraq's repopulation of Kuwait

6 Details of the war are largely taken from a diary of events in the *Army Quarterly and Defence Journal*, vol 120, no 4, October 1990; vol 121, no 1, January 1991, vol 121, no 2, April 1991; supplemented by *The Times* and *The Economist*

7 *The Times*, 27 February 1991

15 Patterns of Future Conflict

1 *The Times*, 3 March 1992

2 For a fuller discussion of the Deir Yassin massacre, see Note 1 to Chapter 9 on p. 258. It must be reiterated that the massacre was denounced and disowned by the embryonic government of Israel under Ben Gurion, and by the majority of Jews inside and outside Palestine. But it was a very nasty example of ethnic cleansing which has thrown a shadow over Israel ever since

3 *The Times*, 6 November 1992

4 A concise and lucid exposition of the history and nature of Islam and Islamic law can be found in the *Encyclopaedia Britannica*, 1981, vol 9, pp. 926–43; vol 15, pp. 341–5

5 *The Economist*, 19 September 1992, p. 76

6 Ibid. Among the 200 others arrested in that week was SL's Chief Coordinator, one of the few people who knew the true identity of cell members operating under war names

7–9 See list of abbreviations on pp. xiii–iv
10 *The Economist*, 'Survey of China', 28 November 1992

16 Keeping the Peace

1 Dr Hans Mark, Chancellor of the University of Texas System, in a faculty seminar in Austin, Texas, on British Studies (18 October 1991) examined the possibility of a Pax Americana. He concluded that the US performance in meeting the 'new and difficult military challenge . . . of tribal wars' would decide whether the dominant US military and economic status would make conflicts more likely or less so.
2 Hans Mark, 'After Victory in the Cold War: The Global Village or Tribal Warfare?', in J.J. Lee and Walter Korter (eds) *Europe in Transition*, University of Texas, LBJ School of Public Affairs, 1991, pp. 19–27
3 Peter Calvolcoressi, *World Politics since 1945*, London, Longman, 1982, pp. 354–65
4 *The Economist*, 25 January 1992
5 *The Times*, 12 May 1992
6 United Nations Advisory Mission in Cambodia
7 *The Economist*, 7 November 1992
8 *The Economist*, 27 June 1992
9 *The Economist*, 18 July 1992
10 *The Economist*, 15 August 1992
11 *The Economist*, 14 November 1992
12 *The Economist*, 10 April 1993
13 *The Economist*, 22 February 1992
14 *The Economist*, 18 July 1992
15 *The Economist*, 12 September 1992
16 *The Economist*, 1 August 1992
17 *The Economist*, 12 September 1992
18 *The Economist*, 17 November 1992
19 *The Times*, 28 November 1992
20 *The Economist*, 27 March 1993; and *The Times*, 29 March 1993
21 *The Economist*, 26 January 1991
22 *The Independent on Sunday*, 18 April 1993
23 *The Economist*, 30 January 1993
24 *The Economist*, 5 September 1992, in a 24-page 'Survey of Defence in the 21st Century', propounds an interesting and comprehensive plan. It proposes the formation of a 'High Command of the Democracies' developed from NATO. 'The Democracies' would include those who 'have discovered by experience that their views of the world are broadly similar, and that they can work together in putting these ideas into practice'. This would certainly include all the NATO countries, Australia and New Zealand, and probably a number of other Central, North and East European democracies. Japan would be included on a qualified basis: she would not, for the time being, be

willing to commit her troops overseas, though she would probably be ready to contribute financially. *The Economist* proposes that the members should earmark contributions towards an expeditionary force of seven divisions, with their supporting troops, logistics, command and control, intelligence, 200 fighter and 400 ground attack aircraft, 150 or more transport aircraft and 20 fast sea-lift ships. They based this order of battle on what was needed to defeat Saddam Hussein, whose attack in 1990–91 is probably as powerful as any likely to be met. Members would retain the right to decide whether or not their part of the force should be used, but would not have the power of veto over the others. (This is roughly the situation in NATO.) The force would of course also be available to take part in smaller operations, such as peacekeeping and disaster relief, and would produce good value for money for national defence budgets.

17 Crisis Management

1 See figures in Note 35 to Chapter 3, pp. 251–2

Bibliography

BOOKS AND ARTICLES

AMERICAN HERITAGE, *The Civil War*, New York, Doubleday, 1960

ANGELL, NORMAN, *The Great Illusion*, London, Heinemann, 1912

ANGELL, NORMAN, *After All*, London, Hamish Hamilton, 1951

ASCOLI, DAVID, *The Queen's Peace*, London, Hamish Hamilton, 1979

ASPREY, ROBERT, *War in the Shadows*, vol II, New York, Doubleday 1975

ASPREY, ROBERT, *The German High Command at War*, New York, William Morrow, 1991

AVERY, HEIDI, 'Industrial Sociey and International Order: Sir Norman Angell's Analysis', unpublished Master of Studies Thesis, Faculty of Modern History, Oxford University, June 1990

BAILEY, SIDNEY D, *Four Arab–Israeli Wars and the Peace Process*, London, Macmillan, 1990

BARNETT, CORELLI, 'Total Strategy and the Collapse of British Power', *Royal United Services Institute Journal*, Winter, 1991

BEGGS, ROBERT, *The Cuban Missile Crisis*, London, Longman, 1971

BELL, CORAL, *The Conventions of Crisis*, London, Oxford University Press, 1971

BIRCH, R C, *Britain in Europe 1871–1939*, London, Pergamon, 1966

BIRCH, R C, *Britain in Europe 1789–1871*, London, Pergamon, 1969

BRECHER, MICHAEL, et al, *Crisis in the 20th Century* (vols I and II) London, Pergamon, 1987

BRINTON, CRANE, *The Anatomy of Revolution*, New York, Vintage, 1957

BROWNE, MALCOLM, *The New Face of War*, London, Cassell, 1965

BURNET, MACFARLANE, *Dominant Mammal*, Harmondsworth, Penguin, 1971

CALVERT, PETER, *The Falklands Crisis*, London, Frances Pinter, 1982

CALVOCORESSI, PETER, *World Politics Since 1945*, London, Longman, 1982

CHURCHILL, WINSTON S, *The Second World War*, London, Cassel, 1954, vol vi

CHURCHILL, WINSTON S, *A History of the English Speaking Peoples*, London, Cassell, 1958, vol iv

CLEVELAND, HARLAN, 'Crisis Diplomacy', *Foreign Affairs*, New York, July, 1963

CLUTTERBUCK, RICHARD, *The Long Long War*, London, Cassell, 1967

CLUTTERBUCK, RICHARD, *Riot and Revolution in Singapore and Malaya*, London, Faber & Faber, 1973

CLUTTERBUCK, RICHARD, *Industrial Conflict and Democracy*, London, Macmillan, 1984

CLUTTERBUCK, RICHARD, *Conflict and Violence in Singapore and Malaysia, 1945–83*, Singapore, Graham Brash; Boulder, Colorado, Westview, 1985

DE VRIES, LEONARD, *History as Hot News*, London, Murray, 1973

DOBSON, CHRISTOPHER, MILLER, JOHN, and PAYNE, RONALD, *The Falklands Conflict*, London, Coronet, 1982

DONELAN, M D, and GRIEVE, M J, *International Disputes: Case Histories 1945–70*, London, Europa, 1973

DOUGHERTY, JAMES E, and PFALTZGRAFF, ROBERT L, *Contending Theories of International Relations*, Philadelphia, Lippincott, 1971

Encyclopaedia Britannica, 1981

Europe: The Revolution of 1990-92, The Economist, London, 1992, p. 19

FALL, BERNARD, *Street without Joy*, Harrisburg, Stackpole, 1961

FORWARD, NIGEL, *The Field of Nations*, London, Macmillan, 1971

GILBERT, MARTIN, *Russian History Atlas*, London, Weidenfeld & Nicolson, 1966

GILBERT, MARTIN, *Recent History Atlas, 1860 to 1960*, London, Weidenfeld & Nicolson, 1967

GILBERT, MARTIN, *The Arab Israeli Conflict: Its History in Maps*, London, Weidenfeld & Nicolson 1976

GIRLING, JOHN, *People's War*, London, Allen & Unwin, 1969

The Gulf Crisis: The First Sixty Days, Manchester, *Guardian*, 1990

HARE, J E, and JOYNT, C B, *Ethics and International Affairs*, London, Macmillan, 1982

HILSMAN, ROGER, *To Move a Nation*, New York, Doubleday, 1969

HOBBES, THOMAS, *Leviathan* (1651), Harmondsworth, Penguin, 1968

INSIGHT TEAM, *The Yom Kippur War*, London, *Sunday Times* and André Deutsch, 1975

JACKSON, ROBERT, *South Asian Crisis*, London, Chatto & Windus, 1975

JOB, BRIAN L (ed) *The Insecurity Dilemma: National Security of Third World States*, Boulder, Colorado, and London, Lynne Rienner, 1992

JOLL, JAMES, *Europe since 1870*, Harmondsworth, Penguin, 1976

KHADDURI, MAJID, *The Gulf War*, New York, Oxford University Press, 1988

KITSON, FRANK, *Bunch of Five*, London, Faber & Faber, 1979

LAWRENCE, JOHN, *A History of Russia*, New York, Mentor, 1962

LEE KUAN YEW, *The Battle for Merger*, Singapore Government Publications, 1961

MARK, HANS, 'After Victory in the Cold War: The Global Village or Tribal Warfare?', in J J Lee and Walter Korter (eds) *Europe in Transition*, University of Texas, Austin, LBJ School of Public Affairs, 1991

MILLER, J D B, *Norman Angell and the Futility of War*, Hong Kong, Macmillan, 1986

MORRIS, DESMOND, *The Naked Ape*, London, Jonathan Cape, 1967

NORTHEDGE, F S and GRIEVE, M J, *A Hundred Years of International Relations*, London, Duckworth, 1971
PALMER, ALAN, *Metternich*, London, Weidenfeld & Nicolson, 1972
RICE, E E (ed) *Revolution and Counter-Revolution*, Oxford, Blackwell, 1991
SHANKS, MICHAEL, *What's Wrong with the Modern World?* London, The Bodley Head, 1978
SIDDIQUI, KALIM, *Conflict, Crisis and War in Pakistan*, London, Macmillan, 1972
STERN, J P, *Hitler: The Fuhrer and the People*, London, Fontana, 1975
STOESSINGER, JOHN G, *Why Nations go to War*, London, Macmillan, 1990
TAYLOR, A J P, *War by Timetable*, London, Macdonald, 1969
TAYLOR, A J P, *How Wars Begin*, London, Hamish Hamilton, 1979
TERRAINE, JOHN, *The Mighty Continent*, London, BBC, 1974
THOMPSON, SIR ROBERT, *Defeating Communist Insurgency*, London, Chatto & Windus, 1966
TOCQUEVILLE, ALEXIS DE, *The Ancien Régime and the French Revolution* (Paris, 1852), London, Fontana, 1971
TROTSKY, LEON, *The Russian Revolution*, New York, Doubleday, 1959
TUCHMAN, BARBARA, *The Guns of August*, New York, 1962
WHITTAKER, BEN, *The Police in Society*, London, Eyre Methuen, 1979
WILLIAMS, PHIL, 'Crisis Management', *International Affairs*, May 1973
WINDSOR, PHILIP, *City on Leave: A History of Berlin, 1945–62*, London, Chatto & Windus, 1963

JOURNALS AND NEWSPAPERS

Army Quarterly and Defence Journal
The Economist
Foreign Affairs
Guardian
International Affairs
New York Times
Sunday Times
The Times
World Almanac 1981

Index

Where acronyms are shown in the list of abbreviations (pp. xiii–iv), the acronym rather than the full title is normally used in this index.